STORM
WARNING

STORM
WARNING

WHETHER GLOBAL RECESSION, TERRORIST THREATS,

OR DEVASTATING NATURAL DISASTERS,

THESE OMINOUS SHADOWS MUST BRING US BACK TO THE GOSPEL.

BILLY GRAHAM

THOMAS NELSON

Since 1798

NASHVILLE   DALLAS   MEXICO CITY   RIO DE JANEIRO

Published in Nashville, Tennessee. Thomas Nelson is a registered trademark of Thomas Nelson, Inc.

Thomas Nelson, Inc., titles may be purchased in bulk for educational, business, fundraising, or sales promotional use. For information, please e-mail SpecialMarkets@ThomasNelson.com.

Unless otherwise noted, Scripture quotations are taken from *The Holy Bible, New International Version* (NIV). © 1973, 1978, 1984 by International Bible Society, used by permission of Zondervan.

Scriptures noted NKJV are taken from THE NEW KING JAMES VERSION. © 1982 by Thomas Nelson, Inc. Used by permission. All rights reserved.

Scriptures noted ESV are taken from THE ENGLISH STANDARD VERSION. © 2001 by Crossway Bibles, a division of Good News Publishers.

Scriptures noted NASB are taken from NEW AMERICAN STANDARD BIBLE®. © The Lockman Foundation 1960, 1962, 1963, 1968, 1971, 1972, 1973, 1975, 1977, 1995. Used by permission.

Scriptures marked AMP are taken from THE AMPLIFIED BIBLE: NEW TESTAMENT. © 1958 by the Lockman Foundation. Used by permission.

Scriptures noted RSV are taken from the REVISED STANDARD VERSION of the Bible. © 1946, 1952, 1971, 1973 by the Division of Christian Education of the National Council of the Churches of Christ in the U.S.A. Used by permission.

Scriptures noted PHILLIPS are taken from J. B. Phillips: THE NEW TESTAMENT IN MODERN ENGLISH, Revised Edition. © J. B. Phillips 1958, 1960, 1972. Used by permission of Macmillan Publishing Co., Inc.

Scriptures noted KJV are taken from the King James Version of the Bible. Public domain.

ISBN 978-0-8499-4641-7 (trade paper)
ISBN 978-0-8499-4691-2 (IE)
ISBN 978-0-8499-4864-0 (TBN Ed.)

Library of Congress Cataloging-in-Publication Data

Graham, Billy, 1918–
  Storm warning : whether global recession, terrorist threats, or devastating natural disasters, these ominous shadows must bring us back to the gospel / Billy Graham.
     p. cm.
  ISBN 978-0-8499-4813-8 (hardcover)
  1. Four Horsemen of the Apocalypse. 2. Bible. N.T. Revelation VI, 1-8—Criticism, interpretation, etc. 3. End of the world—Biblical teaching. I. Title.
  BS2825.52.G72 2010
  236'.9—dc22

                              2010005668

Printed in the United States of America

14 15 16 17 RRD 15 14 13 12 11 10

Contents

FOREWORD

by Franklin Graham

He stilled the storm to a whisper.
—PSALM 107:29

Storms have captivated the imagination since the beginning of time. Some people are frightened by them; others are fascinated. Daredevils taunt them; children hide from them. Many simply ignore them. The word itself bursts with thrill or hovers in doom. People gather at windows to behold the storm's might; others huddle in shelters to escape its fury.

The word excites the guru who chases after the latest techno gadget when it hits the market with headlines that sprawl across the business section of the daily newspaper:

APPLE IPHONE *Storms* WORLD

Who would have guessed when my father first wrote this book, *Storm Warning*, that a cordless, handheld telephone could capture a raging storm by photo or video seventeen years later?

Though the word *storm* is a simple little noun, it packs a big bang when it enters the atmosphere of human intrigue. It demonstrates its power and appeal when people stay glued to their television, laptop, iPod, or shortwave radio to follow the latest killer storm. As it approaches, newscasters make wild predictions, weathermen attempt to track its movement—and some thrill seekers actually run after them with camcorders buffeted by ferocious winds and pelting hail.

This is certainly the case with Warren Faidley, known to the world as the "Storm Chaser." He documented his adventures in a book by the same name and it became an overnight hit, making the best-sellers list on Amazon.com a few years ago. Public interest drove his popularity off the Richter scale with his dramatic conquests broadcast on the Weather Channel.

As president of Samaritan's Purse, a relief and evangelism organization, I have spent more than thirty years reacting to storms on behalf of its victims. As the frequency and magnitude of storms intensified, I learned something about getting ahead of the storms: position teams of workers at the threatened sites in advance so that the response can be swift. No matter how prepared we may be, storms have a way of turning and twisting. Adapting to the changes is of great consequence.

I have been in blinding sandstorms in the deserts of the Middle East; tropical storms on the continent of Asia; choking dust storms in Sub-Saharan Africa; torrential rainstorms in Europe; biting windstorms right here in Boone, North Carolina; and icy snowstorms in the Alaska wilderness.

However, I've never experienced a storm on a raging sea—but I know Someone who has.

"Without warning," the Bible says, "a furious storm came up on the lake . . . but Jesus was sleeping. The disciples . . . woke him, saying, 'Lord, save us!'" (Matthew 8:24–25).

I love this story for three reasons. First, it demonstrates human fear that overcame the disciples. Second, it shows that these burly men knew Who to run to for salvation. And third, it reveals their faith in the storm Maker to protect them. That may surprise you, but even in the storms, we see the Creator at work. God's Word tells us that "it is the LORD who makes the storm clouds" (Zechariah 10:1). It tells us that Jesus predicted the storms when He walked earth's dusty roads (Matthew 16:3). And Scripture pulls back the curtains of the sky, proclaiming, "His way is in the whirlwind and the storm" (Nahum 1:3).

These well-preserved verses are given to us for multiple reasons, but the two most important are that God will bring storms into our lives to warn us of the impending doom for disobedience to His Holy commands; and that God will be our shelter in the time of storm, just as the prophet Isaiah said, "Lord you are a shelter from the storm" (25:1, 4).

This is precisely the theme of my father's book that you hold in your hands. Originally written in 1992, we felt that in light of recent developments since 9/11, it might be helpful to reprint the book, bringing it up to date since the turn of the century.

My father has added nearly two decades to his life since then and has lived through a few more storms. At ninety-one years of age and after sixty-four years of marriage to my mother, who died in 2007, he lives alone in the home my mother created for him and our family at Little Piney Cove. As he looks back over his life and contemplates what lies ahead, he senses the uneasiness around the world, he feels the foundation of America crumbling, and he hears the sound of hoof-beats—perhaps on the fringe of heaven itself.

For the same reason God created the storms—whether to quench our thirst with His spiritual water or to drench our wayward eyes with tears because of our disobedience—my father wants to take you through just one small but very significant part of the Revelation of Jesus Christ in hopes that it will drive you to the foot of the cross for salvation or perhaps send you to the ends of the earth, where millions of souls are thrashing about in the stormy commotion of uncertainty, disappointment, and sin, warning all to prepare for eternity before the four horsemen thunder to earth to bring about the end of this age. These events will usher in the glorious presence of the great white stallion carrying the King of kings to reign forevermore.

We trust you will open your heart as the Revelator—the apostle John—shares the intensity of events revealed when Jesus breaks the seven seals of the heavenly scroll. The storms that will batter life on earth will yet give opportunity for mankind to consider where they stand before the One who holds the book of life. He, the Author of life itself, one glorious day will open it in the presence of every soul that belongs to Him. I pray that your name will be found written there.

—Franklin Graham
Boone, North Carolina
March 2010

INTRODUCTION

*We . . . will be swept up . . . into the clouds
to meet the Lord in the air.*
—1 Thessalonians 4:17 Phillips

S itting on the porch one summer evening with my son Franklin, we talked about Ruth's passing just weeks before. We felt her absence. She loved evenings like that, especially when a storm was gathering in the distance. The gentle breeze began to whistle; the tree limbs started to sway. Franklin and I listened to the powerful sounds of nature and watched the squirrels scramble for cover. Stretching for miles from my log home on the side of the hill overlooking the Swannanoa Valley, we saw lightning bolts pierce the clouds, their razor tips striking the mountain peaks, and the rumble of thunder sporadically cracking like dynamite on the Fourth of July.

As we studied the Carolina sky, we talked about the storms of life. As I reflected back to my childhood, I thought about the enormous changes I have seen in our country and around the world. The world I once knew as a boy has changed dramatically . . . I don't even recognize the world we live in today.

The world we are experiencing in the first decade of the twenty-first century is vastly different from the security of my childhood, when everyone—including the children—worked hard all day and had no difficulty falling asleep at night. I have not seen such widespread anxiety and depression in people's hearts as I do today. While battles rage around the world and storms gather in the human spirit, depression steals rest from our souls. "Depression" today not only describes the hard economic state of affairs sweeping our world but the human state of mind. I see this unfolding phenomenon as one of the many storm clouds hovering over a lost and dying world. Their thunderbolts can grip our hearts with indescribable fear. Our society is caught up in a powerful windstorm that has already caused massive destruction, with the full impact yet to come.

The Centers for Disease Control (CDC) have reported that antidepressants are now the most prescribed drugs in the United States. In an interview on CNN, one physician stated, "It's hard to believe that [so many] people are depressed, or that antidepressants are the answer." I agree with this wise doctor. Drugs are not the answer to man's troubled condition. There is only one answer to the travail of this present age, and it is found in the ageless pages of God's Word, the Bible.

I was first compelled to write *Storm Warning* in 1992, following the fall of Communism in Eastern Europe and the Gulf War. Trouble brewing in the Middle East especially heightened interest in what the Bible had to say about the end days. People began to wonder if there might really be something to the ancient prophecies spoken by God's prophets, and confirmed by His Son, the Lord Jesus Christ. Scripture speaks of earthquakes, wars, and rumors of wars, and warns us with urgency to prepare for the storms to come. The Bible says, "Be on your guard—see to it that your minds are never clouded." "You will hear of wars and rumors of wars, but see to it that you are not alarmed. Such things must happen . . . [the]gospel of the kingdom will be preached in the whole world, . . . and then the end will come" (Luke 21:34 PHILLIPS; Matthew 24:6, 14 NIV).

Now, at ninety-one years old, I believe the storm clouds are darker than they have ever been. The world has dramatically changed. This book has been revised and updated to encompass recent events—some that literally dropped out of the sky, warning a distracted nation and a mute world of impending doom.

Just as a laser pen helps focus attention on vital aspects of a business presentation, in this book I hope to use God's Word—His laser beam—to shed light on His revealed plan to save the human race from the explosive clouds rumbling through our world. Benevolent hands reach down from heaven to offer us the most hopeful warning and remedy: "Prepare to meet your God."

—Billy Graham
Montreat, North Carolina
February 2010

1

THE WINDS
OF CHANGE

He makes winds his messengers, flames of fire his servants.
—PSALM 104:4

KILLER EARTHQUAKE ROCKS HAITI—230,000 DEAD!

QUAKE HITS CHILE—TSUNAMI ROARS ACROSS VAST PACIFIC OCEAN.
TRIGGERS TSUNAMI ALERTS FOR UNITED STATES. ALARMS SOUND
ACROSS HAWAII.

HURRICANE FLATTENS NEW ORLEANS PARISHES: THOUSANDS
IGNORED WARNING!

TORNADO RIPS THROUGH CANADIAN CAMPSITE: SEARCHING
FOR THE MISSING AND DEAD.

These are samples of catastrophic headlines.

Cyclones, monsoons, twisters, typhoons—raging winds that part the waters—storm shocks that reduce the earth to rubble. Camera lenses snap like lightning bolts, capturing the aftermath of catastrophe.

We've heard about them. We've seen them. We've felt for those caught up in their wrath. At one time or another, we have all been warned of an approaching storm. Many live in fear that the earth will shake beneath their feet suddenly—without warning.

Human nature reacts differently. Some head straight to the grocery store at the first hint of a winter storm. When the meteorologist warns of thunderstorms, people scurry to locate their umbrellas. When the Weather Channel posts a warning to take cover because a tornado has been spotted nearby, parents hurry their children to shelter, snatching flashlights and candles in case the electricity goes out for hours—even days.

These are responsible reactions. These are people who *heed* the warnings. Yet how many times have we watched and waited as the snow clouds moved another direction, or the showers sprinkled just enough to calm the dusty air, or the sky abruptly changed complexion—and the warnings turned out to be nothing more than a distraction, an interruption to the activity of life? After a while, one false alarm after another, people become complacent—until it's too late, because at some point the warning is real.

WINDS OF WARNING

I have watched these cycles most of my life. Repeatedly, I have heard of people who faced oncoming storms with defiance, refusing to pay attention to the warnings or prepare for catastrophe, only to be caught in the storm's fury.

I can remember as a boy on our dairy farm that storm warnings were taken with great seriousness. We didn't have technology to track storms by the minute. We didn't have the benefit of forecasters to tell us with precision the exact hour a storm would hit, but that didn't prevent Mother Nature from sending her warnings—in the wind, in the falling temperature, and by darkened clouds in the sky.

My father taught me how to watch the sky and listen to the winds for those warnings. He knew that a power-packed storm could wipe out a year's crop, and gale-force winds could scatter a barn across the fields like a stick of dynamite. One violent storm could destroy the livelihood of families and communities for years. Joy could overcome the losses if physical life was spared, but the loss would still be great.

Jesus said, "When you see a cloud rising in the west, immediately you say, 'It's going to rain,' and it does. And when the south wind blows, you say, 'It's going to be hot,' and it is. . . . You know how to interpret the appearance of the earth and the sky. How is it that you don't know how to interpret this present time?" (Luke 12:54–56).

The truth is, we don't like our lives disrupted. We have important things to do: ball games to watch, work to finish, concerts to attend, trips that have been arranged and perhaps paid for months in advance.

This was the case as Labor Day 2005 approached. Families were making plans for a cookout, a beach trip, or visit to the amusement park. Plans were altered for many travelers who were riveted to any outlet reporting weather conditions. Why? What began as a little storm over the Bahamas gathered strength as it moved across Florida and into the Gulf of Mexico. Hurricane Katrina became a major threat, with ominous news reports warning that it might strike New Orleans and even wipe it off the map. Some cautious travelers cancelled their holiday plans to visit the city. Others gambled with the wind and headed right into the height of hurricane season, figuring the storm would diminish before landfall. They were wrong. The winds grew stronger.

As the storm warnings loomed, officials struggled to evacuate the shoreline cities—particularly New Orleans—and highways became choked with vehicles bumper to bumper. Many who lived along the coastal waters in jeopardy opted to weather the storm rather than battle the traffic moving at a snail's pace. The rest of America watched anxiously as the satellite images documented the hurricane's relentless march toward land. Many moaned as they watched the conflict between the rights of citizens to remain at their own risk and the responsibility of civic leaders to protect lives. Some watched with chagrin as the rebellious owners of Bourbon Street's bars refused to leave or even fortify their establishments, but instead geared up for hurricane parties. As the storm bore down on the helpless city, the nation watched in horror as thousands jammed the city's famed Superdome, desperately seeking shelter. After the ferocious storm breached the levees protecting New Orleans, large portions of the city flooded, making Hurricane Katrina one of the deadliest and most destructive natural disasters in American history.

I couldn't help but think of another group of people who defied Hurricane Camille thirty-six years earlier, in Pass Christian, Mississippi. Warnings had gone out. But instead of boarding up and escaping the city, there were those who actually prepared for a "hurricane party." How could they be thinking it was party time? Were they ignorant of the dangers? Did they believe their egos and pride could overcome nature's unpredictable fury? We'll never know. They didn't discern the warning blowing in the wind and paid the deadly price.

What we do know is that the wind was howling outside the posh Richelieu Apartments when Police Chief Jerry Peralta pulled up sometime after dark. Facing the beach less than two-hundred and fifty feet from the surf, the apartments were directly in the line of danger. A man with a drink in his hand came out on the second-floor balcony and waved. Peralta yelled up, "You all need to clear out of here as quickly as you can. The storm's getting worse!" But as others joined the man on the balcony, they laughed at Peralta's order to leave. "This is my land," one of them yelled back. "If you want me off, you'll have to arrest me."

Peralta didn't arrest anyone, nor could he persuade them to leave.

He wrote down the names of the next of kin of the twenty or so people who gathered there to party through the hurricane. They scoffed as he took their names—and ignored the warning.

When the front wall of the storm came ashore, it was 10:15 p.m. Scientists clocked Camille's wind speed at more than 205 miles per hour, the strongest on record at the time. Raindrops hit with the force of bullets, and waves off the Gulf Coast crested between twenty-two and twenty-eight feet high.

Reports later showed that the worst damage occurred in the little settlement where the party of twenty came to an end—literally! Nothing was left of the three-story apartment structure but the foundation; the only survivor was a five-year-old boy found clinging to a mattress the following day.

WINDS THAT BATTER

In the midst of a world in chaos—battered by everything from natural disasters to financial hurricanes that threaten the very foundations of our societies—we must never forget the personal suffering and fear that grip the hearts of those who have been caught in the aftermath of these events. I've maneuvered through the rubble of such disasters around the world. I've looked into the eyes of the brokenhearted standing in the midst of life turned inside out. No one is ever prepared for the aftershocks, and our hearts should be filled with compassion for the victims.

You may have found yourself touched by events like this—events that were outside your control but still caught in their grip. This certainly was the case when I toured south Florida in 1992. Hurricane Andrew had carved a path of devastation more than thirty miles wide. It was a picture of absolute chaos as far as the eye could see. Not a single house or building had been spared.

Florida governor Lawton Chiles invited me to join him for a

meeting with the people in the hardest-hit areas of the state, especially Homestead and surrounding communities where Andrew's destructive power severely damaged everything in its path. My son Franklin, president of Samaritan's Purse, was already there with a team working in the shambles of what had been home to tens of thousands. The governor called Floridians together and asked me to lead them in a prayer service in the aftermath of this killer storm. My heart ached as I looked into the eyes of the assembled crowd. Just days earlier, these same people had been routinely going about their lives, unconcerned about the dark clouds that satellites had detected somewhere off the west coast of Africa.

At first, it was just another tropical depression. But it began to grow in size and momentum, slowly moving westward across the sea. Forecasters noted that it was the season's first hurricane, but quickly added that it was too far from land to cause concern.

That assessment changed radically over the next three days as the storm approached Caribbean waters. The winds howled. Weather advisories became more ominous: small craft warnings, gale warnings, tropical storm warnings, and finally warnings of a major hurricane. Andrew's initial landfall was in the Bahamas. Four people were killed on the island of Eleuthera, and property damage was the most extensive in the island's history. Four hours later, the palm trees in south Florida began to dance in the wind as the first gusts from Andrew arrived.

My daughter Gigi called that evening from her home near Fort Lauderdale. "I'm sitting here waiting for Andrew," she said. "No one is exactly sure where it's going to hit, but it should be here within the next four hours." Gigi's family was taking what precautions they could, having decided to stick it out at home. Her words gave the storm a new sense of drama and urgency for Ruth and me. Hurricane Andrew was no longer just the lead story on the news; it had become personal.

Farther south, near Florida City, seventy-eight-year-old Herman Lucerne was also preparing to ride out the storm. A former mayor of

Florida City, Herman was a renowned outdoorsman and fishing guide. He was known to many people as "Mr. Everglades," because that great swampland was his stomping ground. He had lived there all his life. When he heard the storm warnings, he took his usual precautions, just as he had done for countless other hurricanes. He had seen so many in the past that he was convinced he could withstand another.

Hurricane Andrew crashed into south Florida around 4 a.m. During those long and terrifying hours, it unleashed a fury of wind and water of incredible proportions. For the first time, a hurricane passed directly over the National Hurricane Warning Service Center in Coral Gables, ripping the radar array from the top of the six-story structure. The Center's anemometer was destroyed shortly after recording 164-mile-per-hour winds, with wind gusts off the scale. The fierce winds that blasted the tip of Florida left thirty-three people dead, destroyed more than sixty-three thousand homes, left 1.3 million people without water or electricity, and did more than $30 billion in damage.

But it didn't stop there. Nineteen hours later Hurricane Andrew crossed the Gulf of Mexico and struck the coast of Louisiana, where it killed again, leaving fifty thousand people homeless and hundreds of thousands without water or electricity.

Ruth and I kept dialing our daughter, but for some time the phone lines were dead, and our concern (and prayers) increased. When we finally made contact, we learned that 100-mile-per-hour winds had battered her neighborhood, knocking down trees and light poles, causing further damage to homes. Thankfully her family survived unharmed, but they assured me they would never try to ride out another hurricane. They had learned their lesson and were grateful for a second chance—and God's protecting hand upon them.

Tragically, in Florida City, Herman Lucerne would never get another chance. He didn't survive Andrew. This time, the storm overcame his vast experience.

WINDS OF UNCERTAINTY

Hurricanes and other natural disasters aren't the only storms that batter our lives, however. As I write these words, the world is in the grip of another type of storm, the most devastating economic crisis since the Great Depression of the 1930s. Millions have lost their jobs, and home foreclosures and business bankruptcies have soared to record levels. "Our economy is on life support," one economist said, referring to the massive amounts of money that governments across the world have injected into their financial systems. Not a single strata of society has been untouched, and many fear that soaring governmental debt could threaten the financial security of the world for generations to come. No one can predict the long-term outcome of these events, but fear and uncertainty about the stability of the world's financial foundations have become hallmarks of our age. Who among us knows what the future holds—for us, and for our children and grandchildren?

Risk is inevitable in financial markets, but what has brought us to the brink of financial ruin in recent times? Why have these things happened? The answers are many, but overshadowing them all are greed, self-indulgence, and financial irresponsibility—not just on the part of individual consumers, but government and industry as well. Today we read of nations with multi-trillion-dollar debts—a figure that is almost incomprehensible. On an individual level, citizens by the thousands walk away from their homes because they no longer can pay the mortgage, while millions face unemployment and the threat of personal bankruptcy.

The great flaw in the American economic system has finally been revealed: an unrealistic faith in the power of prosperity rather than in the ultimate power and benevolence of God. The American Dream became America's god; wealth and abundance have become the measure of America's success. But—as recent events have shown—we have been living an illusion. Journalist Robert J. Samuelson summarized this well in *Newsweek* magazine. He wrote:

Every age has its illusions. Ours has been this fervent belief in the power of prosperity. Our pillars of faith are now crashing about us. We are discovering that we cannot, as we had once supposed, create prosperity at will . . . Worse, we are learning that even great amounts of prosperity won't solve all our social problems. Our Good Society is disfigured by huge blemishes: entrenched poverty, persistent racial tension, the breakdown of the family, and staggering budget deficits. We are being rudely disabused of our vision of the future. The result is a deep crisis of spirit that fuels Americans' growing self-doubts, cynicism with politics, and confusion about our global role.

This was not written in 2010. It was printed on March 2, 1992. The lesson is clear: instead of learning from the past, we have only repeated its mistakes.

We see America's disappointment and despair not just in the current financial crisis, but in other areas also. We were shocked by the violence and looting in Los Angeles sparked by the unpopular verdict in the Rodney King case more than a decade ago. Since then we have almost grown numb to protests and hostile confrontations over a host of crucial social issues, from environmental concerns to abortion. Moral and ethical standards that were once taken for granted have not only been called into question but cast overboard by millions. The mentality to "do your own thing" has had devastating effects. Instead of bringing us peace and stability, it has only caused confusion and disillusionment. The world asks, how can this happen in America? Unbridled selfishness can never bring peace to the human heart, much less to society.

Some years ago, an Associated Press reporter interviewed Americans from California to Florida, and he discovered a deep sense of anxiety and uncertainty, including feelings of despair over the future. A man in Louisiana spoke of a "nameless, shapeless dread." A World War II veteran from Wisconsin sensed the "forewarning of revolution." A lawyer from Washington State spoke of his growing concern over government mismanagement and abuses of power. A nun in Florida spoke of the "floating anxiety" among the people she meets.

At the turn of the twenty-first century, the sheer momentum of such changes robbed many Americans of their joy and optimism. Instead of hope, the new millennium ushered in the same old baggage: lost jobs, broken lives, ruined careers, bankruptcies, shattered marriages, physical and emotional abuse, and a thousand other tragedies that invaded America's homes and people's hearts. What remains is the somber, joyless, unromantic reality of a nation in deep, deep trouble. And it is only too clear that such an emotional roller-coaster ride of the past three decades has been tragically complicated by the moral and spiritual bankruptcy of our society. Truly, we live in a time of trouble. What does it all mean?

WINDS OF FEAR

America is not the only troubled spot today. The entire world is in turmoil. While the population of the planet continues to swell, millions are dying from epidemics, war, poverty, famine, starvation, drugs, crime, and violence. We are living in a time of enormous conflict and cultural transformation. The political and social revolutions of our time stagger the imagination and strike man's heart with fear.

On the world political scene, shocking events seem to bear the unmistakable stamp of destiny. We have been stunned by political and cultural changes in nation after nation around the globe. Some have brought hope and freedom to millions of people, such as in Eastern Europe. However, in spite of the outbreak of democracy and the reported death of Communism there, that part of the world still faces enormous problems and tensions, with few solutions on the table, if any.

No sooner had the world witnessed the tragic deaths of young pro-democracy students in 1989 at Tiananmen Square than we witnessed the equally emotional news of democratic victories in Romania, Poland, Czechoslovakia, Bulgaria, and other former Communist states. In many places, the promoters of change offered a grand vision of world unity. Some optimists asserted that the world had come to the threshold of unparalleled peace and global oneness. In his highly publicized address in Fulton, Missouri, Mikhail Gorbachev called for a strong central government of democratic nations: a new world order to replace the old idioms and stratagems based on nuclear conflict. But while the world applauded his remarks, and perhaps even his sentiments, there was justifiable caution in most quarters. The bloodbath in Yugoslavia in the 1990s is just one example of the hostile tensions unleashed by these changes.

But such turmoil should not be entirely unexpected. Even today while the globalists and international affairs specialists continue their chant for "peace, peace," we are reminded that the Bible says that there can be no lasting peace until Christ returns. So the world remains restless and uncertain. While we are expectant and hopeful—and while the world continues to applaud men when they speak of peace—our fears are not so easily resolved.

As we enter a new decade of the twenty-first century, we see accelerated growth of unrestrained greed and corruption on Wall Street, financial mismanagement in the halls of government, and fraud and perversion at the highest levels of both church and state. While keeping an eye on the showdown that many observers feel may be brewing even now between the financial superpowers of Europe, the Middle East, Asia, and North America, many people sense the possibility of an even greater unraveling in the world.

As we hope and pray for peace and for new opportunities for prosperity, we are constantly confronted by the realities of longstanding and tangled problems and conflicts. While government takeovers of American industry and banking should cause us great concern, nothing should burden our hearts more than the outrageous immorality that is welcomed into homes and minds around the world via television and the Internet.

Should we be surprised that our nation—and the world—has come to this? When we see corruption at every level of our society and in every sector of public life, can anyone expect to continue in the mistaken belief that humanity is somehow perfectible without the intervention of God?

WINDS THAT SHIFT

Storm warnings of a different sort cannot be ignored—storm warnings from the Bible urging us to pay attention to the crises in our world, leading us to the final events that must take place before Jesus Christ comes again. These storms, the Bible says, will be of apocalyptic proportions—disasters that will shatter even the foundations of human society. While it may be easier to judge the potential danger of a hurricane or assess its damage, how does one discern the shifting winds endangering a society already in chaos?

Are we approaching those days of which the Bible speaks? Are the events of our time meant to warn us of even greater disasters— disasters predicted by the Bible that will be harbingers of Christ's coming judgment and rule?

Jesus said, "For nation will rise against nation, and kingdom against kingdom. And there will be famines, pestilences, and earthquakes in various places. All these are the beginning of sorrows" (Matthew 24:7–8 NKJV). The apostle John also spoke of this terrible time: "The sky receded like a scroll, rolling up, and every mountain and island was removed from its place" (Revelation 6:14).

The purpose of this book is to look into God's Word for the answers—to review the state of the world in troubled times and to examine the circumstances confronting us today in the light of the only reliable standard: the Bible. It is not my intent to arouse groundless fears or to make unfounded charges; rather, I hope to raise some important questions and turn to Scripture for the answers. Can we find any hope in the current world situation? Will there be lasting peace? How should we live in the face of our nation's new challenges and the magnitude of the world's crises? These are important—even vital—questions, and I invite you to come with me as we discover the answers God has given us in His Word, the Bible.

2

THE RISING STORM

Behold, waters are rising . . . and shall become an overflowing torrent.
—JEREMIAH 47:2 ESV

Who can forget September 11, 2001? In a matter of hours, the optimistic hopes at the dawn of a new millennium were shattered. America and the world had missed the signs carried by the winds of a rising storm. The dark clouds brooding on the horizon turned into plumes of deathly smoke rising from the rubble of the most terrifying attack on American soil.

As I watched the shocking scenes flash across the television set, I recalled many other instances of international terrorism our nation had endured in recent years: the 1983 bombing of the U.S. Marine barracks in Lebanon; the explosion of a car bomb in the basement of the North Tower of the World Trade Center in 1993; the 1998 truck bombing of the American embassy in Nairobi, Kenya; and the attack on the USS *Cole* in Yemen in 2000.

I also recalled the occasion when my longtime friend President

George H. W. Bush invited me to the White House. Not until that evening did I learn the reason for his invitation—when he announced to the American people the start of Operation Desert Storm, a massive campaign designed to liberate the nation of Kuwait from Iraqi dominance, following Saddam Hussein's invasion the previous summer. The President knew well the seriousness of the steps he had ordered and asked me to pray with him and for him. I prayed not only for wisdom for our leaders and divine protection for those going into combat, but also for a swift end to the hostilities and a new period of peace in that part of the world.

I thought back to the many wonderful times the President and I had shared. This occasion, however, was one of the darkest. Declaring war meant deploying U.S. troops to Kuwait, and this action opened our nation to a different kind of war, heightening tensions in the Middle East. The United States and its allies gained victory with brilliant air power displayed in Desert Storm. However, the storm proved to be a precursor to a greater threat that would rumble throughout the decade and explode during the infancy of a new century.

President Bush, in his 1992 State of the Union Address, spoke of the undeniable awareness that something profound and unusual was happening in the world; "big changes," he called them. Mr. Bush applauded the death of Communism and the West's apparent victory in the Cold War, but then he added, "In the past twelve months, the world has known changes of almost biblical proportions."

Midway through his address, the President warned of the dangers still ahead with striking words: "The world is still a dangerous place. Only the dead have seen the end of conflict. And though yesterday's challenges are behind us, tomorrow's are being born."

The President's remarks had a prophetic tone, but I am certain he never guessed that less than ten years later, his own son—President George W. Bush—would find himself commanding a nation in peril. Tomorrow's challenges dropped from the sky in the form of flying bombs leveling the Twin Towers of the World Trade Center. That fateful day in September 2001 has led to prolonged military actions in Iraq and Afghanistan.

"No matter how hard we try," I stated at the National Cathedral in Washington three days after the 9/11 attacks, "words simply cannot express the horror, the shock, and the revulsion we all feel over what took place in this nation. . . . My prayer today is that we will feel the loving arms of God wrapped around us, and will know in our hearts that He will never forsake us as we trust in Him."

But were those terrible events harbingers of even greater turmoil and upheaval in our world? Could they even be the beginning of the final days of history spoken of in the Bible—days that will lead up to Christ's promised return and a new era of peace? In any case, how should we respond as individuals to the threats and insecurities our world faces today?

WINDS UNKNOWN

More than forty years ago, in my book *World Aflame*, I spoke of the 1960s as a time of anger and outrage, and as a warfare of conflicting ideologies and lifestyle. While the circumstances of our own time have changed superficially, I am convinced that the greater social dimensions have not really changed at all. In fact, we are still paying the price for the recklessness of the free-thinking sixties. More than ever, our culture is caught in a web of irresponsibility and self-centeredness. Our society is still trapped in the same conditions of desperation and fear that have been propelling us downward, relentlessly, into an emotional inferno.

Just a decade ago, as the clock ticked closer to the end of the twentieth century, the world seemed to be spinning faster and faster. Technology and time were racing past us at dizzying speeds. We asked, Who can keep up? Where will it end? Are there any answers for the crises of our time? Is there still hope for us—or is it as bad as we often fear?

WINDS OF THE RISING STORM

The image of an approaching storm captures well this sense of fear and uncertainty. In the midst of every kind of political struggle, a storm of resentment and insecurity already resides in the hearts of many people. There is a tempest of rage brewing in our young people. Too often they realize they have been cheated and exploited, not only by the commercialism of this consumer age, but by educators and sociologists who have stripped them of moral values, family relationships, and the sense of a greater purpose in life. I see too many young men and women whose virtue has been abused and whose faith in marriage and commitment has been shattered. Many of them have grown cynical over our political process and express little confidence in our elected officials. One newspaper called the first decade of the twenty-first century "The Decade of Dread." Millions are filled with confusion and fear as they look to the future.

Storm warnings surround us no matter which way we turn. The generation that lived through the Great Depression knew hard times. But my children, part of the baby boomer generation, did not experience that kind of hardship growing up, nor did their children. For the first time, they are seeing the effects of a demoralized society.

Some respond by figuratively burying their heads in the sand, refusing to think about what is going on, or else blithely saying, "It'll all work out somehow." Others find themselves paralyzed by fear or seek to escape from their fears through drugs, alcohol, sex, or some other self-destructive "solution."

Books by sages of every stripe claim to offer instant wealth and wisdom. For some, the answer is fitness; surely a perfect body will bring happiness. For others, the answer, they believe, will be found in psychological and emotional well-being, or in making contact with their inner "spiritual" self. Others try to persuade us that our rights have been violated in some way, and the way to happiness is to take matters into our own hands and cast off all social norms.

None of these ideas can bring us the lasting and authentic peace we seek. The sickness is deep within the soul of our society—and that has always been God's exclusive territory. God calls that sickness sin. Our greatest problem is spiritual in nature, caused by our alienation from God—an alienation caused by sin. That is why we need Christ, for only He can change us from within by His Spirit, and only He can bring us hope for a better life as we follow Him. Yes, there is hope for all who will peer into the Scriptures and seek God's truth about how we should live in the midst of life's uncertainties.

WINDS OF MORAL CHANGE

Perhaps you remember reading several years ago about a man named Joseph Markowski, an AIDS-infected drifter who had been charged with attempted murder for selling his blood at a Los Angeles plasma center. He was a down-and-outer who said he needed the money, and he admitted he didn't care that he might be killing others with his tainted blood. His story was a tragic illustration of the immorality of a self-centered life. Unless we turn to the morality of Jesus Christ, who shed His blood to save lives, the example of Joseph Markowski is the best the world can expect.

The world today is in desperate need of moral leadership, based upon the foundational values and personal character our society once understood and respected. We need moral leadership that teaches the difference between right and wrong, and teaches us to forgive one another even as we are forgiven by our Father in heaven. We need moral leadership that teaches love for people of every race and nation and tribe; a morality in which material abundance is not the final goal of a society, but merely the result of its strong work ethic, ingenuity, love of others, and abiding by the principles of Almighty God.

The world needs moral leadership that respects the rights of all men and women—rights that God designed for our benefit and to give us the greatest potential for leading happy and productive lives. In His final days on earth, Jesus said, "If anyone loves me, he will obey my teaching. My Father will love him, and we will come to him and make our home with him" (John 14:23).

We need a morality that guarantees respect for mothers who mother, for fathers who father, and for all those who live and work together to fulfill God's commandments to pursue our individual destinies as His privileged children. We need families who stay together and pray together. We do not need a new moral order; the world desperately needs the tried and tested moral order that God handed down in the Ten Commandments at Mount Sinai, which He proved through the prophets and patriarchs of old and which He expressed most perfectly in the life, death, and living presence of His own Son, Jesus Christ. This is the kind of moral leadership the world needs.

WINDS OF INSTABILITY

In reality, however, this kind of moral leadership is rare today—and the trends are not encouraging. Two decades ago, in a lecture at Yale University, U.S. Secretary of Health and Human Services Dr. Louis W. Sullivan called for a "renewed sense of personal responsibility" in this country. He portrayed the toll of tobacco and alcohol use, both in terms of loss of life and in the dollars-and-cents cost to taxpayers: "A high percentage of the disease and disability afflicting the American people is a consequence of unwise choices of behavior and lifestyle." The result, he said, is blighted, stunted, and less fulfilling lives for our citizens, and outrageously high medical costs.

But he also spoke of the broader toll of America's unwise choices concerning morality and our national sense of values. He said, "I am troubled by diminishing confidence in our willingness and ability as a society and individuals to make sound judgments about healthy human behavior and lifestyles. Linked to this declining faith in ethical and value judgment is an erosion of those institutions that have generated, shaped and sustained our ethical and cultural standards— family, neighborhood, church, school, and voluntary associations. As a consequence of this institutional decline, we have fewer sources of instruction in healthy, constructive behavior."

Secretary Sullivan went on to describe the way these conditions contributed to anger, violence, and hostility in our streets: "All about me, I see the toll of our ethical dilemma, the tragic price of our cultural indifference. So many of these problems have their roots in the alienation, isolation, and lack of direction that follow from the collapse of societal standards, and the institutions that generate them."

Sullivan described his Yale address as a plea for a revitalized "culture of character." In fact, the Secretary said he was pleading for a return to such old-fashioned virtues as "self-discipline, integrity, taking responsibility for one's acts, respect for others, perseverance, moderation, and a commitment to serve others and the broader community."

Twenty years later, our failure to follow these moral principles is not only still with us, but it has become even more prevalent—and dangerous.

WINDS OF STRUGGLE

As we have seen, political, social, and economic storms in increasing measure buffet our world and threaten our very existence. But other storms buffet our lives as well—personal storms that come to us all, threatening to rob us of our peace and knock us off balance. In some cases, these storms have always been with us; every generation faces them, and every generation must cope with them. But to be honest, that may not be much help to us as individuals; for even if other people have experienced some particular problem, there is always a first time for us. How will we react? With anger? Denial? Despair? Or faith—faith in the living God, who loves us and wants to give us the wisdom and strength and hope we need to meet life's trials and tribulations?

As I have grown older, I have come to appreciate the complexity of life's storms in a new way. I have come to grips with storms of illness in my own life, and I never thought that my wife, Ruth, would precede me in death. When I had to let go and say my final good-bye to her in 2007, it was a stormy time for me—and it still is, for I miss her beyond words.

No life is without its own set of problems. Jesus never promised our paths would always be smooth. When any Bible teacher over-sells either the material or the spiritual benefits of the Christian life, I believe he or she is in danger of deception that leads others astray.

When I think of physical struggles, I remember a brave young man who came to one of our crusades in a wheelchair. He was suffering the last cruel stages of terminal cancer, and he was angry and bitter about it. He had read too many books promising health to the believer. Too many well-meaning Christians had promised him miraculous healing—if he only had enough faith. When healing did not come, however, he grew more and more uncertain.

His well-meaning parents lovingly carried him from one faith healer to another, and each one prayed for dramatic healing, but to no avail. The young man had prayed and fasted, and he sincerely believed God was able to heal him—but still no miracle had taken place. Instead, he was unquestionably dying. Our crusade would be the last public meeting that young man would ever attend.

Our youth speaker that night was Joni Eareckson Tada. Most people know that Joni was crippled in a diving accident as a young person. She, too, had prayed for healing. Yet she remained confined to a wheelchair as a quadriplegic. When she wheeled herself to the microphone that night, she did not oversell the Good News. She confessed her own early anger at remaining crippled, after praying and believing in a miracle.

Then she told how Christ—who knew from personal experience what it was to suffer—met her in the midst of her pain and brought comfort to her heart. He gave her a new purpose for living, and through her pain she was able to point others to Him. She has faithfully done this around the world. Joni dared to tell it like it is—and the Holy Spirit, through Joni's moving testimony, set that dying young man free. Letting go of his bitterness and anger, he stopped seeing himself as a failure, as one who did not have enough faith. Instead, he came to see Christ as the all-sufficient One. Not long after that meeting the young man died, but his parents were able to rejoice that he had not died angry and bitter. Released from his earthly pain, he had gone to be with the risen Lord in heaven, where there is no suffering, but only perfect peace. In the twilight of death, he learned what life was meant to be.

WINDS OF HOPE

This does not mean that God never heals in miraculous ways; I am certain that at times He does. But there are also many times when He does not. We cannot understand why some people appear to glide effortlessly through life, while others always seem to be in the throes of pain and sorrow. We cannot explain why some withered bodies are healed, while others suffer and die. We cannot know why some prayers are answered the way we hoped they would be, while others seemingly go unanswered. We cannot pretend that life in Christ will always guarantee us victory and material success as defined by human standards.

On the other hand, when we tell only the stories of victory, we tell just a part of the truth. When we imply that the Christian faith involves no yoke and no burden, we tell less than the whole truth. Half-truths and easy answers are the weapons of deceit. Sometimes God brings healing, either through modern medicine or through miraculous means. But sometimes He doesn't—and His way is always best, because He loves us and knows what is best for us. Never forget: for the Christian, this life is not all, nor should our physical well-being be our life's highest goal. Christ is our life, and someday we will go to be with Him for all eternity.

In a time of stress and uncertainty in his life, the apostle Paul wrote to the church at Philippi, "I have learned in whatever state I am, to be content: I know how to be abased, and I know how to abound. Everywhere and in all things I have learned both to be full and to be hungry, both to abound and to suffer need." Then he added these stirring words: "I can do all things through Christ who strengthens me" (Philippians 4:11–13 NKJV).

This is the secret to living a life of happiness. As long as we have the assurance that Jesus Christ is in control, no trial is so great, no tempest so overwhelming, no crisis so crushing that He will not supply what is needed to weather the storm. There are winds of change ahead, for the better or worse, for all of us. How will we respond?

FACING THE WHIRLWIND

Life's daily storms—its nagging problems and worries—preoccupy all of us, and that is understandable. And when they do, we need to heed afresh the words God spoke through the apostle Peter: "Humble yourselves, therefore, under God's mighty hand, that he may lift you up in due time" (1 Peter 5:6).

But the Bible (as we will see in greater detail) points us to even greater storms—to those events that will take place in the world as Satan unleashes his final fury against Christ, and the world is convulsed with upheavals and conflicts and judgments that will make our present troubles seem insignificant by comparison. Have we already entered those days? The Bible cautions us against speculation about this—but one reason it does so, I am convinced, is those evils are already in the world, and we are called to understand them and be on our guard against them, no matter where we are in God's timetable of final events.

I have asked people from various parts of the world what they think of our chances for the future. Most of them are pessimistic. Editorials in the international press often are even gloomier than those in American papers. Repeatedly, the words *Apocalypse* and *Armageddon* are used to describe events on the world scene.

Many people who use these words don't even understand their meaning. Webster's Dictionary defines *Apocalypse* as "a symbolic depiction of the ultimate destruction of evil and triumph of good; a prophetic disclosure or revelation; a cataclysmic event; a sudden and violent end to the world."

What about the word *Armageddon*? There is actually a place in Israel by this Hebrew name. It is about sixty miles north of Jerusalem in the plains of Megiddo, stretching out from the Jezreel Valley, not too far from Mount Carmel, where Elijah encountered the prophets of Baal, when fire fell from heaven (1 Kings 18). I have thought about that great battle between the God of heaven and the gods of idolaters. Images fill my mind as I consider the future in light of Scripture, for this is the place where the last battle between the forces of good and evil will be fought (Revelation 16:16).

Most of what follows in this book will focus on what the Bible says about these terrible days, particularly in Jesus' words in Matthew 24 and in the apostle John's vision of the latter days in Revelation 6. I want to shine a light on Jesus' words in Matthew 24 as He explains to His disciples the signs of the end times. I hope to set a magnifying glass upon the breathtaking passage in Revelation 6 concerning what are often called the "four horsemen of the Apocalypse." These vivid images depict the dangers of what is to come, while at the same time culling out the warnings meant for us today.

Horses are among the most beautiful and intelligent animals of God's creation. But the four horses and their riders in John's vision are anything but beautiful. They are terrible and terrifying. In my view, the shadows of the four horsemen can already be seen galloping throughout the world. I not only want to look at these four symbols of events yet to come, but also put an ear to the ground and to detect their hoofbeats, growing louder by the day. (It is interesting to note that the four horses described in Revelation 6 correspond to the first four signs of the end of the age that Jesus spoke of in Matthew 24:4–9.)

The first horse symbolizes deception through counterfeit religion and secular, anti-God, and anti-Christian belief systems. It is a white horse, seemingly pure but bent instead on conquest. In Jesus' words, "Many false prophets will appear and deceive many" (Matthew 24:11).

The second horse brings war and violence upon the earth: subjects that address current world conditions keeping biblical parallels in view. "Its rider was given power to take peace from the earth and to make men slay each other" (Revelation 6:4).

The third horse signifies famine and pestilence—plagues from the beginning of time that will have no rest until the end of time: "There will be great earthquakes, famines and pestilences in various places, and fearful events and great signs from heaven" (Luke 21:11).

The fourth horse represents the trauma of death and the foreshadowing of judgment and hell: "Its rider was named Death, and Hades was following close behind him" (Revelation 6:8).

These are not meant to be meaningless or vague images, but a divine revelation of the realities of the age before Christ's return to earth. Together, these images of the four horsemen represent all the varieties of fear and crises we are encountering in the here and now. Today's headlines ring with the warnings of approaching storms, and the language of John's prophetic writings has never seemed so contemporary.

Admittedly the figurative language of the Apocalypse (as the book of Revelation is called) is indeed complex and profound and, at times, difficult to fully understand. In covering these chapters I will be as specific and literal as possible. I have provided commentary from scholars wherever I thought they might help clarify certain terms and concepts. My purpose is not to dwell on specific theological issues concerning the Second Coming of Christ, or to offer personal exposition of events such as the Rapture of the church, the Tribulation, or the Millennium. My hope is to examine the witness of Scripture in relation to the events of our time and to highlight the words of our Lord concerning His expectation of those who follow Him today.

Regarding these passages—the images of the Apocalypse in Revelation and the teachings of Jesus in Matthew 24 concerning the coming end of the age—my purpose is to interpret the text in the most practical and logical way possible. Even though there are portions of the text that employ challenging language, the passages are dramatically relevant to our age and to the problems of a changing world.

So this is the backdrop for the four horsemen of the Apocalypse and the cataclysmic event that will take place at Armageddon.

This compels me to review the remarkable passage about the four horses that ride forth upon the earth, as recorded by the apostle John in Revelation 6:1–8. To examine this account and discover God's revealed truth about the end times is not only thrilling but insightful, particularly in light of the troubles beyond the horizon. I trust that as we look together at what the Bible has to say about these times, your heart will be filled with hope and great assurance knowing that God is still in control.

Let no one make the dreadful mistake of interpreting these words (or any part of God's Word) as fiction or fantasy. In the face of so much hopelessness in every corner of the globe, we need to recognize the Word of God for what it is: *the* Word of God. So my ultimate goal is to explore these passages in light of God's message—a message that brings both judgment and hope. As you ponder these words, may you choose hope—because there is only One who turns hope into certainty: the God-man, the Lord Jesus Christ, the Hope of Glory.

3

SIGNS OF THE TIMES

It is not for you to know times or seasons
which the Father has put in His own authority.

—ACTS 1:7 NKJV

We sometimes wonder where God is during the storms of life, in all the troubles of the world. Where is God? Why doesn't He stop the evil? The Bible assures us that God will abolish evil when Christ returns. Someday He will come with shouts of acclamation, and there will be a joyous reunion of all those who have trusted in Him.

No wonder Scripture tells us that, at that time, "every knee should bow, in heaven and on earth and under the earth, and every tongue confess that Jesus Christ is Lord" (Philippians 2:10–11). If you do not receive Christ as Savior and bow to Him now as Lord of your life, the day is coming when you will bow before Him as Judge.

Jesus did not tell us when He is coming back. He said we were not to speculate. "No one knows about that day or hour, not even the angels in heaven, nor the Son, but only the Father" (Matthew 24:36). The sixth chapter of Revelation gives a strikingly detailed portrait of the end times, but no one knows when these things will occur except the Father in heaven. Not even the angels know. But Jesus said that there would be certain signs to watch for. These "signs of the times" are described in the first and last books of the New Testament, the Gospel of Matthew and the Revelation of Jesus Christ, and many accounts in between.

Taken together, these accounts give us a graphic storm warning of events yet to come and provide clearly identifiable signs of the end times. Jesus' own narrative reveals details of the fall of Jerusalem and the persecution that would follow. Matthew also records Jesus' triumphal entry into Jerusalem when the crowds hailed Him as Messiah. Matthew relates the heartbreaking events of Jesus' trials before the Sanhedrin and Pilate, the beatings, the crucifixion, and then the thrilling account of Christ's resurrection from the grave. These events are prophecies fulfilled.

But one portion of this story deserves to be examined in greater detail. When Jesus went up to Jerusalem for the Passover, He wept over the ancient city. He cried, "O Jerusalem, Jerusalem, the one who kills the prophets and stones those who are sent to her! How often I wanted to gather your children together, as a hen gathers her chicks under her wings, but you were not willing!" (Matthew 23:37 NKJV).

Jesus tried to prepare the disciples for the humiliation He was about to endure—the floggings, the cursing, the mockery, and the shameful death on a cross among thieves—but they did not understand. When He told them He must die and be raised in three days, they were mystified. Surely He was speaking in parables; no man could die and be resurrected by his own command—unless he was God.

As they passed through the city streets, the disciples with Him marveled at the size and grandeur of the temple buildings. But Jesus told them that soon the walls, the temple, and the grand palaces in

Jerusalem would be flattened and "not one stone here will be left on another" (Matthew 24:2).

The disciples were astonished that Jesus would even suggest such a thing. These men were fishermen, tax collectors, and tradesmen from the remote northern region of Galilee, but they could see that Jerusalem was a beautiful, grand city—the very city hailed by the prophets of old. How could such towering buildings ever be flattened? What army, what force, could do such a thing? The Scripture says, "As Jesus was sitting on the Mount of Olives, the disciples came to him privately. 'Tell us . . . when will this happen, and what will be the sign of your coming and of the end of the age?'" (Matthew 24:3). They wanted their understanding enlightened. When Jesus finished answering their questions, He astounded them more when He said, "The Passover is two days away—and the Son of Man will be handed over to be crucified" (Matthew 26:2). These men who had walked with Jesus must have felt a storm of uncertainty billowing. News such as this must have been impossible to imagine.

READING THE TIMES

From the beginning of my ministry, I have carefully followed the daily news on television and in print. It is not unusual for me to read the *New York Times*, the *London Times*, *Newsweek*, and *Time* magazines, along with many others. Reading these news publications gives me an insight to how people think about religion, politics, and life in general. Some headlines leave me stunned at the degeneration of mankind. But reading the times of which Jesus spoke, is the only truth that sheds light on why people do what they do and think what they think.

So, naturally, while writing this book I was drawn to revisit what Jesus had to say about "the times." He had given the disciples detailed revelations about the end of time, as recorded in Matthew 24:3–37, and the dramatic portrait of the last days of Planet Earth. Jesus revealed the fate of Jerusalem, which was carried out to the letter when it was sacked and burned by the legions of Emperor Titus in AD 70. Jesus spoke of the coming of a godless, secular society, and He spoke of the dangers of heresies conceived by false teachers who would try to pervert the message of truth Christ came to deliver. He said to His disciples, "Take heed that no one deceives you. For many will come in My name, saying, 'I am the Christ,' and will deceive many" (Matthew 24:4–5 NKJV).

The rest of the passage speaks to the troubles of our own times: "And you will hear of wars and rumors of wars. See that you are not troubled; for all these things must come to pass, but the end is not yet. For nation will rise against nation, and kingdom against kingdom. And there will be famines, pestilences, and earthquakes in various places. All these are the beginning of sorrows" (Matthew 24:6–8 NKJV).

There has never been a time in history when so many storms have come together as they have in our lifetime. The continent of Africa is devastated by turmoil, famine, and every kind of disease. South America has been in political and social chaos. Europe has gone through a time of enormous change and uncertainty, and war rages throughout the Middle East.

In America, we see continued racial division, homelessness, crime, physical and sexual abuse, and the disintegration of the traditional family. And these storms are further complicated by plagues of many kinds, including AIDS and sexually transmitted diseases. Alcoholism, drug addiction, pornography, and other dangerous behaviors are eating away at society. All of these are combined with earthquakes, physical storms, and natural disasters of many kinds across the land. But Jesus said these are merely warnings of things yet to come—the beginning of sorrows.

Jesus warned that in the end times, the price of believing in Him would be high. Mockery, laughter, persecution, even death would be common, but many would refuse to pay such a price to follow Christ. To the faithful He declared, "They will deliver you up to tribulation and kill you, and you will be hated by all nations for My name's sake. And then many will be offended, will betray one another, and will hate one another. Then many false prophets will rise up and deceive many. And because lawlessness will abound, the love of many will grow cold. But he who endures to the end shall be saved" (Matthew 24:9–13 NKJV).

I believe this is a realistic portrait of our times. We have been shocked by scandals in the church, in government, in education, and at every level of authority. We have seen graphic images of police officers beating citizens—and rebellious citizens killing police officers. We have seen top officials of government and business convicted of cheating, lying, and fraud.

We have seen moral and religious leaders, men who claim to be followers of Jesus, fall into disgrace in the eyes of God and man. And worst of all, we have seen the Gospel of Jesus Christ twisted and distorted by false teachers to accommodate the destructive morals and secular behavior of these times. Warnings from the Gospel of Matthew are not parables or myths; they are the very headlines of our day. They are the evidence of Christ's prophecy fulfilled before our eyes.

But the true church would grow through persecution, Jesus said. It would spring forth from darkness and neglect, even as the churches of Romania, Bulgaria, and East Germany have sprung full-blown from the soil of despair. "And this gospel of the kingdom will be preached in all the world as a witness to all the nations," Jesus said, "and then the end will come" (Matthew 24:14 NKJV).

The Bible tells us that the desecrations will not end for the defamers and desolators. They will defile the altar of God and slander Christ and His people. Jesus said, "Therefore when you see the 'abomination of desolation,' spoken of by Daniel the prophet, standing in the holy place (whoever reads, let him understand), then let those within Judea flee to the mountains. Let him who is on the housetop not go down to take anything out of his house. And let him who is in the field not go back to get his clothes." (Matthew 24:15–18 NKJV).

Just what the nature of that abomination will be is not certain, but it will be a desecration and sacrilege of enormous consequence that will bring about the wrath of God. Then Jesus says,

> And pray that your flight may not be in winter or on the Sabbath. For then there will be great tribulation, such as has not been since the beginning of the world until this time, no, nor ever shall be. And unless those days were shortened, no flesh would be saved; but for the elect's sake those days will be shortened. Then if anyone says to you, "Look, here is the Christ!" or "There!" do not believe it. For false christs and false prophets will rise and show great signs and wonders to deceive, if possible, even the elect. See, I have told you beforehand. Therefore if they say to you, "Look, He is in the desert!" do not go out; or "Look, He is in the inner rooms!" do not believe it. For as the lightning comes from the east and flashes to the west, so also will the coming of the Son of Man be. For wherever the carcass is, there the eagles will be gathered together. (Matthew 24:20–28 NKJV)

THE SIGNS OF HIS RETURN

When the work of the church is nearing fulfillment on earth, Christ told His followers there would be physical and visible signs that the final days of Planet Earth had come. "Immediately after the tribulation of those days," Jesus said, "the sun will be darkened, and the moon will not give its light; the stars will fall from heaven, and the powers of the heavens will be shaken" (Matthew 24:29 NKJV).

The good news for Christians who have remained faithful through trials and persecution will be bad news indeed for everyone who has denied Christ, slandered His people, and followed after false gods.

Jesus told them, "Then the sign of the Son of Man will appear in heaven, and then all the tribes of the earth will mourn, and they will see the Son of Man coming on the clouds of heaven with power and great glory. And He will send His angels with a great sound of a trumpet, and they will gather together His elect from the four winds, from one end of heaven to the other" (Matthew 24:30–31 NKJV).

This is what Jesus told His followers in vivid detail. He was not speaking figuratively; this was the unvarnished truth. Jesus illustrated this by using facts about His own creation:

> Now learn this lesson from the fig tree: When its branch has already become tender and puts forth leaves, you know that summer is near. So you also, when you see all these things, know that it is near—at the doors! Assuredly, I say to you, this generation will by no means pass away till all these things take place. Heaven and earth will pass away, but My words will by no means pass away . . . No one knows, not even the angels of heaven, but My Father only. But as the days of Noah were, so also will the coming of the Son of Man be. (Matthew 24:32–37 NKJV)

Jesus illustrated that what He had told them about the end of the age was to be considered as a statement of fact. In those stunning images we have a glimpse of what the final storm will look like in Christ's own words. Though no one had believed Noah's revelation that the Flood would come and destroy the world, so in our time the unbelieving world refuses to embrace the literal return of Jesus Christ. But He *will* come at a time known only to God.

Imagine how shocking and unsettling these words must have been to the disciples. Their hearts must have been struck with fear. Surely they did not fully understand the implications of what Jesus had told them. I suspect that John, the beloved disciple and author of the Apocalypse, came to a greater understanding during his exile on the isle of Patmos. But six decades earlier, in AD 33, such comprehension would have been utterly inconceivable. Even today, many people have difficulty believing these words.

THE SIGNS OF LIFE

For me, the importance of this stirring passage is not that it gives such vivid detail of the end times, but that it assures us of the eternal security of those who put their trust in Jesus Christ. Suffering and death are nothing to look forward to, but death is not really the issue here; Jesus was talking about the ultimate promise of eternal life with God. This is the same truth discovered by the young man who came to our crusade on youth night in his wheelchair. He could not avoid suffering and death in this life, but he came to believe the thrilling certainty of life with Christ ever after.

Every person has the responsibility to respond to the Gospel before death closes the door to life on earth. There is a door to heaven and there is a door to hell. God, in His compassionate mercy, has provided that door to heaven for us through Jesus Christ's death and resurrection. Will we accept His gracious gift of salvation by turning to Christ in repentance and faith?

Life resounds with the reality of death—it is all around us, and it is inevitable in every lifetime. The distinguished British author C. S. Lewis once wrote that war does not increase death. As tragic as armed conflict truly is, Lewis pointed out that war does not increase the amount of death in the world, because with or without war, death is universal in every generation. Everybody dies.

The Bible says, "It is appointed unto men once to die" (Hebrews 9:27 KJV). The moment we are born, we begin the process of dying. All of nature is in the process of dying, yet most people are living their lives as if they will never die. All over the world, men and women are living for today with barely a thought of eternity.

Nature teaches that everything has a beginning and an end. The day begins with a sunrise, but the sun also sets; the shadows gather, and that calendar day is crossed out, never to come again. We will never be able to repeat today. It is gone forever. The seasons come and go, the decades pass, time moves on, and we grow steadily older. One day, each of us will die. That is the promise of the natural world.

Nations rise, they flourish for a time, and then they decline. Eventually every empire comes to an end; not even the greatest can last forever. Time and tide and the ravages of sin take their toll on the noblest achievements of man. This is the decree of history and the way of life on this planet.

The Bible teaches that the world system as we know it shall come to a close. We read in 1 John 2:17, "The world and its desires pass away." And in 2 Peter 3:10, we read, "But the day of the Lord will come like a thief. The heavens will disappear with a roar; the elements will be destroyed by fire, and the earth and everything in it will be laid bare."

You may ask, then, why are the words of Jesus Christ good news for a world in crisis? Because He gives us the Gospel of hope—the Good News that God loves us. He is *the* God of mercy. He provides grace that is greater than the sin of mankind. If we will only confess our sin, forsake our sin, accept His forgiveness, and walk with Him by faith, we can know the joy of His presence, even in the midst of life's storms.

SIGNS OF THE END

While the message of Christ promises hope in troubled times, it also proclaims that the world's days are numbered. Every cemetery testifies that this is true. The Scriptures tell us that life is only a vapor that appears for a moment and then vanishes. Life is like the grass that withers and the flowers that fade. The words of the prophet Isaiah ring in triumph, foreshadowing the coming of Christ:

But those who wait on the LORD
Shall renew their strength;
They shall mount up with wings like eagles,
They shall run and not be weary,
They shall walk and not faint. (Isaiah 40:31 NKJV)

Someday soon the end will come. That doesn't mean an end to life, but the end of a world that has been dominated by greed, evil, and injustice. The Bible speaks often, and in graphic detail, about the end of the world. God's Word warns man of what is coming and calls man to be reconciled to Him. "Repent, then, and turn to God, so that your sins may be wiped out, that times of refreshing may come from the Lord, and that he may send the Christ, who has been appointed for you—even Jesus. He must remain in heaven until the time comes for God to restore everything, as he promised long ago through his holy prophets" (Acts 3:19–21).

The Revelation of Jesus Christ and His teachings in the Gospel of Matthew tell us that the present world system will pass away and come to a dramatic end. These passages also tell us that Jesus Christ will come again and set up His kingdom of righteousness and social justice where evil and death will no longer exist. Jesus Himself promised the end of the present world system and the establishment of a new order—the kingdom of God.

Jesus used images that were dramatic and compelling, but He did not engage in fantasy. He told His followers, "I am the way and *the truth* and the life. No one comes to the Father except through me" (John 14:6, emphasis added). He is truth and veracity personified. Jesus indicated that when certain things come to pass, we can be assured that the end is near. He indicated that only those who have spiritual illumination and discernment from the Holy Spirit can hope to believe the facts of history and the hope of the future.

The Bible plainly indicates that certain conditions will prevail just before the end. For example, the prophet Daniel said, "Until the time of the end; many shall run to and fro, and knowledge shall increase" (Daniel 12:4 NKJV). Today there is more knowledge about everything than at any other time in history. We have more scientists and engineers today than ever before. Our high schools, colleges, and universities turn out millions of graduates every year. The information highway seems endless.

While our young people are gaining knowledge, they are not always acquiring wisdom to use that knowledge. In every area of life people are floundering, suffering from neuroses and psychological problems on a scale we have never known before. Our heads are filled with knowledge, but we are confused, bewildered, frustrated, and without moral moorings.

SIGNS OF POWER WITHOUT PEACE

Another condition that the Bible says will be present at the end of the world system is power without peace. Joining the war on terror are many civil wars taking place all over the world, not to exclude the fact that the world is still very much under the threat of nuclear war.

As we watched the stunning capture of Saddam Hussein after 9/11, many remember in 1992 when the United Nations battled with the Iraqi dictator to isolate and destroy his nuclear capabilities. Never would we have imagined his demise ten years later, only for other dictators to take up the charge. With the proliferation of nuclear arms lying in wait, it is not hard to imagine that somebody could push the wrong button. In a matter of seconds, our world could be plunged into a third world war.

Though the United Nations attempts to mediate hostilities in dozens of nations, the world is still an armed camp. Billions of dollars, rubles, marks, and euros are spent for weapons that quickly become obsolete or are replaced with newer ones that cost even more. The United States alone spends hundreds of billions of dollars on armaments. In short, the atmosphere of the world is still threatening. While the world cries, "Peace, peace," there is no peace (Jeremiah 6:14).

People often ask, "Why is there so little peace in the world when we have such unprecedented knowledge and unlimited potential?" The answer is clear: we are trying to build a peaceful world, but there is no peace within people's hearts. "'There is no peace,' says my God, 'for the wicked'" (Isaiah 57:21). Jesus spoke of peace to His disciples as He warned them of the coming storm: "In this world you will have trouble. But take heart! I have overcome the world" (John 16:33). He told them that He is the source of peace: "I have told you these things, so that *in me* you may have peace" (John 16:33; emphasis added). So the Bible assures us that we cannot build a new world on the unregenerate hearts of people. The new world will only come about when Jesus Christ, King of kings and Lord of lords, reigns supreme.

Many of us are familiar with these memorable words from Handel's famous oratorio, *Messiah*, taken from the writings of the prophet Isaiah:

For unto us a Child is born,
Unto us a Son is given;
And the government will be upon His shoulder.
And His name will be called
Wonderful, Counselor, Mighty God,
Everlasting Father, Prince of Peace.
Of the increase of His government and peace
There will be no end,
Upon the throne of David and over His kingdom,
To order it and establish it with judgment and justice
From that time forward, even forever.
The zeal of the Lord of hosts will perform this. (Isaiah 9:6–7 NKJV)

These words are the best promise of peace and security in a world of tension and turmoil. The Bible says that the King of kings is the hope of every man, woman, and child of every tribe and nation.

The signs of insecurity and the shouts of revolution heard around the world are perhaps the death rattle of an era in civilization—perhaps they signal the end of civilization as we have known it. Many believe that God is silent, even perhaps that He is unmoved by the degrading acts of men, but Scripture promises that when the fullness of time comes, He will act dramatically. He will send His Son, Jesus Christ, back to earth "to rescue us from the present evil age" (Galatians 1:4). He is the Lord of history; He is the Lord of the future; and most important for those living now . . . He is Lord today. Where do you stand now with the One you will someday bow to as Judge or Savior?

The storms of change in the world are no surprise to God; nothing we see in the headlines takes Him by surprise. Events are moving rapidly toward a climax, but it will be according to God's timing. The most victorious headline one day will read:

My Son Has Returned as the Rightful Ruler of the World

Before that time comes, however, God wants to first rule in our hearts.

SIGNS OF PEACE IN OUR HEARTS

The apostle Paul told the church at Colosse, "Let the peace of Christ rule in your hearts" (Colossians 3:15). The Bible says that sin shall not have dominion over us if Jesus Christ is in our hearts as Lord and Master. Either self will reign in our lives, or Jesus Christ will reign. "No one can serve two masters," Jesus said (Matthew 6:24). The Bible challenges us, "Choose for yourselves this day whom you will serve" (Joshua 24:15 NKJV).

Solomon wrote in the Proverbs, "There is a way that seems right to a man, but in the end it leads to death" (Proverbs 14:12). If you want to have peace with God and find security for these times of trouble, you must answer one very important question: *who is the ruler of your life*? Are you trying to be the master of your own fate? Are you trying to be the captain of your own soul? Do you believe you can navigate life's storms without the Master at the helm? Is the kingdom of God even within you?

Jesus Christ can come into your heart right now if you will turn from your sins and receive Him as Savior. He loves you. He knows you by name, and He wants to forgive you. You can enter the new kingdom, the new world that will be born under His leadership when He returns. There is no doubt that the world to come will be a theocracy, but it will be a joyous, exciting, incredibly beautiful place with Jesus Christ in complete and loving control. When we all reach the end of our earthly journey, we will have just begun. Eternity hangs in the balance.

The bad news is that men at their best fall short of God's standard. Left unchecked, it leads to chaos and destruction. The good news, however, is that God is standing by to pick us up and set us on a path that leads to forgiveness and eternal fellowship with Him. But this can only happen when we set aside our plans and live in total obedience to Him. For He alone is the Keeper of the signs of the times.

4

A CHANGING LANDSCAPE

The city had no need of the sun or of the moon
to shine in it, for the glory of God illuminated it.
—REVELATION 21:23 NKJV

O ne of the most world-changing events in my lifetime was the collapse of Communism in Eastern Europe and the re-formation of the once-powerful Soviet Union. The Berlin Wall that symbolized a dividing line between Christian and anti-Christian beliefs painted a picture of the moral and philosophical dilemma in the latter years of the twentieth century.

The suddenness of these changes baffled scholars, Soviet observers, diplomats, and even the CIA. In a matter of days, our history books, maps, encyclopedias, and textbooks were invalidated. After August 1989, the world was no longer the same.

In my travels throughout Eastern Europe and the Baltic States, I saw aspects of the trend toward change that had been developing for some time, though obscure to many. While no one could have predicted precisely how the changes in Russia, East Germany, Romania, and the other Communist countries would come about or when they would occur, I sensed along with many others, a yearning for change in people's hearts.

Tensions were high in Europe during my first crusade in Berlin in 1954. During those emotional years following the end of World War II, the Cold War was born, but the term *Cold War* hardly expressed the deep uncertainty and fear felt by most Europeans at that time.

When I met the people of Berlin, I could feel their anxiety. Consequently, I was not surprised when the Berlin Wall was erected in 1961. The hostility between the democrats in the West and the Communists in the East was just too intense. Considering the nature and consequences of their ruthless doctrines, it was inevitable that the Soviets and East Germans would eventually have to lock democracy out.

Before the wall went up, disagreement and discord between the United States and the Soviet Union—and military adventures such as the American-sponsored Bay of Pigs invasion in Cuba in April 1961—seemed to bring the world to the threshold of war. While Soviet premier Nikita Khrushchev and president John Kennedy stood toe-to-toe, each daring the other to blink, thousands of East Germans were fleeing into West Berlin. The mass exodus was an embarrassment and provoked the Communists to lock their doors. In August of that year, Khrushchev ordered the Germans to build the wall.

The Berlin Wall was more than just concrete and barbed wire; it was a grim metaphor of mankind's capacity for hatred, stretching twenty-nine miles through the heart of the German capital and another seventy-five miles around the city, encompassing the entire frontier. Guard stations with lookout towers and machine-gun posts along its length monitored no-man's-land between East and West, making West Berlin more like a prison camp than a civilized European city. For nearly three decades, hundreds of men, women, and children were gunned down by Communist guards as they tried to cross that hostile killing field to freedom.

In the shadow of president Ronald Reagan's famous 1987 "tear down this wall" speech, the world watched with relief and fascination when the wall finally came down in 1989. It was precipitated by the flight of more than 120,000 East Germans into Hungary and then across the border into Austria. Once more, the flight from Communism was an enormous embarrassment to the East German government. Tens of thousands of skilled workers fled, confirming the disappointment and unhappiness of life under the Communist regime. Ultimately, the humiliation was too much for the East German government to handle, and their repressive attempts were unsuccessful in the face of a sudden groundswell of resistance.

The world watched as the Berlin Wall came down. I suspect a large part of shock expressed by the world was not because the hideous wall had at last fallen, but because the emotional and political barriers to peace were being taken away, stone by stone. When the announcement came that the Wall would no longer serve as a barrier between East and West, it was the beginning of the incredible cycle of events that ultimately led to the reunification of the two Germanys in 1990.

Erich Honecker, a German Communist credited with building the Berlin Wall, was driven into exile in the Soviet Union. He had invited Mikhail Gorbachev to Berlin in October 1989 to join in the celebration of the fortieth anniversary of the founding of Communist East Germany. But the people in the streets of Berlin, Dresden, and Leipzig demanded reforms and threatened to march against Gorbachev. The government spread rumors of Tiananmen Square–type repression if the people did not remain calm. In reality, the government no longer had the muscle to support such threats. The Soviets refused to help them, and ultimately Honecker, the last hard-liner, was overthrown.

CHANGING OF THE GUARD

I vividly remember our rally in 1960 in Berlin, just one year before the wall went up. More than one hundred thousand people attended our weeklong crusade. We saw a desire for openness and a concerted effort to communicate between the different organizations and churches in Germany at that time, but even so, the more extravagant hopes and ambitions of the people were often stifled. I could see then that the political divisions in Germany and Eastern Europe were growing deeper and more troubled.

Since 1945, dialogue between people, nations, and the churches of East and West was severely restricted. During our crusades, we found communications difficult, and widespread cooperation was sometimes difficult to obtain. But that didn't stop us. From 1954 to 1990, I was privileged to hold eight crusades and rallies in Germany. Each time, we sensed the fear and worry in the people, combined with their hunger for truth and meaning in their lives.

During those thirty-six years, God allowed me to address more than a million people in ten East and West German cities, including three crusades in Berlin. In addition, from 1977 to 1990 we held meetings in every Eastern Bloc country except Bulgaria and Albania.

One of our most pleasant surprises was the 1954 meeting in Berlin, when eighty thousand people came to hear the Gospel— many from the Eastern Zone. They didn't know much about me or my ministry at that time. They had read stories in the newspapers about the success of the London Crusade, and they came perhaps out of curiosity. When the invitation for people to receive Christ was presented, it looked as if the whole audience was coming forward. The Lord blessed the preaching of His Word in that place, and for weeks after, we received more than sixteen thousand letters—an indication of deep spiritual hunger. From there we went across Europe and saw God's hand move in the hearts of people longing for truth—God's truth.

EXCHANGING FEAR FOR HOPE

During a trip to Berlin in 1990, I met privately with the leaders of the East and West German republics and asked about the possibility of holding an all-Germany crusade in 1992. We were greeted enthusiastically by representatives of the German Evangelical Alliances from East and West. Two Protestant bishops—Dr. Martin Kruse from West Berlin and Dr. Gottfried Forck from East Berlin—along with many others, came to offer support and prayer.

These leaders agreed that the German people were desperate for the Good News. They said that on both sides of the ideological wall that still separated the two Germanys, men and women were living between fear and hope, and they pleaded for us to come to Germany, not in 1992, but right then in 1990.

So we did. We hastily changed our itineraries, and on March 10, 1990, we set up our microphones at the Platz der Republik, the great open area in front of the Reichstag, the former parliament building next to the Brandenburg Gate. At that historic site, where the evil ambitions of the Third Reich were born, where Nazis once paraded by torchlight, marshaling ethnic bitterness and hatred, we preached the Good News of the Gospel of the Lord Jesus Christ, and many exchanged fear for hope as they responded to the invitation to let Jesus Christ break down the wall of sin that separated them from God.

In the very place where the Nazis had promised the German people a thousand-year regime of military power and awful judgment, I had the glorious privilege of telling them about God's forgiveness and love. It was a message for a people struggling between the failures of history and ideology and their hopes for peace and security.

When I consider the changes that have occurred in the last few decades of my life, I marvel at the hand of God in world affairs. The Bible says,

The kings of the earth take their stand and the rulers gather together against the LORD and against his Anointed One. "Let us break their chains," they say, "and throw off their fetters." The One enthroned in heaven laughs; the Lord scoffs at them. Then he rebukes them in his anger and terrifies them in his wrath, saying, "I have installed my King on Zion, my holy hill." (Psalm 2:2–6)

The Scriptures declare, "Look at the nations and watch—and be utterly amazed. For I am going to do something in your days that you would not believe, even if you were told" (Habakkuk 1:5). The mighty claims of the Lord give us a hint of the power that God will unleash at the close of the age. The events that have transpired on the continent of Europe since the summer of 1989 help us to understand just how awesome God's plans for the world really are.

EXCHANGING HOSTILITY FOR PEACE

The very place I stood to address the German people on that afternoon in March 1990 was only yards away from a shattered section of the Berlin Wall where workers with saws and torches were ripping out the bars that supported the barriers. I told the crowd that the world was watching them by satellite and that Christians everywhere were praying for them. By a show of hands, I learned that more than half of the fifteen thousand to seventeen thousand people who had come to brave the wind and rain were from East Germany.

"How can you find meaning and happiness in your life?" I asked. "How can you become free of guilt? What will happen after death?"

The crowd grew quiet as I spoke of their hopes and fears. They listened attentively and hopefully. A sense of peace filled the air. Smiles shined on faces once sullen and drawn.

When I held a press conference, reporters asked many questions of their own, including this one: "Does Billy Graham regard the dismantling of the Iron Curtain as an answer to prayer?"

Without hesitation, I said, "Yes! Christians in the East and the West have been praying for decades for this day. The prospect of liberation, reunification, and the freedom to worship God has made this the happiest hour for Germany.

"We can never thank God enough for what has happened here," I continued, "but there is another dangerous storm looming on Germany's horizon: the loss of moral and spiritual values. Pornography, prostitution, drugs, violence, and other signs of moral decay are already in evidence throughout West Germany, and now they threaten the East as never before."

I recalled speaking at the wall a day or two earlier to a group of wide-eyed East Germans who told me they were both hopeful and frightened. They were hopeful that peace and freedom would improve their way of life, but they were frightened by the scenes of greed and materialism they saw in the West. They said they would rather remain behind the wall, in poverty and bondage to Communism, than to discover that "freedom" was nothing more than moral decadence, corruption, sin, violence, and greed that characterize much of the West today. I thought those were incredibly wise and stirring sentiments from people who had already suffered so much.

EXCHANGING OPPRESSION FOR REVIVAL

Throughout my ministry, I preached more often in Germany than in any other non-English-speaking country. My prayer was that the German people would not be cheated by hedonism and materialism. Such things cannot satisfy the longings of the soul—only God can do that.

While in Berlin, we held a rally for a thousand church workers in the famous Gethsemane Church in the Eastern sector. Men and women of every class and vocation gathered to encourage one another, to seek God's blessings, and to protect the dissidents who dared speak out against the repressive Communist regime.

I read to them from the books of Isaiah and Ephesians and told them of my belief that God had given them an opportunity to spark revival in Germany. "This divided city longs for a church that is a living answer to the message of Christ," I said. "Let us look at its people with mercy and love. Let us learn to pray together, no matter what political background we come from."

Many great men of faith were born on German soil. Faith-believing teachers and preachers lived and taught in this country. Martin Luther launched the Protestant Reformation at Wittenberg. With deep conviction I said to them, "I believe that a strong revival can spring from Germany . . . I pray Germany does not miss the chance."

There was, indeed, a sense of renewal and revival in that church. When Jürgen Wohlrabe, president of the West Berlin Parliament, addressed our gathering, he said, "Your words touch hearts because you convey the message which was given to us two thousand years ago and which we have forgotten or ignored. You point out to your audiences that today the words of the Gospel are as valid as ever."

Referring to the change in political climate, the statesman said, "Our personal and social life is not determined by material values. We should find orientation and direction for our lives in the Christian faith and in our personal responsibility."

Throughout our time there, we saw the hand of God at work in Berlin. A taxi driver who carried people to the various events told us he wasn't interested in our message, but as he heard my remarks from the loudspeakers, and as he saw the genuine love and brotherhood in the faces of our workers and helpers, he realized that what we had spoken about was what he needed.

A young Hungarian told us his life had been changed a year

earlier when I spoke at the People's Stadium in Budapest. Another man told how he had been arrested at the border while en route to our crusade in 1960. Two soldiers of the East German People's Army made a special trip to fellowship with other Christians.

There were many such stories. One dear lady reached out to me as I was arriving for the service and handed me her card indicating that she had accepted Jesus Christ. She had completed the card with the only marker she had, her lipstick.

Through the years I gained a deep sense of compassion and affection for the people of Eastern Europe. It was humbling to have shared in their hopes, their joys, and their sorrows.

CHANGING VENUES

Of the many opportunities I have had to preach in the East, the chance to speak from the pulpit of the Moscow Baptist Church in May 1982 stands out as a personal highlight and an answer to years of prayer. In those days, no one dared to dream of the changes that would take place. During the spring of that year, there were hotly debated political battles over nuclear proliferation and other volatile issues. So when I went to Moscow to preach and deliver an address at a religious conference on the subject of peace, many Westerners apparently thought I had lost my mind, and they said so.

Leaders at the conference represented most of the major religions of the world, and they were considering a wide variety of issues. The possibility of a nuclear holocaust had been weighing heavy on my heart, and since war is primarily a moral and spiritual issue, I felt the need to speak about it and offer a Christian perspective. The world press was generally divided. I was misquoted on occasion, which led some Christians to scold me or call me naive. Others were more sympathetic and seemed to have a better understanding of the opportunity for the Gospel message.

CHANGING RUSSIAN HEARTS

As I look back, I believe those remarks were instrumental in opening the eyes of many Eastern Europeans to the Good News of Jesus Christ and the message of peace He offered. On my many trips to the Soviet Union, Hungary, Czechoslovakia, Poland, and Germany, people told me that my Moscow address made a profound impact on their lives. In part, I stated:

> The whole human race sits under a nuclear sword of Damocles, not knowing when someone will push the button or give the order that will destroy much of the planet. The possibility of nuclear war, therefore, is not merely a political issue. . . .
>
> The nuclear arms race is primarily a moral and spiritual issue that must concern us all. I am convinced that political answers alone will not suffice, but that it is now time for us to urge the world to turn to spiritual solutions.

Other religious figures were speaking out about nuclear annihilation, calling on humanity to make a moral about-face. But, I continued,

> The question that confronts us is, how can this happen?
>
> Man has far exceeded his moral ability to control the results of his technology. Man himself must be changed. The Bible teaches that this is possible through spiritual renewal. Jesus Christ taught that man can and must have a spiritual rebirth.
>
> I am convinced one of the most vivid and tragic signs of man's rebellion against God's order in our present generation is the possibility of a nuclear war. I include here the whole scope of modern weapons capable of destroying life—conventional, biochemical, and nuclear weapons. I know that the issue of legitimate national defense is complex. I am not a pacifist, nor am I for unilateral dis-

armament. Police and military forces are unfortunately necessary as long as man's nature remains the way it is. But the unchecked production of weapons of mass destruction by the nations of the world is a mindless fever which threatens to consume much of our world and destroy the sacred gift of life.

From a Christian perspective, therefore, the possibility of a nuclear war originates in the greed and covetousness of the human heart. The tendency toward sin is passed on from generation to generation. Therefore, Jesus predicted that there would be wars and rumors of wars till the end of the age. The psalmist said, "In sin did my mother conceive me" [Psalm 51:5 KJV]. Thus, there is a tragic and terrible flaw in human nature that must be recognized and dealt with.

The word *peace* is used in the Bible in three main ways.

First, there is spiritual peace. This is peace between man and God.

Second, there is psychological peace, or peace within ourselves.

Third, there is relational peace, or peace among men.

Sin, the Bible says, has destroyed or seriously affected all three of these dimensions of peace. When man was created, he was at peace with God, with himself, and with his fellow humans. But when he rebelled against God, his fellowship with God was broken. He was no longer at peace with himself. And he was no longer at peace with others.

Can these dimensions of peace ever be restored? The Bible says yes. It tells us man alone cannot do what is necessary to heal the brokenness in his relationships—but God can, and has.

The Bible teaches that Jesus Christ [is] God's unique Son, sent into the world to take away our sins by His death on the cross, therefore making it possible for us to be at peace—at peace with God, at peace within ourselves, and at peace with each other. That is why Jesus Christ is central to the Christian faith. By His resurrection from the dead, Christ showed once and for all that God is for life, not death.

The Bible states, "For the wages of sin is death, but the gift of God is eternal life in Christ Jesus our Lord" [Romans 6:23]. The ultimate sign of man's alienation is death; the ultimate sign of God's reconciling love is life.

Throughout all Christendom you will notice there is one symbol common to all believers—the cross. We believe it was on the cross that the certainty of lasting peace in all of its dimensions has been made.

The Bible says about Christ that "God was pleased to have all his fullness dwell in him, and through him to reconcile to himself all things . . . by making peace through his blood, shed on the cross" [Colossians 1:19–20]. The Bible again says, "For he himself is our peace, who has made the two one and has destroyed the barrier, the dividing wall of hostility. . . . He came and preached peace to you who were far away and peace to those who were near" [Ephesians 2:14, 17].

The Christian looks forward to the time when peace will reign over all creation. Christians all over the world pray the prayer Jesus taught His disciples: "Thy kingdom come. Thy will be done in earth, as it is in heaven" [Matthew 6:10 KJV]. Only then will the spiritual problem of the human race be fully solved.

The Bible teaches that there will be a universal judgment. Christ will come again to judge the living and the dead [1 Peter 4:5]. Then the kingdom of God will be established, and God will intervene to make all things new. That is our great hope [and confidence] for the future.

But in the meantime God is already at work. The kingdom of God is not only a future hope but a present reality. Wherever men and women turn to God in repentance and faith and then seek to do His will on earth as it is done in heaven, there the kingdom of God is seen.

CHANGING KINGDOMS

If I were preparing this address over again, I would probably expand this point to say that those who are members of God's kingdom live in an alien world as pilgrims and strangers. The kingdom is "already" present in the lives of the believers who glorify Him by word and deed in the church and in society. But the world is "not yet" the kingdom, for, as we have already seen, the world is under the rule and reign of the prince of this world—Satan. Nevertheless, King Jesus has conquered Satan, and all those who have accepted Christ as Savior and Lord have been reconciled to God. Is Christ the King of your life?

Jesus dwells within the believer through His Holy Spirit. The crucified and risen King has received all authority, and His indwelling Spirit is greater than Satan and his demon powers. "The one who is in you is greater than the one who is in the world" (1 John 4:4). Believers alone have been "rescued . . . from the dominion of darkness and brought . . . into the kingdom of the Son he loves, in whom we have redemption, the forgiveness of sins" (Colossians 1:13–14).

It is true that believers bear fruit in every good work upon the earth, but believers cannot change the world into the kingdom. Only the return of the King to rule upon the earth can result in His will being done upon earth as it is in heaven. With this inward hope and this indwelling power of the kingdom to come, is it any wonder that Christians strive to extend the kingdom in the hearts of people and work toward peace, provided through the power of the Gospel?

God reigns supreme over the world, leading it providentially toward the day of the kingdom to come (Acts 1:6–7). This is the day of grace for the world. Humanity now lives between the times of Christ's ascension to the Father and His return "on the clouds of the sky, with power and great glory" (Matthew 24:30).

The signs of the kingdom are not political, although they may have political implications. Jesus' signs were given to lead people to faith, not to political reform. Jesus, by His Spirit, draws sinners to the cross, leading men and women to reconciliation with God, which then produces peace in the hearts of those who believe in Him.

FLAMES OF CHANGE

The result of mankind being reconciled to God has always been my motivation to go anywhere to preach this great Gospel message. When I was invited to hold other crusades across Europe in 1982, I had the opportunity to meet with various political and religious leaders. Preaching from Martin Luther's pulpit in the City Church of Wittenberg, where Luther posted his Ninety-Five Theses in 1517 and sparked the Protestant Reformation, was particularly memorable. My sermon cited Luther's writings and teachings based upon God's Word. I sensed a bond of friendship with the East Germans— especially those in Wittenberg. Many accepted Christ upon hearing the Gospel clearly proclaimed.

Later I went on to Dresden, where I had been asked to preach in the great Church of the Cross, which had been gutted by the bombings of World War II and restored in subsequent years. The church was filled with more than seven thousand people. I was startled at how many young faces there were in the crowd. Someone estimated that 85 percent of the audience was thirty years of age or younger. At the invitation, thousands raised their hands indicating their desire to receive Christ.

Still today, I hear of people who attended these meetings and became the spark that ignited the flames of change in that part of Europe. Some were evangelical activists who met at Gethsemane Church; others formed prayer vigils fostering the hope of freedom through Christ in the East. These were God's people seeking His righteousness and preparing for His return.

When I put this into perspective in light of Scripture, my heart is warmed by the flames of change; for as Jesus said, "as the lightning comes from the east and flashes to the west, so also will the coming of the Son of Man be" (Matthew 24:27 NKJV). Some glorious day He will break through the clouds. John reported that he saw "heaven opened, and behold, a white horse. And He who sat on him was called Faithful and True. . . . His eyes were like a flame of fire, and on His head were many crowns . . . and His name is called The Word of God" (Revelation 19:11–13 NKJV).

It is the Word of God that breaks through the storm clouds of life that engulf us. The light of God's presence in our lives is a purifying flame that will draw us near to Him. We don't have to fear the sound of hoofbeats if we fasten our eyes to the One who holds the reins.

5

INSIDE THE
APOCALYPSE

*Blessed is he who reads and those who hear the words of this prophecy,
and keep those things which are written in it; for the time is near.*
—REVELATION 1:3 NKJV

The book of Revelation has been more neglected, misunderstood, and misinterpreted than any other book in the Bible. In his treatise on Revelation, biblical scholar William Barclay wrote, "The Revelation is notoriously the most difficult and bewildering book in the New Testament; but doubtless, too, we shall find it infinitely worthwhile to wrestle with it until it gives us its blessing and opens its riches to us."

For centuries, the mysterious images in John's book were considered by many too enigmatic and surreal to be understood. But it is surprising how political events of the past few years—from the collapse of the Soviet Union, to the Persian Gulf War, to 9/11, leading to the War on Terror—have shed a new and penetrating light on these seemingly cryptic messages; so today they seem much less fantastic and bewildering than they once did.

Many of the passages I used to think were symbolic I now see as evidence of the approaching storm. The revelations to John have not often been taught or preached in some of our churches because they seemed too esoteric and obscure for most people. But God promises a great blessing to those who will read it and heed its warnings.

We all have traveled the highway of life heeding various warnings and cautions. When we approach an intersection and see a yellow light, we had better prepare to stop to prevent a collision with other travelers. When the Department of Transportation posts signs advising of closed lanes ahead, we know to merge so that we don't run out of pavement. While we may be frustrated to slow our momentum, most people are grateful for advanced warnings because it serves notice, for our good, that there is potential danger ahead. The signs are of no use if we do not look at them, acknowledge them, and adjust our course in response to them. Since the majority of people agree that this is necessary to maintain safety, it is astonishing that many of the same people resent, and disregard, the warning signals from heaven. They are posted inside heaven's atlas—the Bible. God has not failed in posting warnings to mankind to consider what is up ahead. In mercy and grace, He has held back His hand of judgment on a wicked world so that many might forsake sin and follow the Savior. So the warning flashes: Prepare to Meet God.

I recall reading a quote in the newspaper by one of the great literary and political leaders of the day. He used the expression "The time is near" to describe events unfolding at breakneck speed. You may ask, "Near to what?" Near to the fulfillment of the prophecy of the Revelation.

What is this great and mysterious revelation? The events leading up to the glorious return of Jesus Christ to this earth, His final judgment of sin, and the beginning of eternity. The questions for us are, where will we spend eternity? How will we get there? What are the signs we should be looking for?

During my study of the Scripture, spanning more than seventy years now, I have often been intrigued, inspired, and informed by the words of this dramatic book written by the apostle John on the island of Patmos, under divine inspiration of the Holy Spirit. The warning signs are unmistakable. Sitting in my study at home in North Carolina, I have read literally thousands of pages from articles and scholarly works on the book of Revelation. In my personal devotions, I have thoroughly immersed myself in the sound and fury of John's language, listening to the voice of God speaking through him. As I consider all that I have learned about this work—its sinister images, its warnings, and the structure of the Revelation—I am constantly humbled by it.

Many great minds over the centuries have grappled with the meaning of John's visions, but in light of the storm I am convinced is coming, I feel compelled to take another look to discover how it relates to the troubled times in which we live. Perhaps it is because I, like John, am growing older and have a deeper perspective on the events taking place, but there is something ominous in the air, and I am intrigued by both the horror and hope of what lies just ahead.

It isn't always easy to understand ancient literature written from someone else's visions and dreams. But in the case of the Holy Scriptures, we have the assurance that God will open our understanding so that we can be comforted by His promises of a better life to come, or be convicted by its truth and surrender our sinful hearts in repentance. The study of this wonderful and challenging book instructs us not only about the storms to come, but how to endure and come through them with great victory.

These biblical storm clouds seem to create a canopy of haze over us. But just as morning fog can move quickly out of the valleys, so are the storm clouds moving swiftly overhead with each passing day. We find such a metaphor in the word *Apocalypse*, a Greek word combining the verb *calypto* ("to veil," "to cover," or "to conceal") and the preposition *apo* ("from"). Thus, *Apocalypse* means "to remove the veil," "to uncover," "to reveal," and "to make clear." John's storm warnings were clear to Christians in the first century, and they should be even clearer in today's climate.

INSIDE THE VISION

Some years ago, in the Louvre Museum in Paris, I stood at arm's length from a large impressionistic painting by Renoir. Globs of paint seemed splattered incoherently across the canvas. I was not impressed. "What in the world is that?" I wondered aloud. Ruth said, "Stand back, Bill, and you will see it." I had been standing too close to the masterpiece, and each individual detail, each patch of color, each brushstroke kept me from seeing the effect of the canvas as a whole. I was bogged down in the details. But when I stepped back across the hall, the mystery disappeared, and the beautiful image created by the artist was clearly visible.

I suspect that too many of us have examined the book of Revelation in the same manner, turning this great masterpiece into a series of detailed images and brushstrokes. As a result, we cannot see the grand design of the prophet's vision, and we may also miss the urgency of his warnings.

We cannot afford to lose sight of the big picture. While John's visions often refer to an unseen time and to future events, they are nevertheless real.

Though I have never been banished to a rocky island ten miles long and six miles wide, as the apostle John was, I understand the texture of John's world as bearer of an earthshaking message from heaven. I sense his passion and, yes, compelling desire to obediently proclaim the truth of God's inspired Word.

In contrast to John's exile, I have experienced the sounds of the city and have watched men and women scurry about amid activity and noise. Their lives are seldom quiet enough to hear the sound of alarm. How often do we see drivers ignoring the sirens of emergency vehicles trying to reach those in trouble? I have stood on street corners in New York, Paris, London, and Tokyo, and witnessed the hopelessness, fear, and boredom on the faces of people passing by. On the surface, it would seem that John and I have almost nothing in common. Yet there are times I can almost hear the warnings he heard and wrote about. They compel me to sound the alarm and call people to heed the warnings from the pages of Scripture—blaring sirens from heaven itself.

Before exploring the imagery of the Revelation, let's consider the writer himself. Who was this wizened old man John? Poet, prophet, or pastor? What drove him to write a letter almost two thousand years ago that still boggles the minds of believers and unbelievers alike? The debate about the identity of the author of Revelation has raged over the centuries. But the earliest Christian tradition, preserved by Justin Martyr, Clement, Origen, Irenaeus, Eusebius, Jerome, and other ancient scholars, makes it clear that the author of the Revelation was, in fact, John the apostle, the last living disciple who had known Jesus in the flesh. Modern prophecy scholars—from Dr. John Walvoord to Bishop Robinson—agree with their findings, and so do I.

Most of the small band of men who had traveled with and learned from Jesus for three years were dead—having been martyred for their faith in the risen Christ.

Many have suggested that John's long life, which included the burden of receiving and documenting the mysterious revelations, may actually have been a far greater price for John to pay than dying a martyr's death. John was often called the disciple whom Jesus loved (John 21:20). The great missionary Amy Carmichael wrote that John the beloved disciple "was entrusted [with] the long martyrdom of life."

INSIDE A PRISON CAVE

Can you imagine the storm that ignited John's last years on that lonely island? Surely the entire revelation he received from heaven was like a lightning bolt that struck without warning. That wrinkled old man whose hand trembled as he scratched out countless Greek letters onto scraps of parchment in his prison cave was once a youthful Galilean fisherman who dropped his nets and, filled with hope, followed after Jesus to become a fisher of men. Years later, as an exiled old man, squinting by candlelight at his growing manuscript, he bears little resemblance to the youth who once stood with Jesus on the Mount of Transfiguration. He hardly remembers the time when, flushed with the aura of Christ's miracles and power, he asked for a prominent seat next to Jesus when He set up His kingdom in Jerusalem (Mark 10:35–45). Now he was being struck by the lightning storm of divine revelation.

The aged visionary, who sprawled exhausted on the rough-hewn table in his cell, once stared at a wooden cross upon which his Master hung helplessly alone. Numb with sorrow and inner despair, John saw his dreams die that day when Jesus drew his last breath. John's aching body, now roused by surly guards to begin another day of hard labor, had once stood in the empty tomb of Jesus and experienced hope born again in him!

After breakfasting on a bowl of gruel, John was roughly herded from the prison cave and marched by Roman guards up the steep, winding trail to the quarries. Perhaps John stashed his pile of parchment pages in a secret hollow beneath his straw mat. One day those pages would be smuggled off the island. One day Christian brothers would copy faithfully what John wrote and deliver the Revelation of Jesus Christ to the churches of Asia. And from those churches, the Apocalypse of John would spread around the world and through the centuries to you and to me.

Controversy would grow! Large church gatherings would be held to test Revelation's place in the growing body of sacred Christian writings. Questions would be raised: Is this vision inspired? Is it authoritative? Is it trustworthy? How is it to be interpreted? Some would rise to condemn John's vision to the fire. Others would rise to speak on its behalf. But when the dust settled, the words written by John in his damp cell would be given an esteemed place in the canon of Scripture. In that act, they would be recognized forever as a word not limited in time and space, not limited by language or culture, but the word "God-breathed . . . useful for teaching, rebuking, correcting and training in righteousness, so that the man [and woman] of God may be thoroughly equipped for every good work" (2 Timothy 3:16–17).

It is ironic how the debate about the Revelation has boiled throughout the centuries like a continual rumble of thunder. Even more ironic is that the angelic voice anticipated this controversy when speaking to John on Patmos. Twice at the end of Revelation John recorded the voice as saying, "Write this down, for these words are trustworthy and true" (Revelation 21:5); and again, "The angel said to me, 'These words are trustworthy and true. The Lord, the God of the spirits of the prophets, sent his angel to show his servants the things that must soon take place'" (Revelation 22:6).

INSIDE THE VEIL

This faithful apostle wrote, "I, John, your brother and companion in the suffering and kingdom and patient endurance that are ours in Jesus, was on the island of Patmos *because of* the word of God and the testimony of Jesus" (Revelation 1:9; emphasis added).

It is one thing to believe that John's words are "trustworthy and true," but it is another thing to understand their full meaning. There are word pictures in Revelation that leave me breathless with their beauty, and others more difficult to fully grasp. But that is no cause to neglect the study of this marvelous *Master piece*.

We need to know several important things about John. First, he was an apocalyptist. That is, he wrote Revelation in a certain type of poetic language known as *apocalyptic language.* An apocalyptic writer—such as John—was one who used vivid imagery and symbolism to speak about God's judgment and the end of the world. Among Jewish people in biblical times, writers often used an apocalyptic style. Some parts of the Old Testament (such as portions of Daniel and Ezekiel) made use of apocalyptic language.

The difficulty, of course, is that this style of writing, using vivid word pictures and symbols, is quite foreign to us today. Undoubtedly most of John's first readers had little difficulty understanding what the symbols stood for—and discerning which were symbols and which were not. It takes careful study for us to understand some of the more obscure parts of his message (much of it quoted from the Old Testament).

Again, this does not mean John's message is lost to us today. The opposite is true. We will be richly rewarded when we delve into the thrill of exploring the treasures of Revelation. Don't think of John's symbolic language as a barrier to understanding; see it instead as the way he painted the picture of God's plan for the future in vivid strokes of color.

As an apocalyptist, John concentrated on one overpowering theme: the end of human history as we know it and the dawn of the glorious messianic age. His message is always of warning and hope—warning of the coming judgment, and hope of Christ's inevitable triumph over evil and the establishment of His eternal kingdom.

We need that message today: sin does not go unpunished, and God will judge. There is hope for the future when we are in Christ. A battle scene in Francis Ford Coppola's *Apocalypse Now* shows a messenger wandering into the front lines, looking at the chaos, and asking, "Who's in charge here?" No one answers his question. Many people today are looking at the chaos and evil of our world and wondering if anyone is in charge of this universe. John's message in Revelation answers clearly, yes—God is!

I always appreciated my friend and colleague George Beverly Shea singing before I got up to preach. Many times he belted out the words to "How Big Is God," a song written for him by the late Stuart Hamblen, the Hollywood actor and songwriter who was saved during our Los Angeles crusade in 1949. With Bev's baritone voice amplified through the stadium, the words of a mighty message were heard: "He's big enough to rule this mighty universe, yet small enough to live within my heart."

God is the Ruler of His mighty creation. There is no reason to despair, because He holds in His hands the whole world, while His Spirit is able to fill the void in man's heart.

As we look at God's message, my prayer is that God will convict men and women of the reality of His judgment to come and that they will accept God's forgiveness through the love of His Son, Jesus Christ.

INSIDE THE CALL

Second, John was also a prophet. Apocalyptists despaired of the present and looked to the future expectantly. The prophets, on the other hand, often held out hope for the present—hope that God's judgment could be delayed, thereby giving people the chance to repent and turn to God in faith and obedience. That does not mean that the prophets offered an easy way out of difficulties, as if somehow all problems would vanish if people would just profess their faith in God. It would not be easy to serve God and fight against the evil of this present dark and sinful world, yet the prophets knew that God would be victorious in the end, and His people would ultimately share in His victory.

As a prophet, John was calling his generation—and ours—to

repentance, faith, and action. He knew that we could never build the kingdom of God on earth, no matter how hard we might try. Only God can do that—and someday He will, when Christ comes again. But John also knew that God's judgment on this world could be delayed if we would repent and turn to Christ.

That sinewy old man on Patmos, chosen by God to receive and declare His special message, was therefore both apocalyptist and prophet. Why shouldn't he be both? After all, as a young Jew he had learned from the Old Testament of God's eventual judgment on the earth and the coming reign of the Messiah. He also had no doubt studied the call of the prophets—Amos, Isaiah, Jeremiah, and the others—who urged men and women with all their strength to turn back to God. Then one day John heard the call of Jesus Christ and responded by following Him. In Jesus, he discovered that the message of the apocalyptist and the prophet were united. In Him the apocalyptist's declaration of coming judgment and ultimate victory was certain. Joined with the prophet's message of repentance and obedience to God in the face of present evil, John was faithful in delivering God's Word wholly.

Again, we need to hear John's message as that of a prophet, declaring a message not only of the future but of the present. We need to hear his call to repentance and his challenge to live for God, taking our stand for purity, justice, and righteousness no matter what others may say or do.

INSIDE THE MESSAGE

Third, John was also an evangelist. He was concerned about people's lost souls because he knew God loved them and had sent His Son to die for them.

The word *evangelist* comes from a Greek word meaning "one

who announces good news"—in this case, the Good News of the Gospel. To some, John's message of the future may have sounded gloomy and depressing. John knew, however, that the worst thing he could do would be to assure people that everything was all right and that there was no need to be concerned about the evil in the world, or God's judgment. But John's message is ultimately a message of salvation in Jesus Christ.

Our chaotic, confused world has no greater need than to hear the Gospel truth. John's message in Revelation focuses not just on events that will happen in the future, but on what can happen now when Jesus Christ becomes Lord and Savior of our individual lives. John's message focuses supremely on Jesus, the Son of God, who died for our sins and rose again from the dead to give us eternal life. What John declared at the end of his Gospel can also be applied with equal force to his words in Revelation: "But these are written that you may believe that Jesus is the Christ, the Son of God, and that by believing you may have life in his name" (John 20:31).

I look back on my many years as an evangelist and wonder, *Have I made the Christian faith look too easy?* Even before I heard the expression, I have constantly borne in mind what Dietrich Bonhoeffer called "cheap grace." Of course it is "by grace you have been saved, through faith . . . not by works, so that no one can boast" (Ephesians 2:8–9). Of course our salvation is a result of what Christ has done for us through His life, death, and resurrection; not what we do for ourselves. We must trust Him to complete in us what He has begun. But in my eagerness to tell the world about the greatest gift that comes only from God, I ask myself if I have comprehended the price He paid for our freedom. Have I adequately explained the price we must pay in humbling ourselves, turning our backs on pride, and sacrificing our earthly desires out of obedience to the Lord? This is part of the Revelator's message to us.

INSIDE THE SOUL

John was also a pastor. His concern was not with a sterile message having no power to influence lives. John was concerned about people's souls. He was concerned with the daily problems they faced as they sought to be faithful to God. He was concerned with the pressures and persecutions many of them encountered as Christians.

Revelation was the apostle's last letter to the people he knew and loved best: those who made up the Body of Christ—the church—the seven groups of Christians scattered across Asia Minor. It is evident that John knew his people well and deeply loved them. Try to feel his fear for them and for those who would come after him.

Picture how those first-century Christians began new life in Christ. I have preached in more than eighty nations of the world. I have seen thousands of people listening to the Good News of Jesus' life, death, and resurrection. I have watched many literally run to accept Christ as Savior and Lord of their lives. I have witnessed their enthusiasm and been thrilled by their early and rapid growth. Then, just as John did, I have watched their first love die. I have seen men and women eagerly embrace the faith and then slowly abandon it, giving in again to immorality, idolatry, and self-destruction. I have witnessed others who accepted Christ and remained faithful to the end but found terrible suffering and sacrifice along the way.

INSIDE THE BATTLE

John worried about his flock as he wrote out his vision of *this world* (where evil reigns) and of *the world to come* (where God will restore righteousness and peace again). He wrote of the war between the worlds and of the men and women who will fight and die on the battlefield. At the center of his vision, he wrote of Jesus, the Lord of the world to come, who entered this world to rescue mankind.

Revelation is not an academic paper produced for some scholarly meeting. It is not a poem crafted by a gifted wordsmith to entertain and divert. It is not the diary of a senile old man driven to wild hallucinations by his isolation and loneliness. Revelation is a pastor's letter to his floundering flock, an urgent telegram bearing a brilliant battle plan for a people at war. It reflects all the realistic horror and heartbreak of a battlefield strewn with the dead. It is frank and it is frightening, but it is a plan for victory.

I hear the distant thunder. I see lightning striking in many places of our world; thus, I know that the coming storm will someday engulf the whole world. I see the storm clouds mounting in the lowering sky. For the length of my days, I will always be sending out the call of an evangelist to proclaim hope that redemption—new life—can be found in Christ and to sound the alarm that there is serious trouble ahead for our world and for all who live in it. These are the elements that make up the images of the Apocalypse—a storm warning that carries a booming jolt of truth—TROUBLE AHEAD; PREPARE TO MEET THY GOD!—followed by the voice of the Gentle Shepherd—COME!

6

THE BLINDING VISION

His countenance was like the sun shining in its strength.
And when I saw Him, I fell at His feet.
—REVELATION 1:16–17 NKJV

W e don't have to be on the battlefields of the world to experience strife and conflict. We need only to open our eyes each morning and read the headlines, we need only to turn a keen ear when our phones ring with bad news, we need only to open our hearts to those next door—and maybe even in our own homes—to notice those with grieving hearts.

The safety of home no longer exists as it did just one generation ago. Too often, precious children are violated and abused by their own parents; others are deserted, left home alone, or ignored so that they grow up bitter, angry, and emotionally disturbed. Far too many young men and women coming of age today have no spiritual or emotional roots. They have been deprived of values by an agnostic and contemporary culture.

The actions of some government leaders, public officials, and educators are outrageous and offensive. The morality of the current generation has fallen to the lowest level in the history of this nation. Many times our society makes heroes and idols of celebrities whose immorality is widely publicized. Where is the moral compass that once guided us? Where is the faith that built our country and gave people meaning to life?

In my book *Hope for the Troubled Heart*, I dealt with many such issues, pointing readers to a practical plan for restoring hope that I have used in my own life. I know it works. The plan is right from the pages of the Bible. For people who do not know where to turn, hopelessness grows into despair. Personal worries engulf our lives, and daily burdens grow larger than most of us are able to manage. Jesus gives us this warning: "Be careful, or your hearts will be weighed down with . . . the anxieties of life, and that day will close on you unexpectedly like a trap" (Luke 21:34).

Dr. John Walvoord, who has written many widely read books on various prophetic biblical passages, wrote that he believes the world has entered a time of dramatic change. He said:

> The present world crisis is not a result of any one factor, but a concurrence of causes and effects which combine to set the world stage for a conflict which may quickly bring an end to hundreds of years of progress in western civilization and establish new centers of international power. Whatever the future holds, it is going to be dramatically different than the past. In this dark picture only the Scriptures chart a sure course and give us an intelligent explanation of world-wide confusion as it exists today.

Dr. Walvoord's view accurately reflects what the Bible says. It should be convicting to all Christians when we realize that much of the confusion in the world is coming from the church itself. There was a time when the church upheld a unified standard of values and beliefs from Scripture. Living separated lives has been exchanged for going the world's way. The devil has successfully fooled many churches, convincing them to follow the world. Biblical standards have been compromised by convenient social theories. Instead of clinging to the only Lifeboat that can save, we have tossed overboard biblical truths in the name of living on the edge of life, like the man who rides the parameter of a hurricane, daring it to sweep him away.

HALF A VISION

In numerous churches, the Bible is treated as a collection of fairy tales and fables written by uneducated men from an ancient time. While it offers challenging spiritual myths and wholesome encouragement, some "modern" churches seem to feel that no one should go to the Bible expecting to find absolute truth.

Such teaching is an abomination before God. Nothing could be more destructive to true faith and peace on earth. The fiercest storm is taking place in some of our churches—the unbelief and disobedience of God's Word. In the face of such a growing storm, our changing world desperately needs moorings, and God has given us that anchor in His Holy Word—the Bible—His unchanging truth.

Dr. Walvoord goes on to say:

> The significance of the present world crisis is that it contains practically all the elements which are a natural preparation for the end of the age. . . . The present generation may witness the dramatic close of the "time of the Gentiles" and the establishment of the kingdom of heaven upon the earth, thus bringing to fulfillment one of the great themes of prophecy—the divine program for the nations of the world.

The Bible declares,

"You must no longer live as the Gentiles do, in the futility of their thinking. They are darkened in their understanding and separated from the life of God because of the ignorance that is in them due to the hardening of their hearts. Having lost all sensitivity, they have given themselves over to sensuality so as to indulge in every kind of impurity, with a continual lust for more" (Ephesians 4:17–19).

A FORBIDDING VISION

When Ruth and I were in Europe some years ago, we followed the news in the British, French, and American newspapers. Within a two-week period we clipped a score of articles that used the words *apocalypse* or *Armageddon*. Reporters, commentators, and editors—the men and women working in all the various modern media—seemed fascinated by the notion of the end of the world.

I recall an article in the *London Times* entitled "The Shadow of Armageddon." The story raised the grim specter of a future race war in Britain. Other columns, editorials, news stories, and letters to the editors were permeated by the common fears of nuclear war, economic chaos, the misuse and the overuse of the earth's nonrenewable resources, runaway crime, violence in the streets, mysterious new killer viruses, terrorism, radically changing weather patterns, earthquakes, floods, famines, destruction, and death. Everywhere we went, people asked one basic question: "Is there any hope?" For the follower of Jesus Christ, the answer is that our hope is in Him and Him alone. "Heaven and earth will pass away, but my words will never pass away" (Luke 21:33).

One morning in the woods near our home, I walked with the morning paper in one hand and the book of Revelation in the other. As I read news accounts bound in hopelessness, my heart found comfort in the passages from John's pen while exiled on Patmos. His words were for such a time as this. John's visions ring with hope. While his letters were addressed to the seven churches in the Roman province of Asia, more accurately to the Christian believers who made up the churches in each town, they are also intended for us.

His letter was overflowing with rebuke and hope, correction and love, warning and promise. He wrote honestly to his Christian brethren of the disaster ahead—what to expect and how to face it. We need to take his words to heart. For any way we look at it, the news is both good and bad.

My lifetime has been spent proclaiming one central truth: God's Gospel offered to the world. At the heart of that Good News is Jesus Christ and the love and forgiveness He gives. He is God in human flesh, and the story of His life, death, and resurrection is the only Good News the world will ever hear. Regardless of your past, you can be guaranteed a future worth living and dying for. I like announcing good news, but if I am to take John's revelations seriously, I cannot speak only of good news; for there is bad news as well.

HEAVENLY VISION

I often wonder if John had hoped to spend his last days writing about the past. Imagine the untold stories of Jesus that he could have shared. After all, John was an old man. Elderly folks are known for reminiscing about the past. He could have added to the books he had already written, including the Gospel of John and the three letters he had sent to some first-century Christians. He could have filled his parchment with memories of those wonderful days with the Master beside the Sea of Galilee and in the hills of Judea.

John was an eyewitness when God walked upon the earth in human flesh, healing the sick, casting out evil spirits, and raising the dead. What wonderful and inspirational stories were left unwritten!

It was not to be. But John was given a new story to write. Jesus Christ came to him through the Spirit of God, foretelling the coming storm and whispering that His peace will reign in the end. To understand John's visions, to understand the warnings and the hope, we must make a journey to Patmos. We must walk the beaches with this aged man and see his visions close up. We must ask what they meant to John and to the small clusters of Christian believers scattered across the empire. Then we must ask what John's vision means to us.

"On the Lord's Day," he wrote, "I heard behind me a loud voice like a trumpet" (Revelation 1:10). From the text we learn that this revelation by Jesus to John began on "the Lord's Day." Perhaps John's Roman captors allowed this Jewish seer his ancient Old Testament practice of keeping one day out of seven holy. Perhaps that day they had already herded the other prisoners to their hot quarry labors and left the old man to walk alone along the Aegean Sea. I can imagine him praying the ancient prayers, singing the blessed psalms, quoting from memory great portions of the comforting words of wisdom, and remembering the new life and meaning Jesus had given to mere men.

A PASTOR'S VISION

As John walked along the beach, perhaps he peered over the sun-kissed water and thought about his many "flocks" on the mainland only miles away, worried about what they would face in the storms of persecution. Perhaps he sang the words King David had penned during his own exile:

> But let all who take refuge in you be glad;
> let them ever sing for joy.
> Spread your protection over them,
> that those who love your name may rejoice in you.

82

For surely, O LORD, you bless the righteous;
you surround them with your favor as with a shield.
(Psalm 5:11–12)

John must have longed for his exile to end so that he could return to the churches with encouragement and exhortation. After all, he had the heart of a pastor. How many men and women, boys and girls assembled for worship had been led to faith in Christ through John's own preaching? He felt responsible for them and for their spiritual growth.

Others who had walked with Jesus and helped establish those churches had been martyred. For example:

- Paul was beheaded with a Roman sword.
- Peter was crucified upside down on a rough wooden cross.
- John's own brother, James, was beheaded by Herod Agrippa.
- Mark was dragged through the streets of Alexandria and burned, his body bruised and still bleeding.

Unconfirmed news of the deaths or disappearances of John's close friends must have left him lonely and even more fearful for the future of the churches they had planted together.

At first it had seemed safe and rather simple to be a Christian, in a world dominated by the Roman Empire. The Caesars had granted special privileges to the Jews, and the majority of Christian believers were Jews who shared in those privileges. Under the Pax Romana (the peace Rome built across the world with Roman might and Roman law) the church had spread. Roman authorities had even saved Paul's life in Jerusalem when Caesar's soldiers rescued him from a mob infuriated by his preaching (Acts 21:31–32). Peter had written to the churches that they were to fear God and "honor the emperor," even though the emperor was often evil (1 Peter 2:17 ESV).

But toward the end of the first century, benevolence toward

Christians had ceased. Rome was losing her grip on the world. The emperors and their courts had grown more and more extravagant. The royal treasuries had been drained. New taxes were levied by the Roman senate to help offset their balance-of-trade deficit. When protest and rebellion followed, Rome answered with the sword, and persecution of Christians became a popular sport.

It was no simple task for Rome to maintain an empire made up of so many different races, religions, and cultures. Nationalist movements, political conspiracies, terrorism, and open rebellion grew until the empire was threatened, even from within. Out of the emperor's growing paranoia to maintain Rome's power and keep its subjects in check, one simple test of loyalty evolved. On certain feasts and holidays, row upon row of subjects lined up to walk past the area's Roman magistrate, toss a pinch of incense into a fire in the golden bowl at his feet, and mutter, "Caesar is Lord."

VISION OF IDOLATRY

Most citizens of the empire were glad to pay tribute to the emperor and to the empire that had brought them a period of peace. But for Christians, a greater oath became the center of their faith: "Jesus is Lord," not Caesar. While they were loyal to the admonitions of Paul and Peter—to worship God and honor the emperor—this act of Caesar worship crossed the line. Because of their refusal to put Caesar before Christ, Christians began to be persecuted.

William Barclay wrote, "This worship [of Caesar] was never intended to . . . wipe out other religions. Rome was essentially tolerant. A man might worship Caesar *and* his own god. But more and more Caesar worship became a test of political loyalty; it became . . . the recognition of the dominion of Caesar over a man's life, and . . . soul."

Imagine a village in the suburbs of Ephesus or Laodicea. Christian believers are at work tanning leather, dyeing cloth, harvesting crops, raising families, studying math and history—at worship, at work, or at play. Then, suddenly, hoofbeats are heard clattering up the nearby cobbled streets. The horses are reined in by a Roman centurion and his honor guard. A leather camp table is unfolded. An incense burner is placed upon the table. A flame is lit. Heralds sound the trumpets. There is no place to hide, no time to decide.

Believers must join their neighbors in that line. Just ahead, the village mayor tosses his incense into the flames and exclaims proudly, "Caesar is Lord." Others follow. The line ahead grows shorter. The moment of decision draws near. Will the Christians avoid the conflict and protect their lives and security with the simple act of obedience? Will they mutter "Caesar is Lord" and sneak back home to safety? Or will they recognize this act as blasphemy, refuse the incense, proclaim "Jesus is Lord," and pay the price for disloyalty to the state?

Did John wander up and down the beach at Patmos that Sunday remembering the centurion, the incense, and the decision of ultimate loyalty each believer had to make? Who knows? Perhaps it was in just such a line, surrounded by his neighbors and friends, that John himself failed the emperor's test and, as punishment, was exiled to the island prison. We don't know the charges leveled against the apostle that led him to prison, but we do know why John was there—to write down the vision from God.

Late in the first century, during the time of John's exile, the persecution of the Christian church by the Roman Empire had begun in earnest. It was difficult to keep the faith. There were awful moments before a centurion's blazing fire.

While there are Christians around the world serving the Lord who can relate to persecution because of their faith, Christians in the Western world cannot begin to comprehend the sacrifices made by others who live for Christ abroad. We, who have allowed our standards to fall prey to the world's standards, have no concept of what it means to live sacrificially for Christ. Many Christians give in to various temptations through peer pressure and find themselves surrendering to worldly passions, justifying pleasures the world offers. This was John's fear for his flock.

VISION OF CROSS BEARING

Every Christian in every nation—totalitarian, democratic, or somewhere in between—must decide about their loyalty to Christ. In the United States, we can see clear evidence of a growing intolerance toward Christians and Christian values. It is no longer as accepted to profess Christ as it once was in America. But the Bible commands that we must each take up our cross daily. Compromising and conforming to the world's standard is against God's Word.

No wonder John was anxious. The infant Christians in the churches of Asia lived in a world (not unlike our own) where their belief in Christ often left them at odds with the political powers, the economic realities, and the social norms. The day-to-day choices were difficult and demanding. Great suffering lay ahead. Would they keep the faith? Would they stand firm, or would they give up under the pressure and the pain of following Jesus?

Christians today are faced with the same dilemmas. Will we give in to materialism, selfish pleasures, and the dishonest practices of this present age? What do you do when you face such crossroads? Is your steadfast desire to do God's will, or do you give in to the steady pressures of those around you? The Bible says, "Don't let the world around you squeeze you into its own mold, but let God remold your minds from within, so that you may prove in practice that the plan of God for you is good, meets all his demands and moves toward the goal of true maturity" (Romans 12:2 PHILLIPS).

We can only guess what John's contemplations might have been as he walked along the sandy beach. He must have been startled when he suddenly "heard . . . a loud voice like a trumpet." I cannot explain how these visions came, or in what form they appeared to John. It is certainly possible that the visions took on real form and substance— unlike the holograms in Disneyland's "Haunted House," where specters dance through walls. What John saw, regardless of form, was unlike any human drama ever produced.

THE GLOWING VISION

We must not get so caught up in how the vision came to John, but what the vision revealed. When he heard the trumpetlike voice, John said:

> I turned around to see the voice that was speaking to me. And . . . I saw seven golden lampstands, and among [them] was someone "like a son of man," dressed in a robe reaching down to his feet and with a golden sash around his chest. His head and hair were white like wool, as white as snow, and his eyes were like blazing fire. His feet were like bronze glowing in a furnace, and his voice was like the sound of rushing waters. In his right hand he held seven stars, and out of his mouth came a sharp double-edged sword. His face was like the sun shining in all its brilliance. When I saw him, I fell at his feet as though dead. (Revelation 1:12–17)

John did not recognize the Master—the very same Jesus he saw ascending into the heavens when John was just a young man. John, the beloved—Jesus' close personal friend—did not recognize this giant glowing figure as his risen Lord.

Then, gently, as a mother wakens a child from night terrors, the figure leaned over the panic-stricken John, touched his shoulder, and said, "Do not be afraid. I am the First and the Last. I am the Living One; I was dead, and behold I am alive for ever and ever! And I hold the keys of death and Hades" (Revelation 1:17–18).

WRITE THE VISION

What is going on here? Did John think that perhaps his prayers for the church had dramatically been answered? Was the Lord going to rescue the church and end all persecution? Out of nowhere, it seemed, the Creator and Sustainer of the universe revealed Himself as the One who holds the key, the One who holds the power over the very worst fears that afflict mankind—death and eternal lostness.

Perhaps the Lord lifted John up as He said with urgency, "Write, John!" Then, as He did while on earth, Jesus gave John very clear instructions. I am sure John believed that the Lord had heard his prayers for the churches, because Jesus said, "Write . . . what you have seen, what is now and what will take place later" (Revelation 1:19) and "send it to the seven churches: Ephesus, Smyrna, Pergamum, Thyatira, Sardis, Philadelphia and Laodicea" (Revelation 1:11).

Don't you imagine that John's heart leaped when he heard the Lord refer to the churches by name? The Lord of history stood before John, assuring him, by His very presence, that He is also Lord of the future. He was about to reveal the plan that will unfold at a time known only by God the Father.

As we will see, John's vision brings assurance to the church that God is in control, but it also predicts harsh reality of what will transpire because of unrepentant hearts. Perhaps right now you are facing some particular problem. Maybe you are even at the point of despair. If you will look to Christ, submit to Him, and obey Him, He will give you peace even in the midst of the storms that pummel you. But if you turn your back, the harshness of sin will take its toll, just as the horseman approaching will warn.

The people of John's day were no different than we are today. I am reminded of a natural disaster that hit the state of California some years ago. The West Coast had been through a long and desperate period of drought, punctuated by torrential rains and flooding. A few years earlier, the state had suffered through the worst winter on record. Howling winds had felled power lines and plunged cities into darkness. Seas had bashed and buffeted beachside communities, swallowing houses, piers, parks, and highways in a powerful, murky tide. Rain had overflowed the rivers, drowning people and animals and swamping whole towns and croplands. It was a terrible time, and the news flashed with stories on how to cope with the storm.

The front page of the *Los Angeles Times* warned that worse times were coming. Scientists at the California Institute of Technology told people across the state to expect an earthquake of major proportions. Instructions were dispatched in print and across the airways telling how to brace for the inevitable. The warning was clear: be prepared.

Picture alarmed Californians, wading through the flooded ruins of beachfront homes, hearing the warnings of a soon-to-come earthquake that will tumble the remains into the sea. That is just a small glimpse of the double-edged predicament that faced the Christian believers in the seven churches of Asia. They faced terrible trouble.

In Revelation 2 and 3, John sends the alert to the seven churches. The warning echoes in the calm before the storm. What follows is a second warning—when the seven seals of the scroll are opened, the horsemen will be sent forth on a mission of great peril.

People have often asked me how God can be merciful when He orchestrates such a storm. The answer is obvious. His mercy is evident by the warnings He has given from the beginning of time. He paid the ultimate price, with His blood, to save the world from destruction. That is the Good News. The bad news, however, is that there is a price to pay when His creation rejects His mercy and ignores His warnings. We diminish His sacrifice for us and don't want to sacrifice for Him—but we must. We do not have to swim the stormy current alone. He is in the wind and the water, and His hand extends to us yet today. The Bible says, "Surely the arm of the LORD is not too short to save" (Isaiah 59:1). Will we respond by reaching out to Him—believing His Word—or will we scoff at His high alerts?

It is quite possible that if there had been "high tech" in John's day, these letters would have been sent via e-mail with an alert to open immediately. This was the urgency of his message—it demanded immediate attention—to set their lives in order.

VISION OF WARNING; VISION OF HOPE

The most important signpost of hope is God's Word, which warns of imminent disaster and clearly marks the detour route to safety. God has prepared a plan to rescue His people. We have seen Him do it time and again.

Ruth was born and raised as the daughter of missionary parents in China. She witnessed firsthand how God prepared His church there during times of trouble to withstand even greater troubled times ahead. The Christians in China not only survived years of crises and conflict, but today the church is growing, multiplying, and becoming stronger in spite of persecution. So in the midst of such storms, there is one bright hope for the future—the Bright and Morning Star, God's Son, Jesus Christ, the Savior.

These letters of old—John's warnings to the seven churches—must have terrified them. Many churches today seem unaware that John wrote these letters for the church today, as well, to warn of the coming storms.

The church is the lampstand in Revelation—the only light in a darkened world. Jesus commanded His followers to "go and make disciples" (Matthew 28:19). The Pharisees demanded that Jesus rebuke His disciples for proclaiming Him as Messiah. Jesus answered them, "I tell you that if these should keep silent, the stones would immediately cry out" (Luke 19:40 NKJV).

While we're looking up to see the rainbow—God's promises—we're ignoring floodwaters rising. While we're looking down to see how close we can get to the edge of the world without being trapped by Satan, we're taking our eyes off of Christ. It doesn't take much for our foot to slip on a pebble loosed from the soil. We're so attracted to busyness that we cannot hear the roar of hoofbeats around the bend.

Followers of Christ must look up and warn our fellow man of the storm clouds above. Tunnel vision will disable us. Perhaps we can point others to the only source of Light that will fill their empty souls. We must look at those in our pathway and warn them to watch their footsteps along the rocky path. Perhaps we can lead them to the foot of the cross, the symbol of Christ's greatest suffering for mankind's most gruesome betrayal. When our voices are silenced, hoofbeats will thunder.

7

HE WHO OVERCOMES

To him who overcomes I will grant to sit with Me on My throne,
as I also overcame and sat down with My Father on His throne.
—REVELATION 3:21 NKJV

Mystery novels are a booming business. Travelers dart into the last-stop shop to buy one before boarding an airplane. Audiobooks fill long hours for passengers crisscrossing interstates. Cruise ships heavily stock galley kiosks with the latest whodunit thriller. Our minds are constantly feeding on fiction that momentarily satisfies our appetites for intrigue. When the last page is read, though, what has been accomplished? Passing time? Entertaining the imagination?

I'm not opposed to a good read. Ruth and I always had books at our fingertips. But no book, fiction or nonfiction, can compare with the book of Revelation. It has long been described as a book of mysteries. Its arcane and provocative language challenges the mind. Some feel that the apostle John's narrative elicits more questions than answers. One reason, perhaps, is that John gives us a glimpse of the unseen world of spiritual reality. Every inspired word bursts with truth about things to come and how the knowledge of these revelations impacts us today. This book has stood the test of time because it is divinely inspired by Almighty God, written in ink that cannot be erased by any man, religion, or belief system.

Among the various mysteries discussed by the apostle Paul in his many letters to the churches, was the idea that our world—the world of the visible—is an unreal and impermanent place. The real world, he said, is the unseen world. "We do not look at the things which are seen, but at the things which are not seen. For the things which are seen are temporary, but the things which are not seen are eternal" (2 Corinthians 4:18 NKJV). Though Paul did not live long enough to read John's letters to the churches, by inspiration of the Holy Spirit, Paul's own writings speak prophetically of many aspects of John's writings while in exile.

Paul wrote about the spiritual world existing in our very midst, around us and unseen, but he also warned that decisions we make in the physical world have eternal consequences in the life to come. This was the reality John wrote about when he was overcome by a blazing vision of the unseen world.

When the Spirit of the risen Christ came to John in his barren cell, the aging apostle must have been in awe at the fearsome reality that infiltrated his mind. As a Roman prisoner, half-starved, sometimes beaten, constantly harassed and abused, his life on that barren, rock-strewn island in the Aegean Sea was as real and unmysterious as the cold ground upon which he slept, as real as bread and water. The life he lived was as physical and tangible as the pain in his aching joints and the burns and blisters on his hands and feet.

Tradition tells us that John's face was wrinkled and blackened by the sun. His arms were lean and muscular, and his hands were rough and calloused. As a political prisoner, exiled to a rock off the coast of what is now modern Turkey, John was forced to carry stones chipped from granite cliffs above the sea to a cargo dock below the Roman citadel. The fortress guarded the narrow isthmus between Scala and the Bay of Merika. The gravel John carried on his back was used to build the foundations for the temples and palaces of the Emperor Domitian and to pave Roman roads, which always led to Rome.

We can imagine that John, stumbling under the loaded straw basket strapped to his forehead, used both hands to grasp his staff and pick his way painfully down the treacherous path. Even the Roman guards must have wondered at the determination of this gray-bearded Christian Jew who worked alongside the other prisoners by day and spent his evenings writing mysterious stories.

John was under the compulsion of a great mystery. He was writing to the seven churches at the direction of the Holy Spirit of God, who came to him in waking dreams and visions.

Can you fathom what went through the minds of the early Christians as these letters were read?

Warnings of hoofbeats and horsemen,
Visions of seals and scrolls,
dragons and angels,
manipulators and martyrs,
false prophets and the faithful,
slaying in the streets and singing around the throne,
the lake of fire and the river of life,
plagues and harvest,
rebellion and repentance,
woes and praises,
blasphemies and blessings,
curses and amens,
abomination and adoration,
envisioning war in heaven and proclaiming peace on earth,
the beast and the Judge,
the liar exiled and the Lamb exalted,
Satan defeated

by King Jesus
who
reigns.

So, in his prison cell, John, the seer of the unseen world, spent every free moment recording the seismographic warnings of a world bulging and buckling just beneath the surface—and capturing the truth that there is an escape to safety.

THE OVERCOMING VISION

These stories of urgency and warning, probably written over several harrowing months, were copied and sent as instructed to the seven churches in Asia. Eventually, the Apocalypse of John was titled by its opening line, "The Revelation of Jesus Christ." This letter became the last and perhaps most controversial book in the New Testament.

We don't know the details of what happened when the Spirit appeared to John. In other places, the Bible describes the way God appeared to Moses, Abraham, Jacob, and Paul. The accounts in the first three books of the New Testament of the appearance of Moses and Elijah to Jesus, and His transfiguration in a brilliant cloud of light gives us a vivid image of how God's presence impacted men—they fell on their faces in terror before a holy God.

The apostle John was affected in much the same way. He fell prostrate before the mighty presence of the Lord. Perhaps he shielded his eyes against the blinding light. The great figure whose own eyes shone like fire, the seven lamps blazing around Him, and the sun reflecting off the surf, smashed together in a stunning spectacle of light. John must have rubbed his eyes in wonder as he tried to focus on the scene and grasp its meaning.

Perhaps Jesus moved out of the light, reached down for John's gnarled hand, and gently lifted the old man to his feet. Maybe their eyes met for a moment. In that flash of recognition, John must have seen past the blinding splendor and recognized the Lord—the same Jesus who had walked beside him along the Sea of Galilee. Possibly John felt the same compelling love of Jesus he had known as they walked the trails and hillsides of Judea. Perhaps he felt Jesus' arm on his shoulder as the Lord led him up the shoreline and past the grove of palm trees to his prison cave. Maybe John stumbled in the darkness searching for the oil lamp and lighting it, flattening out a new piece of parchment and inking the end of a freshly shaved quill. He sat for a moment before the driftwood slab that served as his desk and altar, waiting for the Lord to speak the Revelation.

OVERCOMING TOGETHER

You may imagine the details of John's dream another way. The details aren't important. But it helps to see John there with Christ. For whatever form the vision took—whether it was a personal revelation by our Lord in John's mind's eye or a literal experience on a Patmos beach—to get a feeling for this moment, to comprehend what actually happened that day, is to realize the wonder and hope of Christ's revelation. John's vision of Jesus is breathtaking. Should we expect God to give us a vision like that? No. God has given us His Word, the Bible, and that is all we need. Do you want to know God more deeply, more intimately? Do you want to discover His will for your life? Then read and study the Scriptures daily. They are a personal and compelling revelation for all time—whatever storms may come.

John's task at hand was to write the mystery of the seven stars he saw in the Lord's hand and the seven golden lampstands. "The seven stars are the angels [leaders or pastors] of the seven churches, and the seven lampstands are the seven churches" (Revelation 1:19–20). The events of that day elevate the words of those seven letters into God's eternal Word, as trustworthy and authoritative for our times as they were in John's. What we learn from these words grows beyond the words themselves into profound lessons about God.

First, we see that God cares about each of us as individuals. He knows us by name. The Lord cares about each of us personally. I invite you to look at the details in these letters. God named names. He described events. He commended the churches for their successes. He scolded them for their failures. He gave them warm, loving, but confronting counsel. That alone gives me a tremendous sense of hope. He knows us as a mother knows her child. The Lord did not withdraw to some distant corner of the universe; He is present in the spirit of every believer. When we search His Word, when we stop to hear His voice, we will hear from heaven.

Second, He sees us as sharing our lives with other believers in the church. Jesus was concerned about each of those churches in the cities and towns of Asia. He didn't dictate those letters to key leaders across the world or to official gatherings of clergy. He wrote to individual churches, small clusters of believers, leaders and followers together. At the heart of these letters is God's assumption that we belong together at work and at worship in a local church.

Jesus cared about each of the individual churches then as He cares about each of our individual churches now. He cares deeply about how we relate to Him, to one another, to our communities, and to our world. He wants to stand with us through the storms of life. That should give us great hope!

Third, the issues to which the Lord spoke then are the very same issues about which He speaks to us now. Our problems are not unique. Our sins, our temptations, our weaknesses, and our needs are no different from theirs. That, too, gives me hope; for Jesus anticipated the struggles we would face, and the call He gave them is the call we must hear today.

Fourth, although the form of each letter is practically the same, the content of each is unique. He knew that every church was facing specific struggles that reflected what was taking place within the worldly culture that surrounded them, so He addressed each church specifically. We can gain hope from this. His words to them are His words to us, but we must face our own struggles. As we search these letters, we can be assured of finding exactly the right word at the right time to suit our particular need. Jesus said, "The Holy Spirit . . . will remind you of everything I have said" (John 14:26).

The letters to the churches revealed Christ's knowledge of what the future held. He knew the price they would have to pay for their stand against evil. But He also knew those churches were not yet prepared to pay that price; they were not yet strong enough to face their storms. He knew that unless they spent time praying and preparing, they would not survive the winds of destruction. He knew that unless they learned how to overcome, they would be defeated by the oncoming tempest.

There are clues in the letters that we must also follow as we face the blustery storms bearing down on us. The letters are His words of power that will help us survive the evil day to come.

OVERCOMING LUKEWARM

Ephesus was a large seaport city on the Aegean Sea. The apostle Paul helped found the church in this great commercial and religious center. At the heart of the city was the temple to Artemis (Diana), one of the seven wonders of the ancient world, a temple four times the size of the Parthenon in Athens. Paul almost lost his life in his courageous stand against the idolatrous worship of Artemis (Acts 19). He invested two years of his life in the people of Ephesus and the growing young church there, and that investment paid rich dividends for the kingdom of God. Ephesus became the center from which the Good News of Christ spread throughout Asia.

There is a wonderful moment in the book of Acts when the elders from the church in Ephesus met Paul in Miletus to say their last goodbyes to him. Paul was on his final journey to Jerusalem. From there he would go to Rome, where he would meet his death. The elders held on to the apostle and wept as he shared his final thoughts with them, and said, "After I leave, savage wolves will come in among you and will not spare the flock. . . . So be on your guard!" (Acts 20:29, 31). The church at Ephesus saw Christ's servants persecuted greatly for His name's sake. Not only had they lost Paul, but John had been arrested in Ephesus and taken from them fifty miles away to Patmos.

The church had seen the manifestation of Paul's warning. More than half a century later, Christ's letter to them in Revelation indicated that He was pleased that they had been obedient and had "tested those who claim to be apostles but are not, and . . . found them false" (Revelation 2:2). Paul had instructed the church "to help the weak," and in Revelation Christ commended them for "your deeds, your hard work and your perseverance" (Revelation 2:2). Still, in spite of their obedience and their endurance, something had gone wrong. "You have forsaken your first love," He warned them. "Remember the height from which you have fallen! Repent and do the things you did at first" (Revelation 2:4–5).

In many ways, John's ancient world was much like our own—corrupt. While the city of Ephesus was entrenched in sin, the church had been enriched by the Gospel message and was faithfully proclaiming the Good News. The church at Ephesus was very close to John's heart, so, naturally, it grieved him to know that though the Lord commended them for their faithful preaching, He condemned them for forsaking their first love.

Four miles from the Maeander River in Asia Minor, along a major tributary, is the city of Laodicea. This, too, was a prosperous town in the time of John's exile. On the road between Rome and the southern provinces, Laodicea became a center of banking and exchange. A prestigious medical center known around the world for its healing eye salve was another Laodicean claim to fame. Sheep grazed on the hills around the city, and their pure black wool was renowned. The most expensive, stylish clothing of the empire was made from the rich, black fabrics woven here. How symbolic for Jesus to say to the church in Laodicea, "You are . . . poor, blind and naked" (Revelation 3:17).

We don't know the early history of the Christian church in Laodicea, but we know how highly Christ must have valued their potential in kingdom building, for this church felt His wrath in the words of John with a white-hot intensity. "You are lukewarm—neither hot nor cold—I am about to spit you out of my mouth," Christ warned them (Revelation 3:16). Then, in an almost immediate counterpoint, Christ continues with one of the best-known and most poignant invitations in biblical literature: "Those whom I love I rebuke and discipline. So be earnest, and repent. Here I am! I stand at the door and knock. If anyone hears my voice and opens the door, I will come in" (Revelation 3:19–20).

Both the Ephesian and the Laodicean Christians had lost their holy passion. The same thing had happened to Jerusalem in Jeremiah's day when he wrote, "The word of the LORD came to me. . . . 'I remember the devotion of your youth, how as a bride you loved me and followed me through the desert, through a land not sown'" (Jeremiah 2:1–2). In other words, the people of that day had also lost their first love, and God had rebuked them.

The church at Ephesus became known as the "loveless" church. Their "first love" had settled into a type of doctrinal purity. They could probably spot a heretic a mile upriver. But Christ's letter says, "Repent!" Repent of the coldness of your hearts and your lack of zeal. Repent of your lack of concern for others.

And in the case of the Laodicean church, their passion had faded into comfortable prayers of gratitude. But Christ mocked their words: "You say, 'I am rich; I have acquired wealth and do not need a thing.' But you do not realize," He warned, "that you are wretched, pitiful, poor, blind and naked" (Revelation 3:17).

Some years ago, Ruth and I had been invited to the home of wealthy socialites. They had gathered a large group of their neighboring vacationers for a party and asked if I would say a few words. I explained the Gospel simply and briefly, reminding them that pleasures and possessions are not lasting—that only the person who knows Jesus Christ as Savior can know true happiness. As I concluded, an attractive woman known for her casual morals and high lifestyle, young and smartly dressed, laughed and said, "But, Billy, what about those of us who are perfectly happy?"

From God's point of view, that woman was spiritually poor, blind, and naked, as the years ahead soon proved. Christ also says to such people, "Repent!"

OVERCOMING THE LACK OF PASSION

What began with these churches as a wholehearted commitment to Christ and His work had evolved into a passionless faith. We don't have any of the details, only these fragments of historical fact from Revelation.

The first time I saw Ruth, it was love at first sight. I can still remember the excitement I felt. I remember the first time I held her hand. I remember the thrill of our first kiss, our eyes shining with love for each other. First love is wonderful. But the first flames of passion inevitably cool.

The word *love* is an active verb. Love must have an object. To truly love, we must love someone or something. Love should not be confined to the physical. It comes with a lifetime commitment. Before Ruth became bedridden, we would sit on our front porch on a summer's evening without saying a word, but we were communing with each other. The passion of our relationship grew deeper through the years because of our commitment to one another. Over the years we came to know so many couples who did not have that depth of commitment. In some cases, their love was only physical. The flames of the honeymoon faded and the day-to-day routine settled in.

When the passion of their first love died, their relationship died as well. This is what happened to the churches in John's time.

If you are a Christian, perhaps you will remember the moment you first heard of Jesus Christ and believed in Him as Savior and Lord of your life. Perhaps you remember kneeling at your parents' bedside, at a church altar, or around the campfire at a retreat. Perhaps you came forward in an evangelistic crusade. Do you remember joining the church and feeling the loving arms of other Christians reaching out to you? Can you recall your baptism and the joy you felt in that act of faith?

When I accepted Christ, someone handed me a booklet entitled *Biblical Treasure Chest* containing Scripture verses and hymns. I can remember milking the cows on my father's dairy farm, singing those hymns and memorizing those scriptures as I worked. Do you remember the time you made your first generous pledge to the church or joined a small group of brothers and sisters in Christ to sing "Amazing Grace" or to do something for the poor and oppressed in your town? Do you remember your first love for Christ and all those acts of obedience, witness, work, and fellowship that flowed spontaneously from the time of your first love?

Christ pointed the Ephesians and the Laodiceans back to their first love—and away from their passionless, lukewarm religion. They had settled for mere theological respectability and material comfort. Christ wanted them alive and passionate again. He wanted them totally committed to Him, wholeheartedly obedient. For it is in that first-love commitment that they would find the strength to overcome the storms that were already on their way.

OVERCOMING SIN

Perhaps you have never known Christ personally as your Savior and Lord. Perhaps you have never experienced the wonder of Christ's forgiveness for your sins. Before you read further, stop and ask Him to save you.

You may ask, "What do I have to do?"

First: Admit your need. Confess, "I am a sinner."

Second: Be willing to turn away from your sins (repent).

Third: Believe that Jesus Christ died for you on the cross and rose from the grave.

Fourth: Through prayer, invite Jesus Christ, the Savior, to come in and take control of your life.

When you make Him Lord of your life, you enter into the promise of His love and the joy of eternal life with Him. God loves you. Christ died for you. Repent of your sin. Receive forgiveness. Discover the joy of that "first love."

The Old Testament is full of ardent expressions describing God's relationship with His people as a relationship of love. In New Testament terms, the church is the "bride of Christ." He expects us to be faithful to our vows.

Today we need to be reminded that love is more than *feeling*. Love is a commitment; it is *doing*. "For God so loved the world that he gave . . ." (John 3:16). This same John the Revelator was also John the beloved of Christ who had written this verse that envelops the heart of every believer. He also wrote, "Dear children, let us not love with words or tongue but with actions and in truth" (1 John 3:18). You can do the works of first love again and, in the process, rekindle the intensity of that love.

OVERCOMING DARKNESS

When we are truly in love, we want above all to be with the ones we love. We enjoy talking with them and listening to them. This is what the Lord desires from us. Many times I have gone off to a quiet place to talk with God alone, to actually walk with Him as His child.

Many times before our crusades, I have wandered into the woods or the mountains to pray, to talk, and to listen to what God is saying through His Word.

I remember before the London Crusade in 1954, I spent a great deal of time on the front porch of what we (who live in Montreat) call the Chapman Home. It was the old homestead of one of the great evangelists of another generation, J. Wilbur Chapman. This was the place where the famous hymn "Ivory Palaces" was written. Many times I sat on that front porch and poured my heart out to the Lord. He would give me assurance that He was going to be with us in that crusade. We were still young and inexperienced in those days, but we were trying to reach one of the great cities of the world for Christ. The London Crusade was supposed to be a monthlong crusade. We ended up staying three months, and by the end of it, tens of thousands had come to salvation in Christ. The crusade made news all over the world and encouraged Christians everywhere. The Lord answered prayer—not only my prayers, but the prayers of thousands who helped us in that evangelistic campaign.

I also recall the New York Crusade, where we stayed sixteen weeks at Madison Square Garden. I can't tell you how many problems we faced and how many crises came even before the meetings began! I used to walk the trails around my home and pour my heart out to the Lord. In some of the darkest hours, I reached up and sensed the touch of His hand on mine.

When was the last time you set aside an afternoon simply to be alone with the Lord, to walk and talk with Him as you might do with your best friend? From my earliest days of faith, I loved to read, study, and memorize the Word of God. I was eager to learn what Jesus Christ wanted from me; I was eager to know His will. When was the last time you turned off the noises that drown out His still, small voice and took time to read and memorize Bible passages that give life such meaning and hope?

I have always loved to be with the members of my church for worship and fellowship. It's so easy to drop out of regular worship, to move from your hometown and your home church and never find a new community of believers to replace it. How quickly our interest can dry up and our first love cool. Perhaps you remember the joy of sharing your faith in those early days, or teaching, or giving—how easy it is to stop the works that spring spontaneously out of first love. How easy it is to let your first love die!

You may not feel like working at first love. It may seem like drudgery to read and memorize the Word. It may be inconvenient to take time regularly to be alone and pray. It may feel awkward to find and join a church in your neighborhood. You may resist getting involved again. But beware; you have been warned. John wrote in the Spirit. "Repent and do the things you did at first." Unless you get about the business God called you to, you are in danger of "being removed." This storm warning is for the church today.

Dr. Luke wrote about the early church in the book of Acts: "They continued steadfastly in the apostles' doctrine and fellowship, in the breaking of bread, and in prayers . . . all who believed were together" (Acts 2:42–44 NKJV). This is what first love was for the infant church, and this is what the apostle John was admonishing them to do—return to the things of the Lord.

THE CALL TO OVERCOME

North of Ephesus, clustered around the Hermus River Valley, lie three cities in the next group of letters from Revelation: Pergamum (sometimes called the compromising church), Thyatira (referred to as the corrupt church), and Sardis (known as the dead church).

Pergamum, a coastal city, was the capital of the Roman province of Asia. It was a city crowded with heathen temples and the home of the first temple of the imperial cult of Rome, the place where Caesar was worshipped as a god.

Thyatira was inland on the Lycus River, a commercial center on an important trade route. Many trade guilds had their headquarters in Thyatira. Membership in the guilds was necessary to work, and the immorality of the guild banquet orgies was widely known and fully accepted.

Sardis, a wealthy commercial city, was also known for its loose, luxurious lifestyle. The city had twice been captured by enemies as a result of its slackness in spite of its well-fortified hilltop citadel built to guard the city from invasion.

While the Christians at Ephesus and Laodicea were enjoying their season of comfort, the churches at Pergamum, Thyatira, and Sardis were apparently victims of their runaway physical passions that led to idolatry and immorality.

In each case, the Lord first commended the churches before He chastised them. To those at Thyatira, He said, "These are the words of the Son of God, whose eyes are like blazing fire and whose feet are like burnished bronze. I know your deeds, your love and faith, your service and perseverance, and that you are now doing more than you did at first" (Revelation 2:18–19).

To Pergamum, although He had very little good to say, He did promise, "To him who overcomes, I will give some of the hidden manna. I will also give him a white stone with a new name written on it, known only to him who receives it" (Revelation 2:17). In other words, there was a small minority in Pergamum who held on to their first love. He said the same about Sardis: "You have a few people . . . who have not soiled their clothes" (Revelation 3:4).

Christ found something or someone in all three churches to commend. Many people who have studied these passages tend to think of these three churches as being fallen and sinful, with no sign of spiritual life. There was much about these churches that was commendable. Still they were in serious trouble, especially in light of the storms that lay ahead—and they didn't even know it. The parallels between the churches of that day and our own may actually be much too close for comfort.

To the Christians in Pergamum, John wrote, "I have a few things against you: You have people there who hold to the teaching of Balaam, who taught Balak to entice the Israelites to sin by eating food sacrificed to idols and by committing sexual immorality. Likewise you also have those who hold to the teaching of the Nicolaitans" (Revelation 2:14–15).

To the people in Thyatira, he wrote, "I have this against you: You tolerate that woman Jezebel, who calls herself a prophetess. By her teaching she misleads my servants into sexual immorality and the eating of food sacrificed to idols" (Revelation 2:20).

To those in Sardis, he wrote, "You are dead. Wake up! Strengthen what remains . . . for I have not found your deeds complete in the sight of my God" (Revelation 3:1–2).

What is so seriously wrong in Pergamum that the Lord Himself threatens that unless they "repent," He will fight against them with the sword in His mouth? What is happening in Thyatira that causes our Lord to warn, "I will strike her children [the followers of the false teacher in that church] dead." "Then all the churches will know that I am he who searches hearts and minds, and I will repay each of you according to your deeds" (Revelation 2:23). Or what's happened in Sardis that He says to them, "If you do not wake up, I will come like a thief, and you will not know at what time I will come to you" (Revelation 3:3)?

There are clues in John's short letters that will solve the mystery of Christ's anger at these three churches. Balaam was an Old Testament prophet who led God's people off their trail to the Promised Land and into the towns and practices of God's enemy, the Moabites (Numbers 22:21). One commentator describes Balaam as an example of compromise with false religion. The Nicolaitans were first-century followers of a similar false prophet who taught the Christians to give in to the practices of tipping their hats to the false gods of the city and their immoral sexual practices, so that the Gospel might be more acceptable to the people.

Jezebel was a foreigner (a Phoenician princess) who, centuries before, had married a king of Israel and insisted on sacrificing to the idol Baal alongside the worship of the God of Israel. She dared to encourage the people of Israel to worship her false god and practice immoral ways. Now someone in Thyatira whom John nicknamed "Jezebel" was teaching those first-century Christians to give in to the worship of the gods of the city and to their immoral sexual practices. The people were obeying her.

Imagine the predicament of those first-century believers. They lived in towns where many different gods were worshipped. Their neighbors' homes had shrines to various deities; in little nooks and in grand temples stood statues and symbols of family gods, ancestral gods, ancient mythical gods, and the god of Rome—Caesar himself. A Christian couldn't walk through a neighbor's house without passing a pagan shrine. He could hardly buy meat that hadn't first been sacrificed to a pagan god. He couldn't conduct business without walking through the temple of the patron gods of his union or guild. In the market or at business, he couldn't avoid the devout throngs of people before the temples of Diana or Isis. He couldn't cross the city without passing sentries and the priests who tended the place of worship set aside to worship Caesar.

Why offend neighbors by ignoring—or worse, by condemning—their religious beliefs? After all, it would only mean a token offering, an orange placed at a neighbor family's shrine or a pinch of incense at the feet of Caesar's giant marble form. It would only mean standing at the pledge of allegiance or bowing at the prayer or joining in a hymn to the deities of friends, neighbors, and coworkers at a social, political, or commercial event. Why be so rigid? Why not worship the one true God in private while simply nodding good-naturedly in the direction of the false gods on every corner? Was this really so bad?

Why all the fuss about sexual immorality? There was a beautiful sanctuary called Daphne just outside Antioch, the town where the first Gentile church was established. The temples of Diana and Apollo were surrounded by lush green lawns, flower gardens, fountains, and cypress groves. Leading citizens from the business, professional, and political worlds met there to rest, to conduct business, and to worship. Temple prostitutes were provided as a courtesy. What John called sexual immorality was a common practice of the first century—even part of worship for the unbeliever. Men had wives for raising families and concubines for sexual pleasure.

So what was the problem? Why was Christ, through John, angry at their adultery? The temple prostitutes kept their sexual needs satisfied. It kept Christian tradesmen from looking like fanatics—or worse, like fools—during guild parties and initiations. Why were the sexual standards of Christ's revelation to those early Christians so tough, so rigid, and so demanding? Why was Christ so intolerant? This is a picture of us today—worshipping the values of this world (idolatry); giving in to our sexual passions (immorality). We have become so tolerant and accepting of the world's ways that it is hard for many in the church to notice the sin much less answer how it crept in. The church is to be *in* the world, but worldliness is not to infiltrate the church.

Yet we see these signs penetrating the church today. This is no different than the up-and-down history of the people of Israel. God rescued a motley crowd of Jewish slaves and started them toward the Promised Land. Filled with gratitude to God, they "believed his promises and sang his praise" (Psalm 106:12). But almost immediately their gratitude turned to grumbling.

Grumbling and gratitude are, for the child of God, in conflict. Be grateful and you won't grumble. Grumble and you won't be grateful. The psalmist wrote, "They soon forgot what he had done and did not wait for his counsel. In the desert they gave in to their craving; in the wasteland they put God to the test" (Psalm 106:13–14).

When Israel felt passionately about God and His great mercies to them, when they sought His guidance and obeyed His commands, they were victorious over their enemies. But when their holy passion for God waned, they were defeated. When Moses disappeared on the top of Mount Sinai and was gone for so long, they immediately reverted to idolatry and had Aaron make a golden calf from the jewels they had taken from Egypt. When Moses came down from the mountain, he found them in an orgy of idolatry and immorality.

There is only one passion that can help us control the many other passions that plague us; that is the passion to know and obey God. When this primary passion grows cold, we give in to our lower passions. When we get out of touch with Christ, we begin touching the things of the world, trying to fill the void that the human flesh craves.

It is like the prodigal son who tried to fill his stomach with the husks that the pigs were eating. I meet people constantly who are going to one round of parties after another: gambling, drinking, abusing drugs, partaking of a thousand and one things this world has to offer. But nothing satisfies the hunger of the soul.

Many people today, even in so-called Christian countries, are turning to Satan worship to try to fill the longings that only God can satisfy. Not even human love can satisfy the longing for God's love. Instead of turning to the Father's love, we begin a mad, promiscuous search for the perfect human lover. Idolatry is closely connected to immorality. When the natural love of God is perverted, men and women seek substitutes—any substitute.

On the isle of Patmos, Christ sounded His warning to the churches of Asia. He ordered them to stop conforming to the values of the culture around them. "Repent!" commanded John. "Wake up!" he warned them. "Hold on!" he cried. His cry can still be heard today in the pounding of hoofbeats.

Look at the condition of marriage within the context of today's Christian homes and churches. The divorce rate is almost as high among believers as among unbelievers. Almost every day a new revelation surfaces about another leader in the church whose marriage is in shambles. All too often, in both the spiritual and in the marital dimensions of life, it is simply a matter of letting their first love grow cold (the problem of the Ephesians and the Laodiceans) and of giving in to the values of this age and to its immoral practices (the problem of the Christians in Pergamum, Thyatira, and Sardis).

OVERCOMING IDOL WORSHIP

It is interesting, if not frightening, to compare today's churches to the early church. Our lack of passion and practice to know and obey Christ is as evident as it was in John's day. People who passionately follow the Master will be better able to master their passions than those whose first love has died. Invariably, I find people involved in irresponsible, destructive, and debasing practices trying to fill the empty space with other things, even trying to fill the spiritual emptiness with sexual excitement. It will not work! Only God's love can fill the empty space. Human love will always fall short and fail; sex or materialism will not even come close to filling it. The Scripture makes it clear that our first love is always to be for our Lord.

For those who would worship the one true God, the command is clear: "You shall have *no other* gods before me" (Exodus 20:3; emphasis added). God's instructions regarding sexual morality are equally clear. Old and New Testament literature cry out for sexual purity. Hebrews 13:4 says, "Marriage should be honored by all, and the marriage bed kept pure, for God will judge the adulterer and all the sexually immoral." In 1 Corinthians 6, Paul wrote, "Flee from sexual immorality. . . . He who sins sexually sins against his own body. Do you not know that your body is a temple of the Holy Spirit . . . ? You are not your own; you were bought at a price. Therefore honor God with your body" (vv. 18–20).

Adultery (sexual relations with anyone but your own spouse)

and fornication (sexual relations apart from the loving and lifelong commitment of marriage) are expressly forbidden, for they are inevitably destructive, dehumanizing, and demeaning to God's creation. God's Word promises that sexual immorality, though a short-term source of physical pleasure and emotional escape, in the long run will lead to disappointment, heartbreak, and even death. The Bible is clear: "You shall not commit adultery" (Exodus 20:14).

Nearly all entertainment and advertisements give the opposite message. They tell us to enjoy ourselves now, cater to our whims, and ignore the possible consequences. My friend, consequences are not only possible, but they are probable. We've become used to such expressions as "You only live once" or "You only go around once." The late comedian Richard Pryor said, "Enjoy as much as you can. Even if you live to be ninety, that's not as long as you're going to be dead."

When I hear such taunting, my heart swells to realize that people who make such claims do not understand the principle of death—death is only for a season. For all will live eternally—in heaven or hell. The Bible says, "For the hour is coming in which all who are in the graves will hear His voice and come forth—those who have done good, to the resurrection of life, and those who have done evil, to the resurrection of condemnation (John 5:28–29 NKJV). This is not speaking about works of service but accepting or rejecting Christ. If we follow Christ, we will live eternally with Him. If we reject Christ, we will live eternally where Satan abides. Both results have Christ at the center: we follow Him or we turn our backs on Him. We alone seal our fate.

Satanic influences are everywhere, pushing us toward idolatry and sexual immorality. Moral living sometimes demands difficult choices. It requires selflessness. At times it may create tension between what we want to be for God and what we crave for ourselves. In that awful struggle to overcome, friends and family may come to our aid. Pastors and counselors and fellow Christians may assist us. Setting goals, practicing disciplines, building new interests and diversions, creating systems of reward to modify our behavior, all of these may help. But in the struggle for righteousness, there is nothing more helpful than being passionately in tune with Christ through His Spirit and being passionately committed to doing His will. It has been said that in order to tune in to God's voice, we must tune out this world's noise.

The children of Israel got off track when they "tuned God out." They let their first love die. They traded Almighty God for an empty idol, and the consequence was life-changing—they never reached the Promised Land. The Bible says that "their bodies were scattered over the desert" (1 Corinthians 10:5).

The price we pay in broken lives and shattered dreams when we let that first love die goes far beyond what we can imagine. And it happens when we begin giving in to pagan values and practices. Many believe that pagan worship is a thing of the past, but it is ever present—we have just given it a new name: pop culture.

The Bible says, "I, Jesus, have sent my angel to give you this testimony for the churches" (Revelation 22:16). "Blessed are those who wash their robes, that they may . . . go through the gates into the city. Outside are . . . those who practice magic arts, the sexually immoral, the murderers, the idolaters and everyone who loves and practices falsehood" (Revelation 22:14–15).

As you read these words, you may know that you have sinned against God and need His forgiveness. Perhaps you have fallen into sexual sin or you have allowed worldly desires and pleasures to fill your heart and mind. Whatever your sin, take it to the Lord and leave it at His feet. Why carry your burden when He is knocking at your door, asking to come in and help you and strengthen you? Let Him help you overcome.

OVERCOMING SUFFERING

Smyrna, now the city of Izmir, Turkey, was and is one of the great business and trade centers of the Near East. Almost two centuries before Christ, Smyrna welcomed Rome and served Caesar with unquestioning loyalty. The city was perhaps the most beautiful in the entire region. Many religious cults were headquartered there, including the cult of Caesar worship. Although eleven cities bid for it, the Roman senate built a temple to Emperor Tiberius in Smyrna. A great and powerful Jewish minority also lived there and joined with Rome in making life tempestuous for Christians of both Gentile and Jewish background. As a result, the church at Smyrna was a persecuted church.

Philadelphia, due east from Smyrna, was built on a plateau looking out across the valley of the river Cogamus. This prosperous city was called the "gateway to the East," and through its gates passed caravans to and from Rome, the capital of the empire. To them, John wrote, "I have placed before you an open door that no one can shut" (Revelation 3:8). Here, too, the Jewish synagogue was strong and hostile toward the young Christian church. We know almost nothing about either of the Christian churches in Smyrna or Philadelphia except for these two short letters dictated to John by Christ on the island of Patmos.

Interestingly, both churches were faithful and persecuted. There is not one word of criticism in the letters to the Christians in either church. John wrote to Smyrna, "I know your afflictions and your poverty—yet you are rich!" (Revelation 2:9). To Philadelphia, he wrote, "I know that you have little strength, yet you have kept my word and have not denied my name" (Revelation 3:8). Apparently both churches were small; both had few economic resources; both faced hostile environments (John—a Jew himself—scathingly refers in both letters to the "synagogue of Satan"). For both churches, more troubled times were ahead. This should be a wake-up call for the church today: the Bible clearly says that faithfulness and persecution often go hand in hand.

The irony of these two letters is immediately apparent. John wrote to Philadelphia, "Since you have kept my command to endure patiently, I will also *keep you from the hour of trial* that is going to come upon the whole world to test those who live on the earth" (Revelation 3:10; emphasis added).

To the church at Smyrna, John wrote, "Do not be afraid of what you are about to suffer. I tell you, the devil will put some of you in prison to test you, and *you will suffer persecution . . .* Be faithful" (Revelation 2:10; emphasis added).

Smyrna would face terrible suffering. Philadelphia would escape unscathed. All the assumptions we can make about suffering are tested by these two short letters. Both churches seem equally faithful. Yet one would suffer "even unto death." The other would not suffer at all.

This seeming inequality has precedent in the Scripture. In Hebrews 11 we have a long list of people whom God delivered. But in verse 35 the writer said, "Others were tortured and refused to be released." In the book of Acts, for example, James was beheaded, while Peter was delivered.

In these passages we are reminded that suffering has a mysterious component, known only to God. John, too, assumed that suffering is a natural part of Christian faith. He didn't question why one church suffered and another did not. He didn't even expect God to rescue Smyrna from suffering, yet he praised God for protecting Philadelphia from the suffering to come.

John warned the church at Smyrna what they would suffer and what would be gained: "Be faithful, even to the point of death, and I will give you the crown of life" (Revelation 2:10). John told the Philadelphia church, "Hold on to what you have, so that no one will take your crown" (Revelation 3:11).

There are several applications here that we must not overlook in our own times of trouble. First, expect suffering. Don't feel surprised, put upon, proud, or afraid. Suffering is part and parcel of the Christian life. Second, don't compare yourself to someone else's burden or lack of burden. Comparisons are demoralizing either way. Third, recognize that it doesn't take great wealth or social influence to be faithful (note how few resources these two churches had), but it does take obedience and endurance. Fourth, remember that one day all earthly suffering will end and the second death, the eternal death of the spirit, will not touch us. Fifth, keep in mind that when one bears suffering faithfully, God is glorified and honored. The suffering servants of Christ will be honored in a special way and will be given a new name that "no man knows except he that receives it."

Some years ago, the great Canadian photographer Yousuf Karsh sent me a book of his photographs. On the outer mailing wrapper, the customs official had stamped the words "Value of Contents." Under that was written, "Autographed by the author." On the inside page was the photographer's name written by his hand. While the book alone would have been worth perhaps forty or fifty dollars, the autograph raised its value. As believers in Jesus Christ, our value is the fact that we are going to be autographed by the Author. This is a wonderful picture of what lies ahead for those who belong to the Author of life.

I don't understand the reasons for suffering and persecution. I don't know why the churches in one part of the world endure terrible pain and deprivation while other churches are fat and rich and almost pain free. I don't know why some of the young evangelists who gathered at our conferences in Amsterdam over the years carry scars from burnings and beatings they suffered for Christ's sake, while my life has been free from that sort of persecution. I don't know why the late Corrie ten Boom had to watch her sister die in a Nazi prison camp, or why Joni Eareckson Tada is paralyzed from the neck down.

Perhaps you have faced pain or suffering you did not understand. You may even have become angry at God for allowing it to happen while others escaped such problems. Don't let the acids of bitterness eat away inside. Instead, learn the secret of trusting Christ in *every* circumstance. Learn to say with Paul, "I have learned to be content whatever the circumstances. I know what it is to be in need, and I know what it is to have plenty. I have learned the secret of being content in any and every situation, whether well fed or hungry, whether living in plenty or in want. I can do everything through him who gives me strength" (Philippians 4:11–13).

THE OVERCOMING SAINT
AWAITS THE COMING SAVIOR

What I have learned from John's short letters in Revelation is this: Christ commands us to overcome in the strength He alone can supply as we turn to Him in faith, trusting His promises.

"Overcome!" cried the Savior from the island of Patmos. "Overcome!" wrote John at the end of each letter to the seven churches. "Overcome!" cried the leaders of each of the seven churches to their flocks, who then joined the saints and martyrs known and unknown through the ages.

"Overcome!" is a command and warning from the pages of God's Word. We are to join with the suffering of those who have been laughed at and ignored, humiliated, stripped, tried unfairly, imprisoned, beaten, tortured, and killed for the name of the Lord Jesus Christ. The Revelation of Jesus Christ will overcome Satan's grip in the end. For everyone who endures the storm awaits a crown of victory. I long to see the many crowns upon the head of Him who rides into eternity with His church. The joy will be more glorious for the bride of Christ if we will follow Him in obedience today.

John ended his letters to the seven churches with the admonition to "overcome." Jesus Christ ends His Revelation to all with His promise, "Yes, I am coming soon" (Revelation 22:20). I hope you are ready to meet the coming King.

8

STANDING BEFORE GOD

There before me was a great multitude that no one could count,
from every nation, tribe, people and language,
standing before the throne and in front of the Lamb . . .
and they cried out . . . "Salvation belongs to our God."
—Revelation 7:9–10

The most moving moments in my life as an evangelist have been when I stood in the pulpit and invited people to come forward to receive Christ as Savior and Lord. I have watched the brokenness reflected on their faces as the Spirit of God touched their hearts and, one by one, moved them down the aisle to a moment of public commitment. Often, tears of emotion trickled down their faces as they stood, with counselors beside them, praying for forgiveness of sin and surrendering their lives to the Lord. I have seen their joy when they realized that they had been redeemed by Jesus Christ, who purchased their souls with His very blood. They came as lost sinners and left as members of the family of God.

The time of invitation is the most important moment in a crusade. I always said, "You're not coming to a man; you are not coming to Billy Graham. I cannot save you. You are coming to the Man Jesus Christ—He is the only One who saves." It was during this holy moment we witnessed lost souls standing before God.

I believe our Lord was thinking of new believers when He spoke to John on Patmos—not only of the early Christians in Asia but those down through the ages. Christ knew the horror and heartbreak that lay ahead for the faithful in the churches of Asia and in every faithful church around the globe for centuries to come. Christ knew the price they would pay to "overcome." He knew they would need His power in times of struggle. He gave His promise for that day when He said He would wipe away our tears and we would live with Him forever. So as He ends the seven letters to the churches, He gives an invitation not to unbelievers as I do, but to Christians. This invitation from Revelation is, I think, the most beautiful and powerful invitation in the entire biblical account.

Jesus says, "Behold, I stand at the door and knock. If anyone hears my voice and opens the door, I will come in to him and dine with him, and he with Me" (Revelation 3:20 NKJV). What a plea. What a promise.

STANDING AT THE DOOR

It is humbling to imagine that even in His heavenly glory, Christ knocks on the doors of our hearts, asking to come in. If we open that door, we will stand before Him. What a glorious moment. There is an old song that speaks of the comfort we find when we stand before God and with God.

When I stand with God, no raging storm shall ever shake me
When I stand with Him, the cares of life can never break me

For when I'm crying He dries my tears
When I'm frightened He hides my fears
All my sorrows disappear
When I stand with Him.

We have the assurance that in the storms of life, Jesus Himself will be standing with us. He is waiting to share our sorrows and to renew our courage.

We are not alone, my friends. We never shall be. He is there all of the time; all we need to do is open the door to Him. What is your need today?

Do you need comfort in your personal trials? Christ is waiting.

Do you need forgiveness for your sins? He is knocking.

Do you need to make a commitment to serve God with your life? He has work for you to do.

Whatever your spiritual need right now, Christ is knocking at the door of your heart. He is Lord of the universe, and He wants to be Lord of your life as well.

When Jesus was on trial in Jerusalem, the Roman governor turned to the crowd and asked, "What shall I do, then, with Jesus who is called the Christ?" (Matthew 27:22). This is the most important question that has ever been asked. It is also the question you must ask yourself. No one can answer for you. Unless you have made the decision to accept Jesus Christ and follow Him as Lord of your life, you will not share in the promises that follow. Jesus said, "To him who overcomes I will grant to sit with Me on My throne, as I also overcame and sat down with My Father on His throne. He who has an ear, let him hear what the Spirit says to the churches" (Revelation 3:21–22 NKJV).

Try to imagine what went through John's mind as he wrote these words: "Behold, I stand at the door and knock." After this, John saw "a door standing open in heaven." He wrote, "The first voice which I heard was like a trumpet speaking with me, saying, 'Come up here,

and I will show you things which must take place after this.'
Immediately, I was in the Spirit" (Revelation 4:1–2 NKJV).

STANDING IN HIS PRESENCE

If John was worried about the world and its condition, if he was
concerned about the future and how his flock would overcome, and
if he was perplexed about the power of evil and the lack of good on
this planet, the next vision made all the difference. It offers equally
great promise for our time.

"There before me was a throne in heaven with someone sitting
on it," wrote John. "And the one who sat there had the appearance
of jasper and carnelian [a fiery red stone]. A rainbow resembling
an emerald, encircled the throne" (Revelation 4:2–3). John had to
be blinded by the light and glory that encircled the Lord. "From
the throne proceeded lightning, thundering, and voices . . . before
the throne there was a sea of glass, like crystal" (Revelation 4:5–6
NKJV).

Surrounding the throne were twenty-four other thrones. Seated
on them were twenty-four elders dressed in white and wearing crowns
of gold. Around the throne were four living creatures. The first was
like a lion, the second was like an ox, the third had a face like a man,
and the fourth was like a flying eagle. "Each of the four living creatures had six wings and was covered with eyes all around" (Revelation
4:7).

The visual impact of that moment must have been overwhelming. For centuries Bible commentators have analyzed that scene,
describing in detail the names of the elders, usually assumed to be
the twelve Old Testament patriarchs and the twelve New Testament
apostles, and the living creatures, usually seen as seraphim and cher-
ubim, angelic beings created to carry out God's commands.

John didn't bother to analyze what he saw. But what he heard he reported in detail. Those strong, angelic creatures never stopped proclaiming:

> *Holy, holy, holy*
> *is the Lord God Almighty,*
> *who was, and is, and is to come.* (Revelation 4:8)

Whenever the living creatures give glory, honor and thanks to him who sits on the throne and who lives for ever and ever, the twenty-four elders fall down before him . . . and worship him . . . They lay their crowns before the throne and say:

> *"You are worthy, our Lord and God,*
> *to receive glory and honor and power,*
> *for you created all things,*
> *and by your will they were created*
> *and have their being."* (Revelation 4:9–11)

STANDING BEFORE
THE MYSTERY OF HIS MAJESTY

For this one moment in time, the old apostle was ushered into the presence of the Mystery behind the universe. There is no way to describe God. John could only describe the response to God by both the angelic and the human beings before him. Yes, there was a description of color and beauty, of majesty and power, but even as the apostle stood before Him, God remained a mystery to John. He who is the mystery behind creation and the preservation of mankind deserves our glory, honor, and praise.

In spite of rumors to the contrary, we are not creatures abandoned on a planet spinning madly through the universe, lost in galaxies upon galaxies of gaseous flaming suns or burnt-out cinder moons. We are the children of a great and wonderful God who even now sits in power accomplishing His purposes in His creation.

At the heart of this mystery is great hope. The national powers that we see hell-bent for destruction—amassing weapons, killing and being killed—are not the ultimate power. Nor are the individual figures who rule in our lives: mothers, fathers, teachers, pastors, counselors, politicians, diplomats, bankers, police officers, social workers, wardens and jailers, probation officers, tax collectors, dictators and their soldiers, kings and presidents. For the day will come when all shall stand powerless before this God of John's vision.

The Revelation is carefully calculated to rebuke our sin, restore our standing before God, and renew hope in each of us. Almighty God is behind creation, and though in many ways He remains a mystery, I am confident that He has created the planet on which we live, that He has created me, and that what He has created He loves and has a plan to save. If He didn't, He wouldn't be worthy of our praise.

George Ladd wrote about this scene: "However fearful or uncontrolled the forces of evil on earth may seem to be, they cannot annul or eclipse the greater fact that behind the scenes God is on his throne governing the universe."

God is in control! That awesome truth penetrates every chapter John wrote, and it can make the difference for you if it penetrates every area of your life. You can trust your life and your future to God, because He loves you and He alone knows your future.

How do I know He loves you and me? Because He sent His only Son to die on the cross for our sins. "For God so loved the world that he gave his one and only Son, that whoever believes in him shall not perish but have eternal life" (John 3:16). Jesus Christ broke the power of evil and sin through His resurrection from the dead. Christ is alive!

John stood in awe and wonder as God held out a scroll "with writing on both sides and sealed with seven seals" (Revelation 5:1).

A mighty angelic voice trumpeted out the question, "Who is worthy to break the seals and open the scroll?" (Revelation 5:2). Apparently what followed in the silence of that awful moment left John weeping, for "no one was found who was worthy to open the scroll or look inside" (Revelation 5:4).

Why the tears? At that very moment, God Himself was holding out a scroll—a list—and no one was worthy to open it. So John wept. Is there no one who can tell us what is written on the scroll? Is there no one worthy to bear God's message to us?

"Then one of the elders said to [John], 'Do not weep! See, the Lion of the tribe of Judah, the Root of David, has triumphed. He is able to open the scroll and its seven seals'" (Revelation 5:5). Immediately, John turned in the direction the elder was pointing. What did he expect to see? A lion, of course—the traditional Jewish symbol of the conquering Messiah who would come to deliver His people from evil. Instead, John wrote, "I saw a Lamb, looking as if it had been slain, standing in the center of the throne" (Revelation 5:6).

Again, John beheld a mystery. Who was the Lamb standing on the throne? Years before, John himself had transcribed the words of John the Baptist when he identified Christ as the Messiah, saying, "Look, the Lamb of God, who takes away the sin of the world!" (John 1:29). The Lamb was Jesus, the Messiah, God's anointed One, His only begotten Son. Christ had three roles to play in man's redemption. First, He came in the humble form of a man. In that form He suffered and died. Through His sacrifice the penalty for mankind's sin was paid. Second, He rose to life, thereby conquering death and the grave. Third, He would reign as Lord, the promised Messiah and the Lion of David in splendor and in power, and would sit at the right hand of God the Father, making intercession for us.

Now John was watching a vision of that perfect sacrifice, the Lamb of God "in the center of the throne." Suddenly he saw the Lamb reach out and take from the hand of God the scroll no one dared to open.

Suddenly, the elders and the angelic forms fell before the Lamb in a chorus of praise. The heavenly choir sang "a new song":

> *You are worthy to take the scroll*
> *and to open its seals,*
> *because you were slain,*
> *and with your blood you purchased men for God*
> *from every tribe and language and people and nation.*
> *You have made them to be a kingdom and priests to serve our God,*
> *and they will reign on the earth.* (Revelation 5:9–10)

Then John heard "ten thousand times ten thousand" angels encircling the throne and joining in that song of praise to the Lamb, who was bridging the gap of silence between God and His creation:

> *Worthy is the Lamb, who was slain,*
> *to receive power and wealth and wisdom and strength*
> *and honor and glory and praise!* (Revelation 5:12)

The vision widened. The song swelled. John said in wonder:

> *I heard every creature in heaven and on earth and under the earth*
> *and on the sea, and all that is in them, singing:*
> *"To him who sits on the throne and to the Lamb*
> *be praise and honor and glory and power, for ever and ever!"*
> (Revelation 5:13)

And again, the elders all fell down before the throne and worshipped, and the four angelic creatures lifted their voices in a solemn "Amen!"

The presence of God in His glorious splendor blinds us. Without Jesus as our guide, we cannot fully grasp who God is. But in Jesus, the Lamb of God, we see all of God we need to see. Jesus said to

Philip, "Anyone who has seen me has seen the Father" (John 14:9). From Jesus we learn all of God we need to know.

It would be a mistake only to see God isolated, high and lifted up on a throne surrounded by thunder and lightning. What hope would we have in that kind of powerful but impersonal God? That would be about as comforting as the turbines in a hydroelectric dam. But it would be an equally great mistake to see Jesus only as a wonderful man who suffered and died, who gave us an example of what human life should be—a good man who was assassinated, as Lincoln and Gandhi were slain. Jesus was not just a good man. He is God and the Son of God.

In John's vision we see the Father through the life, death, and resurrection of the Son. The Third Person of the Trinity, the Holy Spirit of God, makes all of this known to us.

STANDING ON TRUTH

In the summer of 1989, I was interviewed by a London newspaper reporter who asked if I thought the world would recognize Jesus the next time He comes to earth. "Yes," I said, "because He's not going to come riding on a donkey. He's coming mounted on a pure white stallion as King of kings and Lord of lords."

I have heard people say that Christ would no doubt be crucified even more quickly by today's pagan culture if He were to come now. No matter what you think of Jesus Christ, you should know that He is not coming back as the suffering servant. He is coming as King.

When we read John's attempts in these early chapters of Revelation to portray the glory and majesty of the glorified Christ and the indescribable reality of His great throne of judgment, we know that words are simply not adequate to capture the vision. The majesty of our God is beyond anything our finite minds can conceive. Even the most surreal imagery does not do justice. This is the Christ of power, dominion, and glory who is coming back to this world. In the language of today, He is totally awesome!

A rabbi in Israel once said to a group of visiting Christians, "You know, our two religions are not all that far apart. When the Messiah comes back, we'll just ask him, 'Is this your first or second visit?'" But the humor of that remark cannot disguise the terrible consequences it entails. For when Christ returns, that *slight* difference will make *all* the difference in the world.

Jesus Christ the Messiah has identified Himself time and again as the Redeemer of the world. For twenty centuries He has sent His prophets, apostles, saints, and ordinary believers like you and me into the world to proclaim His name before all generations, and He demands that all hear His voice, acknowledge Him *by faith*, repent, and accept Him as Lord. When we see Him next, face-to-face, it will be too late to decide.

Matthew records some of the most disturbing words Jesus said during His earthly ministry: "Not everyone who says to Me, 'Lord, Lord,' shall enter the kingdom of heaven, but he who does the will of My Father in heaven" (Matthew 7:21 NKJV). In the Gospel of the Greek physician, Luke, Jesus said:

> For many . . . will seek to enter and will not be able. When once the Master of the house has risen up and shut the door, and you begin to stand outside and knock at the door, saying, "Lord, Lord, open for us," and He will answer and say to you, "I do not know you, where you are from," then you will begin to say, "We ate and drank in Your presence, and You taught in our streets." But He will say, "I tell you I do not know you, where you are from. Depart from Me, all you workers of iniquity." There will be weeping and gnashing of teeth, when you see Abraham and Isaac and Jacob and all the prophets in the kingdom of God, and yourselves thrust out. (Luke 13:24–28 NKJV)

What a bleak and heartrending scene that will be. How tragic for those who have been blinded by personal pride, or intellect, or ideas of tolerance, or by believing that Christ's words are meaningless. For two thousand years, His words have been proclaimed over and over. I have proclaimed them thousands of times during the last seventy years. No one in the civilized world can claim he or she has not heard the news that Jesus Christ wants to be Lord of his or her life. No one can claim ignorance.

"God's invisible qualities—his eternal power and divine nature—have been clearly seen, being understood from what has been made, so that men are without excuse" (Romans 1:20).

The Holy Bible is the best-selling book in the history of the world. The International Bible Society, the American Bible Society, and other groups have given away millions of copies, and they haven't even scratched the surface of the demand. No thriller, no romance novel, spy-chaser, cult book, or anything else outsells the Bible. It's not as if the Truth were out of reach. What other excuses are there?

One of the problems, of course, is that Satan is alive and well on Planet Earth. He is a liar and a deceiver who stands behind us, mocking, scoffing, laughing at the Word of God, convincing people that the Bible is just another self-righteous book. *It is so judgmental*, he says. *It's full of holes*, he says. But Satan "is a liar and the father of lies" (John 8:44).

I agree with Paul de Parrie, an author who says he finds it odd that the same people who never think to question the instructions that come with their VCR or microwave "instantly bristle with questions about God's instructions on the most important issues in all of life." If the handbook on their Japanese camcorder warns them to keep it away from water, they do it, but if the Bible, which comes with much greater authority and a lifetime warranty, tells them to "flee fornication," they recoil in horror!

STANDING BEFORE THE NATIONS

Some years ago while in Washington, D.C., at the office of a power-ful and well-known politician, I looked in his eyes and asked, "Sir, have you ever received Christ as your Savior?" He hung his head and didn't say anything. After a prolonged silence, he said, "You know, no one has ever asked me that question before." I asked if he would like to receive Christ right then and have the confidence of eternal security. As I held out my hand, I said, "It means repentance." I explained that it means faith in Christ and Christ alone. He was quiet for a few minutes, and I didn't say any more. Then he held out his hand and said, "I'll receive Him now," and we prayed. He was a church member. He had been exposed to Christianity throughout his life, but he had never repented and surrendered to Christ. Nothing on earth is more important. Nothing.

My mother used to look out the window every morning and say, "Maybe this will be the day when Christ comes again." She lived with that daily anticipation, but the signs of His imminent return have never been greater than now. Everyone outside the family of Christ is under the judgment of God. To share in the rewards of eternal life and security in the presence of the God of Revelation, we must first acknowledge His Son, repent, and receive Him. That is not optional, no matter what your instinct or your faith may tell you.

John wrote, "He who has the Son has life, he who does not have the Son of God does not have life" (1 John 5:12). It cannot be clearer. Without a personal knowledge of Christ as Lord, without confessing our sins to Him, and without surrendering our lives to His Lordship, there is no possibility of peace with God. The clock is running out.

In Revelation, John issues Christ's challenge to "overcome." In his letters, he wrote, "Who is he who overcomes the world, but he who believes that Jesus is the Son of God?" (1 John 5:5 NKJV). Then he added, "He who believes in the Son of God has the witness in himself; he who does not believe God has made Him a liar, because he has not believed the testimony that God has given of His Son (1 John 5:10 NKJV).

Anyone who denies the reality of Jesus Christ as the glorified Son of God is, by definition, *against* Christ. John says that such a person is an *antichrist*.

"Who is a liar," he asked, "but he who denies that Jesus is the Christ? He is antichrist who denies the Father and the Son. Whoever denies the Son does not have the Father either; he who acknowledges the Son has the Father also" (1 John 2:22–23 NKJV). The logic is simple and irrefutable. The Word of God is clear.

John calls for each of us to be faithful to what we have been taught by Scripture. He says, "Therefore let that abide in you which you heard from the beginning. If what you heard from the beginning abides in you, you also will abide in the Son and in the Father" (1 John 2:24 NKJV).

The reward for faithfulness to the teachings of Scripture, John says in the very next verse, is eternal life. Christ is coming for the church. Just as it was my mother's hope until she went at last to be with Him, it should also be our hope. What greater glory can we anticipate than to stand before the throne of God in humbleness, before His great and incomparable majesty?

We must all consider where we stand before God. This is the question He asks when He knocks on the door of the heart. He does not knock as a visitor. He doesn't knock as a passerby. He does not knock and then realize He has the wrong address. He is knocking on just the right door and at the exact time the Holy Spirit is whispering to your soul. Answer the door. Invite Him in. Stand before Him with thanksgiving in your heart. Sit at His feet in worship; praise Him for bidding you to dwell with Him in the place He is preparing forever. Prepare for the coming King, for when the four horsemen are released from heaven, look up. The Lord Jesus will be preparing to mount His horse, ride to the earth in mighty power, and overcome the world.

9

WHITE HORSE LOOSED

I looked, and there before me was a white horse!
Its rider held a bow, and he was given a crown.
—REVELATION 6:2

Horses are magnificent creatures, mighty animals, and man's companion in ancient warfare. From the days of Indians and pilgrims, to the Civil War, to how the West was won, Americans have always had a fascination with horses. There are race horses, show horses, and the least of all glamour—the work horse.

In the Bible, horses are mentioned some three hundred times and are predominantly equated with war. While King Solomon was not a wartime king, he owned twelve thousand horses—a powerful show of strength and majesty. The Old Testament speaks frequently of horses and horsemen: "Couriers, mounted on their swift horses that were used in the king's service, rode out hurriedly, urged by the king's command" (Esther 8:14 ESV). They carried important people and urgent messages. This brings us to the four horsemen of the Apocalypse. They are mounted on four horses: white, red, black, and pale, and their messages have not changed since the time of John's vision.

Older than the Revelation is the story of the beginning when "God created the heavens and the earth" (Genesis 1:1). By His very nature, God creates. He is the Creator, and we discover the essence of Who God is in His creation. We see Him everywhere. The book of Hebrews states, "By faith we understand that the universe was formed at God's command, so that what is seen was not made out of what was visible" (Hebrews 11:3). If we know anything about His creation, we know something of God. Creating is what God does.

In the book of beginnings—Genesis—we read how God made the earth and all that is in it; He spoke it into existence. He made it beautiful beyond expression: the seas, the mountains, the rolling prairies, the mighty forests, and the infinitely varied life forms that populate every part of this planet. He made all these and the universe that surrounds us—it is His handiwork.

Living in the mountains of North Carolina is a daily reminder of God's creativity. Each morning I experience the wonder of sunrise, and each evening sunset seems more spectacular than the last. Until Ruth died, she looked forward to watching the sun come up. I miss sitting with her on the porch as night falls, because she always had a cheery perspective about each day. I relive those moments often through memories.

The world around us abounds with wonders. David, the psalmist, sang, "The heavens declare the glory of God; and the firmament shows His handiwork" (Psalm 19:1 NKJV). If you have ever walked in a forest glade on a misty summer morning anywhere along the Blue Ridge Parkway, you know something of the Creator's originality.

Since men first scratched out rough drawings on hides or papyrus or on the walls of caves, they celebrated the beauty and wonder of God's creation. The world created by God was perfectly designed for human life, with food and game, sparkling mountain streams, and every pleasant thing. It was made to order by a loving God for the enjoyment of the only living beings made in His own image, the man Adam and the woman Eve.

The image we see of paradise in the book of Genesis is brief but beautiful. Moses wrote:

> The LORD God planted a garden eastward in Eden, and there He put the man whom He had formed. And out of the ground the LORD God made every tree grow that is pleasant to the sight and good for food. The tree of life was also in the midst of the garden, and the tree of the knowledge of good and evil. . . .
>
> Then the LORD God took the man and put him in the garden of Eden to tend and keep it. (Genesis 2:8–9, 15 NKJV)

That was the life God wanted us to enjoy forever, but He did something only a loving and benevolent Creator would do: He gave us minds and wills of our own. The Bible teaches that God desires to have fellowship with us, to dialogue with us. He did not make us as robots or mindless creatures but as beings capable of choosing or not choosing, of loving or not loving. What has become of the human race since Creation is the result of the choices we have made by our own free will. Since Adam and Eve were enticed by Satan's charms in the Garden, believing that they might be "like God," humanity has had to scrape out a living in a world less desirable and more threatening than Eden—all because of sin.

SIN LOOSED

What is sin? Theologian and author Dr. Myron Augsburger says:

> Sin is the perversion of the good; it is the cheaper form of something better. Sin is not just things that we have done; rather, it is a perversion at the very core of our being that causes us to deify self and demand our own way. In this self-centeredness, we are

persons formed in our own image, rather than what we were created to be—persons created in God's image.

The answer to our sin is not simply restitution for a few bad things that we have done. The answer is to turn to God and open ourselves to Him. All sin is ultimately against God.

As we move one step closer to the heart of John's vision and the dismal work to be done by the four horsemen of the Apocalypse, it is important to pause long enough to grasp where the human race has come from and how far it has fallen. The image of the horsemen indicates the graphic consequences of sin. Through arrogance, willfulness, and conceit, the world has earned its punishment. We stand deep in the mire of the humanist dilemma.

It is sad and ironic that two centuries of scientific and technological achievements seem to have convinced humanity that God has no part in the creation. Through study and genius, the greatest minds have touched the very edges of God's creation, and some have apparently decided there is no God. I think of a child so absorbed with his paper airplane that he is oblivious to the 747 taking him around the world.

The problem in the world is that people do not do what they know to be right. They seek after their own wills, contrary to the will of God, and in the words of the prophet Hosea, "They sow the wind, and reap the whirlwind" (Hosea 8:7 NKJV). Paul wrote in his letter to the Romans, "For all have sinned and fall short of the glory of God" (Romans 3:23 NKJV). The other half of this declaration, Paul says, is that "the wages of sin is death" (Romans 6:23 NKJV). The cause is our willfulness; the price is separation from God for all eternity.

DECEIVER LOOSED

The four horsemen of the Apocalypse point inevitably to deeper moral and spiritual problems that affect our lives. But each is unique. Each carries his own agenda. In every age, we have seen precursors of the horsemen riding over the earth. They gave warning to the first-century churches in Asia, and their warnings apply to the church today.

Jesus Himself underscored these warnings with a command: "Therefore keep watch" (Matthew 24:42). "Watch out that no one deceives you" (Matthew 24:4). This is representative of the white horse who carries one who imitates Christ and promises a false peace.

"You will hear of wars and rumors of wars, but see to it that you are not alarmed" (Matthew 24:6). This depicts the red horse that takes away peace and brings war.

"There will be famines and earthquakes in various places" (Matthew 24:7). This is the black horse that will wipe out the food supply, leading the nations into severe hunger.

"Then you will be handed over to be persecuted and put to death" (Matthew 24:9). The fourth horse is the only one of the four with a name and a color to match: the pale horse called Death.

When John beheld this fearsome vision, he must have recalled this prophecy that Jesus spoke of as they walked throughout Israel. Now John was writing about the first horseman mounted and ready to ride.

"I heard . . . a voice like thunder," John wrote. "'Come!' I looked, and there before me was a white horse! Its rider held a bow, and he was given a crown" (Revelation 6:1–2). As suddenly as he appeared, the rider kicked the flanks of the white stallion and raced toward the earth "as a conqueror bent on conquest" (Revelation 6:2).

Throughout the centuries, Bible scholars have debated the identity of this rider. The text says he is wearing a crown and carrying a bow of great destruction in his hand. In Revelation 19, Christ is pictured on a white horse wearing many crowns. This has led some to believe that the rider on the white horse in Revelation 6 is also Christ. I do not believe this to be the case. In the Greek text, the crown worn by the rider of the white horse is called *stephanos*, which would refer to the crown of victory worn by a conqueror. The crowns

Christ wears in Revelation 19, on the other hand, are *diadema*, or the crowns of royalty. Although the rider on the white horse bears a resemblance to Christ, his appearance is actually (and no doubt deliberately) deceptive. A closer look reveals his true nature. He is "a conqueror bent on conquest," greedily riding roughshod over all who stand in his way—the rider of the white horse is characterized by his lust for power, destruction, and deceit.

Who, therefore, is the rider on the white horse? He is not Christ, but a deceiver who seeks to capture the hearts and minds of all mankind. He is one who seeks to have people acknowledge him as Lord.

We should always remember that one of the Bible's strongest indictments of Satan is that he is a deceiver, implacably opposed to the truth of God. Jesus said concerning Satan, "He was a murderer from the beginning, not holding to the truth, for there is no truth in him. When he lies, he speaks his native language (John 8:44). In Revelation 20, John speaks of God's final judgment on "the devil, who deceives" (v. 10).

The rider who deceives has been at work in the world since the dawn of human history. He was at work in the Garden of Eden when Satan accosted Adam and Eve. By his diabolical power of deception, he convinced them to turn their backs on God and disobey His clear command. The human race fell from its glory, bringing sorrow and death.

From Eden to Armageddon, there is a worldwide battle raging between the forces of God and the forces of Satan, between light and darkness, between good and evil. Every man, woman, and child alive today is caught in the crossfire. Satan stalks the earth seeking to dominate and to destroy God's creation. At the same time, our Creator, in His love and mercy, works to save that which He has created. The Garden of Eden was "round one" of that battle. It has since escalated into what Dr. Arno C. Gaebelein referred to as "the conflict of the ages." Someday Satan and his works will be completely destroyed and Christ will be victorious; but until that time, stormy battles still rage.

The one who deceives was at work in the animosity between two brothers: Cain and Abel. He sowed dissent among the Israelites as they fled from slavery in Egypt, persuading them that a golden calf could save them or that they should return to the fleshpots of Egypt. He roamed the Sinai wilderness, spreading lies among the children of Israel to make them doubt God's promises and to prevent them from entering the Promised Land. Back and forth the battle has raged: God urging humanity to follow Him to peace and safety; evil darting in and out of the ranks on his white horse, waylaying, luring, lying, and deceiving the careless, and bringing death to those who follow him.

THE LOOSE CULTURE OF DECEPTION

The first horseman storms into our lives today as he has throughout history. The thunder of his coming can be heard growing despairingly louder on the horizon of this troubled world. He promises to do whatever it takes to persuade us to disobey God and join his tragic train of captives plodding to their doom. But if we believe in Jesus Christ, we must do all we can, in God's strength, to resist his alluring deceits.

One of the biggest problems confronting our world is the fact that through years of manipulation and deceit, morality and traditional values are no longer en vogue. The deceiver has betrayed our culture and convinced leaders in government, media, the universities—and even churches—that black is white and wrong is right. The reality of daily life in America, and throughout the West, shows that biblical morality has little place in the lives of most people. By and large, the secular culture will accept any set of values and beliefs and any sort of behavior, so long as it is not noticeably Christian. This, they believe, will bring peace to the world.

Where does that leave us? Secular culture militates against biblical virtues and, sadly, the church follows close behind. As principles and values are crushed, even some Christian leaders are charmed by sin's allure and some have fallen from grace. To each one of us the apostle Peter warned, "Be sober, be vigilant; because your adversary the devil walks about like a roaring lion, seeking whom he may devour. Resist him, steadfast in the faith, knowing that the same sufferings are experienced by your brotherhood in the world" (1 Peter 5:8–9 NKJV). The deceiver on his white horse is already loose in the world. He has succeeded in perverting a huge segment of the population, and he is sporting the victor's crown.

GOD'S JUDGMENT LOOSED

In some ways, God's judgment is like pain in our physical bodies. Whenever we experience pain or discomfort, we generally wait for a while to see if it will go away. But if the pain persists and becomes intense, we go to a doctor to find its cause. At that point, the doctor can generally deal with our problem and relieve the pain. In the beginning, the pain is like an alarm, warning of potential danger. The purpose of the pain was corrective—to let us know something was wrong so we could take action to overcome.

God's judgment is often meant to be corrective in much the same way. It is meant to remind us of our need to get right with God. God can use trials and difficulties to teach us and help us to become better people for His glory. The book of Hebrews says, "My son, do not make light of the Lord's discipline, and do not lose heart when he rebukes you, because the Lord disciplines those he loves. . . . No discipline seems pleasant at the time, but painful. Later on, however, it produces a harvest of righteousness and peace for those who have been trained by it" (Hebrews 12:5–6, 11).

For John, this image must have been unmistakably clear. He had perhaps watched the invading legions of Rome enter Jerusalem with the conquering centurion riding a prancing white steed and carrying in his hand the bow, a sign of victory and of power. Perhaps this is even a flashback to an event that happened in the Roman Empire just before John's exile on Patmos.

The Romans were dauntless and fierce, but they feared their Parthian neighbors who threatened the far eastern borders of the empire. The Parthians rode swift white horses and were deadly accurate archers. In AD 62, a large Roman army had been overrun by the Parthians and forced to surrender. Apparently the Parthians were such skilled bowmen that even from a galloping horse, bow held waist high, an archer could pierce an enemy on another moving horse across the battlefield. William Barclay once stated that there is an old English expression, a "Parthian shot," which means "a final, devastating blow to which there is no possible answer."

LET LOOSE ON THE WORLD

As I review various commentaries on the book of Revelation, I keep coming back to one basic question: are the judgments that John foresees inevitable? Will they definitely happen, or can they somehow be delayed or even completely averted? In other words, are they *conditional* so that they may be avoided by repentance and faith, or are they *unconditional* and will happen no matter what?

This is not an easy question to answer, and I am aware that sincere students of the Bible may not all agree. However, after careful study, I have come to the conclusion that the answer is *both*! God's judgment will come, but Scripture indicates that He will delay judgment in response to the obedience of those who obey His Word. But because men's hearts are evil by nature, there will eventually come a time, known only to God, that thunderous hooves of the four horsemen will storm across the world stage, bringing deception, war, hunger, and death on a scale so massive that it will stagger the imagination.

God will use the four horsemen in an awesome act of judgment on earth, and like a tremendous tidal wave smashing on the shore, nothing will be able to stand against it. The Bible makes it clear that God's judgment is certain—it is coming: "For he has set a day when he will judge the world with justice by the man he has appointed" (Acts 17:31).

Looking at the evidence of judgment already visible in the world, I believe that time may be very near. Perhaps in early stages it is already upon us. Even if that is so, I believe there is hope for a reprieve if God's people react in time and come before Him in humility and prayer. Throughout history there have been many occasions when God delayed or averted His hand of judgment for a period of time because men and women repented and turned to Him in faith and obedience. But I believe sincere repentance is our only hope.

Throughout the centuries, cries of anguish have echoed through the streets of our troubled world. Time after time we have seen disaster in the pages of history—deception, war, hunger, and death. Violent strife and conflict have haunted the human race to one degree or another since the day Adam and Eve first chose to rebel against God.

At those times, death rides through every city and town, bringing suffering and death. But sometimes, just as suddenly, we enter a time of peace and relative calm. Why? I believe it is because there are times when God withholds His judgments, possibly even for several generations, because many have listened to His message of warning and turned to Him in repentance and faith.

A good example of this is seen in God's dealings with the people of the ancient Assyrian capital of Nineveh. They were an evil, pagan people who worshipped idols and often fought against God's people. God sent the prophet Jonah to Nineveh. "Go to the great city of Nineveh and proclaim to it the message I give you. . . . Forty more days and Nineveh will be overturned" (Jonah 3:2, 4). But when the king of Nineveh heard Jonah's message, he repented and ordered the whole people to repent as well. As a result, God's judgment was averted. Only later, when evil increased in the generations after Jonah and the people failed to repent, did God's judgment finally fall on Nineveh. God's judgment is often this way. Someday it will come in all its fullness and finality, but in the meantime it may be that God's hand of judgment will pause when we repent, just as this first horse pauses before being let loose on the world in full measure.

LOOSENING THE GRIP

The world has been corrupt since the fall of man. Society, as a whole, abides by the rules of men: paying our taxes on time, obeying the rules of the road, and so on. If we don't obey them, man imposes penalties, and consequences follow that can seriously alter our lives. Yet people mock when it is suggested that we obey the rules of the One who created everything. We have loosened our grip on the standards God has set before us.

As we look at the four horsemen and their judgments, we must not feel that we are to sit back and do nothing to fight evil just because someday the four horsemen will come with full and final force upon the earth. God alone knows when it is, and until that time we are to learn the lessons of the horsemen and live in such a way that He may be pleased to delay His judgment and allow our world the opportunity to hear His Word and turn to Him.

The first step to overcoming the deceiver is to acknowledge that he exists. The second step is to recognize that he works through deception. The rider's method, first and always, is deception. He promises peace to the world, but he gives only false peace. He will be a superman imposing a supersystem with an iron fist. Jesus said, "I have come in my Father's name, and you do not accept me; but if someone else comes in his own name, you will accept him" (John 5:43). The world that has rejected Jesus Christ will readily receive the devil's antichrist.

The Bible teaches that some time in the future there will be a great superman, called *the* antichrist. As we read in 1 John 2:18, "the antichrist is coming." On the other hand, John prophesied that previous to the actual antichrist's coming, there would be "the spirit of the antichrist" (1 John 4:3), and there would be "many antichrists" (1 John 2:18).

I sometimes imagine this first horseman sitting upon the white horse, reins held tight, struggling to keep the horse from charging full-throttle ahead. Suddenly, the mount loosens his grip, the gate swings open, and the white horse thunders toward us with such great power that many cannot see the difference between this first white horse and the pure white horse that carries the Lord, full of glory and righteous judgment. I trust that as we look at this mysterious rider, you will clearly see deceit for what it is—the first horseman leaves his calling card for us to ponder.

10

THE CULT OF
SPIRITUAL DECEPTION

Watch out that you are not deceived. For many will come
in my name, claiming, "I am he,"... do not follow them.
—LUKE 21:8

One afternoon in Paris years ago, Ruth answered a knock on the door of our hotel room. Two men stood there. In broken English, one explained that the other was "the Messiah" who had come to see me on a "divine errand." After a brief and pathetic encounter, they walked away. Ruth remarked to me, "He claimed to be Christ, but he couldn't even speak to us in our own language."

There is a vast menagerie of masquerading messiahs in the world today—both men and women—claiming to be the Christ. Some of them are mental or emotional cripples. Others scheme and dream with ever more menacing motives. But all are counterfeits.

Deception has become accepted by many who don't really

understand the root meaning. Deception is everything opposite the truth. Our culture will stand in roaring ovations for the illusionists, escape artists, and magicians. Much of it, in the form of entertainment, tricks the mind, causing us to think we are seeing something real when truthfully it is fraudulent. Prisons and jails are filled with con artists—and sad to say, so are many churches.

This is what John's letter to the believers at Smyrna was about: deception in the church. The apostle Paul also encountered this in the Corinthian church. He wrote and warned them: "False apostles, deceitful workers, [transform] themselves into apostles of Christ" (2 Corinthians 11:13 NKJV). The Bible promises that this line of false christs will grow longer until the final embodiment of antichrist appears at the head of the procession. He will be Satan's man. Imitating Christ, he will offer peace, but he is as false as the peace he offers. His golden age will be short-lived.

Some deceivers around us are more obviously in league with Satan than others. They speak directly of the tempting powers of evil and call men and women to worship at the feet of Satan himself. Overt Satan worship is perhaps the easiest deception to see through.

With nearly a million copies in print, the Satanic Bible declares the aims, purposes, and practices of Satan worshippers. Under the guidance of leaders such as Anton LaVey, founder of The Church of Satan, and Michael Aquino, the Satanists persuade thousands of deluded men, women, and especially teenagers to follow them in their hellish practices. As the author of books such as *Satanic Rituals* and *The Satanic Witch*, LaVey at one time was perhaps the best-known, most persuasive Satanist priest in America.

SEEKERS DECEIVED

People are looking for answers in every area of life. Young people, especially, are caught up in whatever appears to be the most bizarre.

They look for truth and settle for folly. The opposite of folly is wisdom; and the Book of Wisdom says, "The folly of fools is deception" (Proverbs 14:8). False religions and the occult are clever in reaching seekers who want to experience a rush of any kind.

Jerry Johnston's book, *The Edge of Evil: The Rise of Satanism in North America*, gives a startling portrait of the real dangers of Satanism and other "black arts" that have become prevalent in our society. Johnston describes the way young people are recruited and introduced to the strange and mystical rituals and practices of Satanism.

What is the danger in such beliefs? In his classic book *Those Curious New Cults*, William J. Petersen, former editor of *Eternity* magazine, says, "The most infamous blasphemy of Satanist ritual is the Black Mass." Petersen describes how, in the Black Mass, the participants try to reverse everything they know about Christianity. The crucifix is hung upside down. The altar is covered in black instead of white. Hymns are sung backward. The rite is performed by a defrocked priest, and whenever the Lord or Christ is mentioned, the priest spits on the altar or worse. To make the blasphemy even more despicable, sexual rites are added. Sometimes a child is even slain. During the ceremony, worshippers acknowledge Satan as Lord, and when the ritual concludes, the high priest closes with a curse rather than a blessing.

Regardless of how obviously evil or repulsive all this may seem, it is not fiction. No one knows how many thousands of Satanists are in the world today, but when the Satanic Bible was published in 1969, some reports indicate that one million copies were sold.

In my travels throughout the world, I have seen innumerable varieties of Satan worshippers. One night in Nuremberg, Germany, we were holding a crusade in the same stadium in which Hitler used to stage his infamous rallies. It was difficult to sit in that place and hear in the echoes of memory the masses shouting, "Sieg, Heil!" We realized that from this place the Third Reich had marched out to wage war on the world and, in the pursuit of its pagan ideologies, to exterminate millions of Jews and other prisoners held for political, religious, and psychological reasons. But we were reaching sixty thousand people a night in that open arena. They were singing Christ's praises, and I was preaching the Word of God. Thousands were coming to accept Jesus Christ as Savior and Lord. The presence of God's people there seemed to exorcise the demons that had stalked those aisles many years before.

Then one night, as I sat on the platform, Satan worshippers dressed in black assembled just outside the stadium doors. Using ancient, evil rites, they tried to put a hex on the meeting. The rumor of their presence spread. Christians prayed, and in answer to those prayers, nothing came of the incident.

Another night in Chicago, three hundred Satan worshippers approached McCormick Place with the intent of taking over the platform and bringing a halt to the crusade service already in progress. They had announced their plan in advance, but I didn't dream they would actually try to storm the platform. We had just sung the second hymn of the evening. George Beverly Shea had sung a gospel song, and Cliff Barrows was about to lead a massed choir in a great anthem of praise. At that moment a policeman rushed to the stage and whispered something to the mayor, who was present that night to welcome us.

Satan worshippers had forced their way past the ushers at the rear of that spacious auditorium and proceeded down the aisles toward the platform. More than thirty thousand young people were in our service that night. Only those seated near the back saw the Satan worshippers enter. The mayor of Chicago turned to me and said, "Dr. Graham, we'll let the police handle these intruders."

"Let me try it another way, Mr. Mayor," I suggested. I then interrupted the choir's song and announced, "There are about three hundred Satan worshippers entering the auditorium. They say they're going to take over the platform. You can hear them coming now."

The crowd could hear the rising chant of the Satan worshippers.

Everyone turned to see them moving down the aisles, making a considerable disturbance as they passed the ushers who were working quietly to restrain them. "I'm going to ask you Christian young people to surround these Satan worshippers," I exhorted. "Love them. Sing to them. Pray for them."

I will never forget that moment! Hundreds of young Christians stood and did exactly as I had asked. Some grabbed hands and began to sing. Others put their arms around the Satan worshippers and began to pray for them. Everyone else sat praying as God's Spirit moved through His people to confound the work of Satan in our midst. I stood watching in silence. I waited and prayed until peace was restored and the service could resume.

It happened again in Oakland, California, in the football stadium. Hundreds of Satan worshippers invaded the meeting to distract and disturb thousands who had come to hear of Christ and His plan of salvation. We did the same thing we had done in Chicago. I asked the young people to surround them in prayer. They did! Later that week, I received a letter from one of the leaders of the Satanist group thanking me for what I had done. He wrote, "I think you saved our lives." The power of those Christian young people came not in the spirit of evil and violence, but in quiet, loving prayer.

Millions of others have been deceived by various belief systems, and where deception exists, disillusionment follows. Disillusionment and deception are the two primary alternatives to true faith in God, and they are the handiwork of the first horseman of the Apocalypse. We have always thought of men in white hats riding white horses as the "good guys," knights in shining armor, but Satan transforms himself into an angel of light. So we must heed the warning of this mysterious white horse.

The deceiver has many options in his bag of tricks; the first is leading susceptible people to ignore religion altogether. When we feel alienated, isolated, unloved, lonely, and adrift in a cold, dark universe, we need God. But the deceiver tells us "there is no God."

The nineteenth-century philosopher Friedrich Nietzsche said, "God is dead." *Do not seek God or Jesus Christ*, the deceiver whispers, *but seek escape.* I would suggest that this is the real reason that drugs are such an epidemic in America today. This is why promiscuous sex runs rampant, why alcohol abuse is commonplace. Without faith in God, men and women are alone. They will do anything to fill the void in their lives, but short of Christ, nothing works. Augustine said, "Thou madest us for Thyself, and our heart is restless, until it repose in Thee."

NEW AGE OF DECEPTION

A second form of deception is false religions. The rise of the New Age movement is such an example. New Age is, in fact, another storm warning indicating man's search for "transcendence" without regard for righteousness. Whether it's Dianetics, est, Unity, Gaea, Transcendental Meditation, Taoism, ufology, crystalology, goddess worship, reincarnation, Scientology, harmonics, numerology, astrology, holistic healing, positive thinking, or any of a hundred "consciousness raising" techniques of our day, the world is on a search for some mystical "divine unity," a search that actually testifies to the failure of modern-day secular humanism to satisfy the spiritual hunger of the soul.

We were designed for a relationship with God. As the body craves oxygen, so the human spirit craves God. We all have a passionate desire to know God and to communicate with Him, but ever since Eden we have been guilty of sin, and nothing but repentance—humbling ourselves before the cross of Christ—will ever bring us into fellowship with Him. The sin nature is born within each of us; we are not born noble, as Rousseau and the philosophers of the Enlightenment declared.

The real disaster of the cult of humanism and its New Age, and other expressions, is not just the foolishness of placing one's trust in such a frail, finite, and limited creature, it also separates man from the authentic source of power and meaning. David's lament recorded in psalms has never been truer than today: "The wicked in his proud countenance does not seek God; God is in none of his thoughts" (Psalm 10:4 NKJV).

Many people have decided that there is no room for God in their lives, no need of Him. The problem, however, is that denying the existence of God cannot make Him go away any more than denying the existence of the Internal Revenue Service can make the tax man vanish. Many people who imagine a god of their own choosing will be horrified when they stand before the true God of heaven. His is the kingdom, and the power, and the glory forever. No pious idealism, no New Age fantasy, and no amount of denial can ever change that fact.

Still another ploy of the New Age is to transform God into something else, or to come to the conclusion, as many have done, that we are gods. On the last page of her book *Out on a Limb*, actress Shirley MacLaine attempted to make herself equal with God when she wrote:

> *I know that I exist, therefore I AM.*
> *I know that the God source exists. Therefore IT IS.*
> *Since I am a part of that force, then I AM that I AM.*

In the eyes of a righteous God, there is no greater blasphemy, but such "abomination" has become common heresy in our day. Even among some churches that consider themselves evangelical, we see individuals in the pulpit preaching a "second blessing" through the prosperity gospel or adding dramatic displays with no scriptural truth. These manifestations are just that: *man-infested* blasphemies against the Holy Spirit of God—another evidence of the rider on the white horse "going out conquering and to conquer" through his deceptions. In essence he says, "I am who I want to be."

The great deceiver has wanted to be God from the beginning,

but the Bible says, "I AM WHO I AM" (Exodus 3:14 NKJV) and the Lord will never relinquish His place—high and lifted up.

POLLUTION OF DECEPTION

In this age of humanism, man is seduced by society with the lie that he can become his own god. The remark attributed to Protagoras, "Man is the measure of all things," is the central tenet of humanist ideology. But it is the ultimate deception of Satan: to rob men of their relationship with the God of the universe through a lie as old as Eden that "you will be like God" (Genesis 3:5).

Because it springs from false theology, and especially because it is inspired by the deceiver himself, the New Age movement is polluted with self and it will never bow before God—at least not until Christ returns. Rather, it tries to manufacture its own infinitely forgiving and fallible god designed on the pantheistic concept of the oneness of man with the universe. When a Hollywood actress claims to be God, she is simply denying that she has sinned and fallen short of the glory of God. New Agers are terrified of their own mortality, and they want to believe that somehow the soul will survive. Of course it will, but not as they imagine.

Someday the New Age gurus will die, just as the founder of the Church of Satan died in 1997. We all must die, and our bodies will return to the earth from which God made them. Then what remains, our eternal spirits, will stand before the true, righteous, and all-knowing God of creation and ponder why they felt compelled to run so hard to escape the God who loved them and gave His Son as a sacrifice.

On that day, sincerity will mean nothing; hard work will mean nothing; good intentions will mean nothing. God judges mankind by the standard of the only God-man who ever lived, Jesus Christ. Jesus, the innocent Lamb of God, stands between our sin and the judgment of God the Father. Without His holy shield, no one is worthy. This is the lesson of the fourth chapter of Revelation.

Author and writer Russell Chandler, in his book *Understanding the New Age*, reports that dozens of American companies (perhaps unintentionally) are indoctrinating men and women into the New Age movement through "consciousness raising" techniques and required "self-improvement" courses. Many Fortune 500 companies regularly send their executives off to remote training centers and retreats to "get in touch with their inner person." In plain language, that means they are being introduced to such New Age practices as meditation, visual imaging, Zen, yoga, chanting, and even tarot cards. All this is done in the name of "success enhancement." What it amounts to is opening up the human spirit to the ultimate source of deception: the father of lies.

DECEPTION TAKES HOLD

Why are the cults and the New Age movement so successful today? Why are so many people willing to be swept away by false teaching and thereby turning their backs on God's truth? There are many reasons, but I fear that we as Christians must confess at times we have been part of the problem because we do not exemplify the marks of the Holy Spirit reigning through our lives. Many people—especially young people—have become disillusioned with the Christian faith and the church, and therefore have been open to deception.

This is not a new phenomenon. Throughout history there have been examples of Christian believers becoming unwitting allies of the horseman who deceives. Rather than standing against the symbol of the white horse whose hoofbeats can be heard, unknowingly we can assist him through our words and actions. For example, some churchmen in Nazi Germany gave their official blessing to Hitler's Third Reich as it wreaked havoc on Europe (although others, like Dietrich

Bonhoeffer, courageously spoke out and even paid for their courage with their lives). Sometimes our sin is displayed as a result of our silence and inaction. These are considered sins of omission.

There are many Christian believers today in danger of helping the rider on the white horse in his work of deception. In his book *Unholy Devotion: Why Cults Lure Christians*, Harold Busséll says, "In our fervor to point out [the cult's] errors of doctrine, we have virtually ignored our own shortcomings and vulnerabilities."

Allow me to briefly illustrate some of the ways people assist in the deception of others:

- Half-truths, easy answers, and lies
- Double standards (saying one thing but doing another)
- Discriminating against certain sins while approving or ignoring other sins
- Inadequate practical teaching on "the inward journey"
- Inadequate practical teaching about the "outward journey"

PROCEED WITH CAUTION OR BE DECEIVED

These are some of the primary reasons young people—and others—reject Christ and follow after the rider who deceives. Christians sometimes use these tactics to "sell the faith." I have listened to too many sermons, read too many Christian books, and seen too many Christian films with happily-ever-after endings. Some even declare that if you become a Christian, you will get rich or always be successful. This is simply false teaching.

In our attempts to share the faith, some have given the impression that, once a person has accepted Christ as Savior and Lord, his or her problems will be over. This, also, is not true. In fact, it is quite often the opposite. Becoming "new" in Christ is a wonderful beginning, but it isn't the end of pain or problems in our lives. It is the beginning of our facing up to them. Being a Christian involves a lifetime of hard work, dedicated study, and difficult decisions. Living the Christian life means striving for holiness. Christ did not teach that a life of faith would be easy, but that the reward for endurance would be great.

The Bible says, "Put to death . . . whatever belongs to your earthly nature . . . since you have taken off your old self with its practices and have put on the new self, which is being renewed . . . in the image of its Creator. . . . Work at it with all your heart . . . since you know that you will receive an inheritance from the Lord as a reward" (Colossians 3:5, 9–10, 23–24).

After the apostle Paul's dramatic conversion on the road to Damascus, I doubt he realized what hardship and suffering lay ahead—even though God had told Ananias, who was to disciple Paul, "I will show him how much he must suffer for my name" (Acts 9:16). In one of his letters to the Corinthian church, Paul recounted some of his sufferings, not in discouragement and complaint, but in joy and victory:

> In great endurance; in troubles, hardships and distresses; in beatings, imprisonments and riots; in hard work, sleepless nights and hunger . . . through glory and dishonor, bad report and good report; genuine, yet regarded as impostors; known, yet regarded as unknown; dying, and yet we live on; beaten, and yet not killed; sorrowful, yet always rejoicing; poor, yet making many rich; having nothing, and yet possessing everything. (2 Corinthians 6:4–5, 8–10)

Then the apostle allows us to catch a glimpse of his personal testimony.

> Three times I was beaten with rods, once I was stoned, three times I was shipwrecked, I spent a night and a day in the open sea, I have been constantly on the move. I have been in danger from

rivers, in danger from bandits, in danger from my own country-
men, in danger from Gentiles; in danger in the city, in danger in
the country, in danger at sea; and in danger from false brothers. I
have labored and toiled and have often gone without sleep; I have
known hunger and thirst and have often gone without food; I
have been cold and naked. Besides everything else, I face daily the
pressure of my concern for all the churches. Who is weak, and I
do not feel weak? Who is led into sin, and I do not inwardly burn?
If I must boast, I will boast of the things that show my weakness.
(2 Corinthians 11:25–30)

Living the Christian life, for Paul, meant suffering. The same
could be said of a multitude of Christ's followers, many of whom
were killed for their faith. So when Christ said time after time that
one must "deny himself and take up his cross daily and follow me"
(Luke 9:23), He was indicating that it will not always be easy to be
His follower. The apostle Paul warned, "Everyone who wants to live
a godly life in Christ Jesus will be persecuted" (2 Timothy 3:12).
Christ did not suffer and die to offer cheap grace. Jesus did not will-
ingly go to the cross so we could have an easy life or offer a faith
built on easy-believism. As someone has said, "Salvation is free, but
not cheap." It cost Jesus His life.

Charles T. Studd was a famous sportsman in England, captain of
the Cambridge XI cricket team. More than a century ago he gave
away his vast wealth to needy causes and led the Cambridge Seven
to China. His slogan was, "If Jesus Christ be God and died for me,
then no sacrifice can be too great for me to make for Him."

During the first decade of this century, Bill Borden left one of
America's greatest family fortunes to be a missionary in China. He
only got as far as Egypt where, still in his twenties, he died of
typhoid fever. Before his death he said, "No reserves, no retreats, no
regrets!"

A generation ago, Jim Elliot went from Wheaton College to

become a missionary to the Aucas in Ecuador. Before he was killed, he wrote, "He is no fool who gives up what he cannot keep to gain what he cannot lose." In some parts of the world, it is still very hard to be a Christian—men and women today are martyred for their faith. In the Middle East, Latin America, Asia, and many places throughout Western Europe, the price of faithful service to Jesus Christ can be humiliation, torture, and death. Even in the United States we have seen Christians killed because they dared to speak the name of the Lord Jesus Christ, as exemplified in the horror killing of students at Columbine High School in Littleton, Colorado, in 1999 when seventeen-year-old Cassie Bernall lost her life.

A study by Barrett and Johnson reported that more than seventy million Christians had died as martyrs since AD 33.

In North America, other factors make it difficult to stand up against the ridicule of secularism and its humanist values. Materialism and self-centeredness are the great vices of our age. But whatever comes your way, know that Christ is in your struggles with you. He knows what it means to suffer, for He, the sinless Son of God, suffered the pangs of death and hell for you. He knows what it means to be tempted, and "because he himself suffered when he was tempted, he is able to help those who are being tempted" (Hebrews 2:18).

In the midst of every situation of life, He can give an inner calm and strength that we could never imagine apart from Him. "Peace I leave with you," He said, "my peace I give you. I do not give to you as the world gives. Do not let your hearts be troubled and do not be afraid" (John 14:27). This, then, is our hope in the storms of life— Jesus will be with us through it all.

The benefits of Christianity are tremendous, but the trials may sometimes overwhelm us and stifle our joy. So when any preacher or teacher of the Christian Gospel oversells either the material or the spiritual benefits of the faith, he is actually aiding the work of the horseman who deceives.

DOUBLE STANDARDS DECEIVE

The rider who deceives is having a field day in churches that proudly employ the double standard. Christian leaders point their finger at cults and cult leaders and accuse them of deceiving their members. But cult leaders say the same about Christians as they observe us saying one thing but practicing another. I like the bumper sticker that reads, "Christians aren't perfect, just forgiven." But that does not give us license to live below God's standard. We need to examine our own history as Christian believers. Too often our Christianity is in our talk—not in our walk. Which of us cannot identify with the words of the apostle Paul, who said, "For the good that *I will to do*, I do not do; but the evil *I will not to do*, that I practice" (Romans 7:19 NKJV; emphasis added)?

Often the unbeliever sees through our facades and calls it hypocrisy. He has heard stories of Christian churches that have been divided by anger and hatred. He knows about the deacon who left his wife to run away with the church receptionist. He knows how some of the Sunday morning faithful spend Saturday night. He knows that Christian believers, too, are human.

We sometimes see Christian books about celebrities who are supposedly converted to the faith. All too often, after the book is released, our celebrity Christian is caught in a scandal with crude details sprawled on the front page. We produce films about the wonderful change Christ makes in a couple facing tragedy. Then, as has happened on occasion, just as the film is released, that same couple announces their divorce. All people, including ministers, deacons, Christian leaders, and celebrities, are vulnerable to sin. Why can't we simply face these problems openly and deal with them without excusing them?

As long as we remain in these mortal bodies, none of us will ever be perfect. None of us lives without occasional sin and failure, and it is hypocritical to pretend otherwise. At the same time, however, we must never grow complacent about sin or simply say, "Oh well, everyone else is doing it too." The Bible commands, "But just as he who called you is holy, so be holy in all you do" (1 Peter 1:15). It also tells us that there is forgiveness and new life when we repent and confess our sins to Christ.

The unbelieving world should see our testimony lived out daily because it just may point them to the Savior. He is our strength in times of temptation. When others look at our lives, they should see Christ in us. I like what D. L. Moody said: "The place for ships is in the sea. But God help the ship if the sea gets in the ship!" If we remain in the world, the storm will swallow us up. Noah was in the Ark—not the Flood. As followers of Jesus Christ, we are not to walk as the world does; we are called to obey Christ. He is the Master of our lives and has washed us in His blood, which cleanses our souls, our minds, and our mouths. The world is watching. What do they see and hear?

PRETENDING DECEIVES

Years ago, Ruth told me a story about the early mountain people near our home. They used wooden cradles with slatted sides to put their laundry in. The cradle was placed crossways in a rushing creek, and as the water flowed through the slats, the laundry was continuously cleansed. I can remember Ruth laughing when she said, "This was probably the first automatic washing machine in North Carolina."

These mountains where I live are filled with stories many will never hear. But Ruth was always collecting them, writing about them, and gleaning a spiritual application. One day a bootlegger who operated in our area was converted to Christ. When he was taken down to the stream to be baptized, he asked if he could please be put crossways to the current so that he would "get washed the cleaner!"

When sin and failure come into our lives, as they most certainly will, we still have the wonderful promise that "the blood of Jesus, his Son, purifies us from all sin" (1 John 1:7). This is a promise written to believers. And the word *purify* means "continuous cleansing." What a great comfort to know that Christ is working in our daily lives in this way.

But we deceive ourselves if we pretend that sin never comes knocking. The important thing is how we respond. As followers of Christ, we are given the strength to run from sin, just as Joseph did in his master's house. But when we do fail, when we cave in to the pressure because we have momentarily taken our eyes off Christ, we have the assurance that the Holy Spirit will convict us of our sin. Immediately we should go straight to the Scriptures, repent, and claim the many promises of God. Memorize them. Psalm 119:11 says, "Your word I have hidden in my heart, that I might not sin against You" (NKJV). Because it was inspired by God for imperfect human beings, Scripture has the remedy for sinfulness. These times in our lives become part of our testimony; not that we spread our sinfulness before others, but that God is there to pick up the pieces. The emphasis is not on us—because we are nothing without Him; rather, the focus is purely on the Lord Jesus Christ. He is the One who shed His blood to cover our sinful disobedience and He will forgive us, discipline us, and love us.

Why must we deceive one another? Why should we pretend things are okay when we are aching inside? Why sport smiles of victory in public gatherings and weep tears of loneliness and anger when we are alone? If your business fails and bankruptcy threatens, let a brother or sister in Christ be aware of your struggle. If your marriage is coming apart at the seams, find at least one or two trustworthy believers to share your pain and help you deal in practical ways with the problems you face. The Bible says, "Carry each other's burdens, and in this way you will fulfill the law of Christ" (Galatians 6:2).

When we admit that we are not perfect—just forgiven—and share the Scriptures, we drive away the rider who deceives. But as long as we pretend to be perfect and live a double standard, we give him room to ride.

Let us pray that God will make us sensitive to sin wherever it is found. We must reach out in Christian love to those whose lives are battered and bruised by sin, point them to the only One who can bring healing and new life, and welcome them into our fellowship. "For it is God's will that by doing good you should silence the ignorant talk of foolish men. Live as free men, but do not use your freedom as a cover-up for evil; live as servants of God" (1 Peter 2:15–16).

The inward journey is that lifelong pilgrimage of spiritual growth and maturity in the believer. Many times pastors and Christian leaders tend to see conversion as the end rather than the beginning of life's struggle to know God and to do His will. Responding to an invitation in a crusade or church to receive Jesus Christ as Lord and Savior is really just the first step of the inward journey.

Ultimately this journey should include a daily study of God's Word, the practice of prayer—communion with God, Bible study and memorization, fellowship with other believers in a sound Bible-believing church, and building up others in the faith. These components are gifts to us and are necessary if we are to grow in the Christian faith. The Bible tells us to "spur one another on toward love and good deeds. Let us not give up meeting together . . . but let us encourage one another—and all the more as you see the Day approaching" (Hebrews 10:24–25).

I'll never forget a pastor telling me the story of one of his most faithful members who did not know how to pray. She had been a hardworking, committed member of the church since her conversion in a crusade. She had taught Sunday school and pledged her financial support. She had even brought neighbors and friends to church. One Wednesday evening, the pastor asked the woman to lead in a closing prayer. After a long and embarrassing silence, she ran from the room in tears. The woman disappeared for a time. She wouldn't answer her phone. She stopped going to church. Sometime later, the woman called the pastor and made an appointment to see him. In his study, she confessed that she didn't know how to pray. She didn't know what to say or how to say it.

The pastor told me that teaching this dear lady the elements of prayer was one of the rewarding tasks of his ministry. She began to gain new insight by learning how to pray before the very throne of God. This is what the disciples learned when they said to Jesus, "Lord, teach us to pray" (Luke 11:1).

Each evening in our crusades, I give the invitation for people to repent of their sin and commit their lives to Christ. After leading them in prayer, I mention four important things that must become part of their daily lives if they are to develop and mature. One of those is prayer. I tell them that they don't have to pray like a clergyman. I encourage them to simply reaffirm their trust in Christ and ask for God's help. The best way to pray is to open the Bible and pray Scripture back to the Lord, claiming His promises and asking that He strengthen them and guide them in obeying His Word.

A word to Christian leaders: we must recognize that the term "babes in Christ" has a very specific meaning. There is an innocence and vulnerability in new believers that the deceiver will exploit. If we do not teach Christian principles to all followers of Christ, we are not equipping them with God's truth that will overcome worldly influence.

Satan is always moving about. He is aware of every new believer and takes the first opportunity to discourage them in their newfound faith in Christ. We can be guilty of leaving infant believers open and at risk to all kinds of "isms" that can quickly overtake them. Satan is masterful at using just enough of God's truth to capture a person's attention and then mix it with his devious potion that will lead them astray. We need to encourage new believers to feed on God's Word—it is nourishment for the soul. It is vitally important for local church leaders to keep in touch with the spiritual state of their members, to discuss their level of biblical knowledge, and to teach them how to study God's Word and pray.

Some time ago, a survey reported that the majority of the seminaries in this country had no classes on prayer. That really shouldn't surprise us when we consider how many local churches offer classes on gardening and the Art of Conversation instead of the study of God's Word and prayer. The rider who deceives gloats when shepherds assume their flocks are alive in Christ and growing in wisdom—when they're not. Often the sowers of deceit are those pushing for a gardening class, not a growing class. He knows when our spiritual growth and maturity are not a primary concern to us. Christ's church is a place to grow people up in the Lord, not to enhance our leisure time.

The rider who deceives also revels when we make faith seem too easy. Faith involves trust in Jesus Christ, commitment to His Lordship and turning away from seeking worldly pleasure. The crowd at the fringe of the cross can easily be led away. But those who mix their blood and sweat with the tears of the martyrs are not easily deceived. The more involved a believer is in communing with the Lord daily and encouraging others to do so as well, the more likely he or she will grow in faith that leads to an effective witness. The less involved, the more likely he or she will be deceived.

David Wilkerson, pastor and author of the book *The Cross and the Switchblade*, preaches a powerful sermon about the lack of commitment and obedience to the Lord in our churches today. He calls believers to prayer and the study of God's Word, challenging Christians to the "passion of anguish" for the lost and how to live our lives before the unbelieving world. How needed this is.

Many sincere people leave the church and join cults because cults make demands. When committing their lives to a belief or cause, people expect guidelines. Generally speaking, people join something because there is an expectation. It is amazing to watch everyday people buy membership to clubs where they are handed a list of rules and regulations. They are giving their money to a group that makes demands on them. Imagine! If they fail to adhere to the guidelines, they can lose their membership. Even golfers adhere to the dress code enforced at the country club.

Likewise, cults often insist that their followers conform to their mandates simply based on their own set of beliefs. Yet these are often the ones who claim that Christians use God as a crutch, never realizing that they are being led down a morbid trail in rusty chains. On the other hand, Christians are becoming disengaged in following the Scripture that tells us not to conform to the world's system.

I am concerned that while churches make an effort to reach out beyond their walls to serve their communities, they are forgetting their "first love." We are commanded to love our neighbors, and the first step in doing this is to show a watching world that Christ reigns within us. The Bible says, "God's word is not chained. Therefore I endure everything . . . that they too may obtain the salvation that is in Christ Jesus, with eternal glory" (2 Timothy 2:9–10).

DECEIVE OR BELIEVE

Storms bring struggles, and struggles often stir passion to persevere. The church should not be pampered but rather prepare for, and expect, persecution—for it is Christ's body on earth. He told us that we would be persecuted because of His name. Church is not for pretenders and performers. Church is a place for pastors to preach principles of the faith in order to prepare believers to face the storms of life on the stage of an unbelieving world. We are, after all, the light of the world—Christ shining through us.

Church is not the place to promote programs but to profess faith. The church is not to be pliable but principled. The church is not to be preoccupied but prevailing. The church is not perfect but predestined. The church is not philosophical but predetermined. The church does not pressure or pollute but pronounces and protects. The church does not prey on the lost; it prays for the perishing. The church does not pollute the mind; it provides food for the soul. The church does not profane the truth; it possesses God's Word. The church is not passive or progressive; it is purging and possessive. The church should not reflect pop culture but portray godly attributes. The church should not seek pleasures but seek after God. The church should not be prideful but princely—we are children of the King. The church should not promote anything—but preach Christ only. The church platform is not a playground but the place of proclamation. The church is not to reflect the world but to be a portrait of Jesus Christ. The church is not a public institution—Christ purchased it with His purifying blood. The church should not work for its own profit; it is Christ's priceless possession. The church's lectern is not a politician's prop but a preacher's pulpit. And finally, the church is a place to pray for those who do not know Christ and to praise the Savior for making a way for salvation if they will only believe.

DECEIVED WITHIN

The church is in turmoil today. It has an identity crisis. We are in the same predicament as the early churches of John's day. Every true believer should be on his or her face before God, interceding for those who make up the true church of the living Christ. This crisis mode is not new. While we are thankful that Christ will never turn His back on the church, we should not presume on His patience. We have already seen the pronouncements on the church from heaven, yet Jesus declared, "I will build my church, and the gates of hell shall not prevail against it" (Matthew 16:18 ESV).

As believers, we should make every effort to protect and cherish Christ's most treasured possession. It is our duty to protect it from being infiltrated by false prophets. The church today needs cleansing. Jesus Christ has entrusted to us what is closest to His heart. And to the leaders of the church, Paul the pastor-apostle said, "Be shepherds of the church of God, which he bought with his own blood. . . . Savage wolves will come in among you and will not spare the flock. Even from your own number men will arise and distort the truth in order to draw away disciples after them. So be on your guard! Remember that for three years I never stopped warning each of you night and day with tears" (Acts 20:28–31).

The church, since the first century, has been tormented by waves of deception. And while many books of the Bible document these struggles, there is a one-page book in the Bible that is often overlooked. It is carefully tucked in between the apostle John's three short books 1, 2, 3 John and Revelation. Nevertheless, the twenty-five verses that constitute the book of Jude are certainly a fitting introduction to Revelation. It is no mistake that this all-important book precedes John's climactic vision, where Christ lifts the blinders from the eyes of the church and reveals the infiltration of carnality in its midst.

Like a freight train pulsating down a track, the Conductor's whistle whines with warning that deceivers have slipped into the sidecar of the church. Here we see Jude, a flagman of sorts, warning the brakemen to throw the switch before the train jumps the track and heads for the barren wastelands—the home of the darkened soul.

Many scholars believe that the author of this power-packed book is none other than one of Jesus' half brothers. The study of Scripture reveals that Jude, also the brother of James, did not believe that Jesus was the Christ until after the miracle of His bodily resurrection. When Jude identified himself in the opening sentence, he did not mention his blood relation to Jesus but rather his relationship under the blood of Christ. He, like the other New Testament writers, called himself "a servant of Jesus Christ."

"Dear friends," Jude wrote, "I felt I had to write and urge you to contend for the faith that was once for all entrusted to the saints. For certain men whose condemnation was written about long ago have secretly slipped in among you. They are godless men, who change the grace of our God into a license for immorality and deny Jesus Christ our only Sovereign and Lord" (Jude 3–4).

We see in this passage a storm cloud hovering over the church. The cloud has not burst open in deluge but is dripping slowly into the hearts of God's people. Jude lowered a haunting blow when he employed the word *Woe!* to describe the apostate teaching that had seeped into the church, causing believers to turn a blind eye to those who were corrupting the apostles' teachings and leading many astray. He said, "These men are blemishes . . . shepherds who feed only themselves. They are clouds without rain, blown along by the wind; autumn trees, without fruit and uprooted—twice dead. They are wild waves of the sea, foaming up their shame; wandering stars, for whom blackest darkness has been reserved forever. . . . These are the men who . . . follow mere natural instincts and do not have the Spirit" (Jude 12–13, 19).

Jude's message emphasizes the urgency of the Gospel. The Lord Jesus never failed to give ample warning to the sinful heart, nor did He fail to speak mercy to a wandering soul. Jude warns the church of the hovering clouds and then bolsters their resolve: "Contend for the faith. . . . Build yourselves up in your most holy faith" (Jude 3, 20).

As the double red signal lights flash at the crossing, cautioning danger ahead, the church must heed Jude's woeful warning not to dismiss the alarm that is sounding. Wake up! Watch out! Beware! Strengthen what remains and is about to die.

I am thankful that Christians are in the service of the One who loves us deep enough to send out a warning of woe. His call is not only to shake us back into submissive obedience but to demonstrate His mercy extended to those who are on the wrong track of life: those who don't know what to believe, those who have been deceived by lies that have not been corrected because of the lack of hearing the Word of God preached in truth, and even those who have been completely entrenched in the seduction of the deceivers.

Jude closed this wonderful epistle with these words: "Be merciful to those who doubt; snatch others from the fire and save them; to others show mercy, mixed with fear—hating even the clothing stained by corrupted flesh" (Jude 22–23). The Lord Jesus Christ is preparing a home fit for all who live for Him, a place designed for the church triumphant. Let's exemplify the work of His hands, for they are busy, on our behalf, building a city large enough to encompass His people of faith—an eternal home for the soul.

11

THE CULT OF SELF

I denied myself nothing my eyes desired; I refused my
heart no pleasure . . . Yet when I surveyed all that my hands
had done and what I had toiled to achieve, everything
was meaningless, a chasing after the wind.
—ECCLESIASTES 2:10–11

S elf. When it leads or follows another word, it is self-descriptive:
Self-absorbed. Self-reliant. Self-indulgent. Self-centered.

There are those who believe them*selves* to be self-starters
and self-disciplined. No matter how the four-letter word is moved
around on the scrabble board it points right back to one's self. If you
turn the four-letter word around and add an "h," the word still defines
itself: FLESH!

Me, Myself, and I has come to be known as the trendy trinity.

This modern-day profile of the individual is punctuated with
"itself." Iconic behavior is self-destructive.

The root word *icon* is described as a religious work of art. With the popularity of the personal computer, however, the word has become part of the language utilized in the high-tech world, symbolizing innumerable images and applications. I am told that MySpace and Facebook pages—the modern-day telegrams—are sprinkled with icons of its users: pictures, messages, and day-to-day narratives—the "tell-all" self-tabloid of the day. You might say it is a bulletin board of personal postings about one's hour-by-hour activity. It connects people to one another electronically but provides a wall—a buffer—so that individuals don't have to personally interact with relatives, friends, and acquaintances yet can stay current with their latest self-proclamations.

From school age on, people are indoctrinated with the secular definitions of self-esteem, self-image, self-realization, and self-actualization propagated by the prophets of selfism. The ideas and principles of Carl Jung, Alfred Adler, Carl Rogers, Erich Fromm, Sigmund Freud, and Deepak Chopra, among others, are better known on college and university campuses than those of Moses, Samuel, Isaiah, Jesus, or Paul.

The focus on self has led our society into a fascination with pleasure, emotional and sexual stimulation, and "personal fulfillment." What Freud described as the liberation of the id (ego) was the first step toward the cult of self.

America's compulsion for "maximum personhood" is evidenced everywhere. Legitimate recreations, from skateboarding to golf, have become obsessions for some. Athletics, jogging, the workout craze, even bodybuilding among both men and women, have taken on the aura and discipline of cultic and mystical rites. Many doctors today prescribe yoga as a helpful stress reliever but would not consider prescribing prayer to the One who calms our fears and anxieties. The focus of our activity is no longer on the heart, the soul, or the mind, but on the body. Feeling good about ourselves is ultimate success.

Certainly I believe in physical fitness. Because of my own travel schedule and frequently exhausting speaking commitments over the years, I have always been a firm believer in the value of conditioning the body. I enjoyed walking, swimming, and physical exercise within reason; it's very important for old and young alike. While it's no longer possible at my age to do most of these things, I do what I can to maintain good health. The Bible says that our bodies represent the temple of the Holy Spirit (1 Corinthians 6:19). At the same time, however, we are not to turn our natural concern for health into an unnatural quest for eternal youth. The Bible says, "For physical training is of some value, but godliness has value for all things" (1 Timothy 4:8).

THE WORLD OF CULTURE

Socializing has a new face today. Until the mid-1950s, Western society had a somewhat more modest opinion of itself. Despite reasonable pride in our technology and industry, most Americans lived simple lives. Fathers and mothers worked hard so their children could have a better life than they did. The motive was good, but the results were devastating. Younger generations developed the attitude that they deserved what they had not worked for.

There was a day when both tradition and religion made it clear that self-centeredness was antisocial and unacceptable. The Bible says that pride comes before a fall, and I believe we have seen this lived out in the past several decades. Parents and schoolteachers taught that "rights" were always accompanied by "responsibilities." Democracy showed us that in America's republic, each person may rise to his level of competence, but nobody owes them a living. The Bible says that to whom much is given, much is required (Luke 12:48).

So the language of self-reliance and self-interest that has emerged did not, at first blush, arouse concern. However, as Floyd McClung points out in his book *Holiness and the Spirit of the Age*, we have taken a giant step beyond the context of the frontier spirit into something much uglier. He wrote:

> Modern individualism, which is divorced from the moral founda-
> tions of Christianity and surrounded by a hedonistic society, has
> produced a way of life that is neither beneficial to individuals nor
> productive to society at large. Individualism used to be expressed
> positively within the context of the family, the community, the
> church, and the government. Personal rights were subjected to the
> overall good of society. But individualism today no longer observes
> such boundaries. The cry is, "I want what I want when I want it!"
> Such selfish individualism weakens the very underpinnings of a
> nation built on strong moral foundations.

In a book published in 1994 subtitled *The Cult of Self-Worship*,
the author wrote, "This book provides a compelling look into the
self-actualization theories first popularized in the 1960s and 1970s.
Self theories are significant because they set the stage for many social
changes—including . . . the increasingly radical redefinition of the
family."

The effects of these theories have morphed into the pop-culture
era that permeates everything from leisure to love, from *SELF* magazine to eHarmony.com.

All of this has helped set the stage for the rider of the first horse.
His game is deceit, and his deceit plays out through those who are
deceived by his clever tactics, convincing us that by lavishing ourselves
with the latest fashion, the sleekest gadget, the most electronic friends,
no-pain exercise gimmicks, online dating, and self-improvement info-
mercials, we will gain personal contentment and thereby live in
peace—at least with our*selves*. We've been warned in Scripture when
Paul wrote, "Do nothing out of selfish ambition or vain conceit, but
in humility consider others better than yourselves" (Philippians 2:3).

But as the world war generations have grown old, the religion of
the material world has gained new ground, changing America's

countenance brushed with hyper gloss and sloppy threads—the more bizarre, the better. The nation's image has become more like a chameleon—accepting whatever trend marketers concoct. Gone are the days of a nation characterized by its rugged individuals who felt the pride of accomplishment by the sweat of their brows. Gone are the days of reverencing a holy God in the church or within ourselves. Yet the Bible tells us, "Happy is the man who is always reverent" (Proverbs 28:14 NKJV).

THE MODERN WORLD

In some sense, each generation has made its contribution to society, whether good or bad. When America recuperated from the devastation of the world wars, our nation quickly immersed itself in "modernism." From the fins of our automobiles to the shrinking swimsuits of Hollywood models, it was apparent that America was making a deliberate turn toward the new, the modern, the materialistic, and the shocking. The music, the movies, and the media of the day pointed people to a virtual sign that read: THIS WAY TO CULTURAL RELEVANCE. Hot jazz, rhythm and blues, and early rock-and-roll hits were slightly off color, and young people took mischievous pleasure in scandalous behavior, shoving it in the face of the older generation. Gone was the day of showing respect to authority.

As GIs, army nurses, and others returned to the campuses, the relatively new discipline of psychology became a major topic of interest. By the mid-1960s, psychology was the hottest major in American universities. This new emphasis was a leading contributor to the shift in values taking place in the American psyche. The principal teaching that made secular psychology so radical was that it introduced a "new way of thinking."

Just as the theories of Charles Darwin had undermined belief in God as the Creator, modern psychology tended to turn people against belief in God altogether. It taught that there was hidden depth and substance within each individual. The outer person was a compromise; the inner person was profound and important. Psychology thus concluded that the true *self*, buried under a false covering of social conditioning and religious prejudice, was struggling to be set free. For some psychologists, therefore, religion was seen as a hindrance rather than a help to improve the human condition.

THE WORLD GOES POP

"Pop psychology" has contributed to the chaos of pleasure-seeking, secularism, and materialism, creating a culture that has especially permeated the baby boomer generation and their offspring. While much of secular psychology emphasizes self-interest as the ultimate reality instead of responsibility to a Higher Being, I have been pleased to see some Christians taking psychology to a higher level with Christ-centered and Bible-based application.

However, the cult of *self* has become an addiction—feeding off the ego of self-glorification. The word *cult* encompasses many movements and ideas, but simply put, it describes a culture of alternative beliefs, fads, and trends, and tampers with just enough truth to knock many off balance. Some analysts have suggested that self-absorption is actually a defensive reaction against the loneliness and sterility of today's depersonalized lifestyles. We have become urbanized and disconnected. Some people lack family roots—many lack a heritage of faith. Consequently, without the old connections and dependencies that gave life meaning, many have lost their sense of belonging.

When my sons were young, they enjoyed cowboy movies: stories about good winning over evil, stories about cattle drives and tough guys living out on the range. When Western territories began to populate, ranchers had to find a way to distinguish one herd from another. The ancient Egyptian practice of branding was employed and somewhat refined by the American West. An iron bar was twisted into a symbol, put into the fire, and when the iron turned red-hot, the iron was applied to the hide of a cow, horse, or other livestock that grazed on the open range. This brand became the owner's symbol. When livestock from various ranches mingled, the cowboys could go through and identify which animals belonged to them by the brand. This prevented range wars and debate concerning true ownership of the stock.

Today, branding has become a big business of its own. Marketing firms are contracted to come up with branding campaigns for companies to attract the consumer's desire to own something of that particular brand. This advertising bonanza has created a culture all its own, from jeans to football, from technology to stock. In some cases, these promotional appeals have been credited for revitalizing a product that was about to die. When marketers are able to reinvent a company's brand, they are often able to reinvent its image.

The architect of popular culture is none other than Satan. He is the chief designer and chief marketer, and he has been branding worldliness since the beginning of time. His methods are shifty and constantly in motion, changing fads and trends to keep the world running in circles, trying to keep up with the latest and greatest. His methods waver depending upon his targeted audience, but his pattern is always the same. Diluting God's standards of right and wrong are at the center of his PowerPoint presentation. His schematic casts shadows by shading the truth; thereby causing chaos and confusion.

His designer brand today has been repackaged and renamed— and at first glance, it seems reasonable. In the twenty-first century, his leading brands are called "acceptance" and "tolerance." He takes God's laws, twists the meaning with the sleight of hand, and tells society there is no consequence to anything that will satisfy our every desire. Satan has slipped this idea into the church under the guise of love and forgiveness, without repentance and transformation. We have turned a deaf ear to the truth. The Bible warns, "Watch out for those who . . . put obstacles in your way that are contrary to the teaching you have learned. Keep away from them. For such people are not serving our Lord Christ, but their own appetites . . . they deceive the minds of naïve people" (Romans 16:17–18).

Centuries ago, Solomon, the wisest king to ever rule, described the world in which we live: "Men have gone in search of many schemes" (Ecclesiastes 7:29). In his final analysis, he concluded, "This too is meaningless, a chasing after the wind" (Ecclesiastes 4:16). All the nations that make up the world are burdened down with riches or poverty, obesity or malnutrition, success or failure. The Bible says, "The man who fears God will avoid all extremes" (Ecclesiastes 7:18).

Much of the world is riddled with disease, hardship, and oppression. I have traveled in parts of Europe, Asia, and the Third World where there is no joy. No one smiles; there is no happiness or celebration. The surroundings are grim and depressing, without hope; it is what some have described as "life in the abyss." For me it is the image—in totality—of life without God. These people look at the Western world and long to experience the happiness we portray, not realizing that much of it is a facade—hiding behind cosmetic surgery while parading sculpted bodies scantly clothed, frowns turned upward with implants and permanent makeup, and Botox treatments to camouflage furrowed brows. And the deception doesn't stop with just the outward appearance—it permeates the need for lewd entertainment, laughing at filth and then drowning out the misery with substance abuse. Our society has traded strength of character for makeovers that deceive. Browse through a teen magazine today and look into the eyes of the "beautiful people" the publisher props up. The photographs often reflect a dissatisfaction of heart. Let's stop pretending that there is nothing we can do about it. The Bible clearly tells us to "find out what pleases the Lord. Have nothing to do with the fruitless deeds of darkness, but rather expose them" (Ephesians 5:10–11).

Some years ago, a dear pastor friend and his family from the

Middle East came to the United States for a visit. They had young children at the time and were sent on a trip to Disney World. Upon their return to North Carolina, a friend asked the pastor, "Did you enjoy the amusement park?" The pastor looked away in distress. Tears came to his eyes when he responded, "I tell you, my friend, I walked through the park and prayed for this blessed country. My heart ached for you Americans." Those standing nearby were stunned. One said, "But I don't understand! Disney World is a happy place—a place of escape even if for a day." The pastor clasped his hands passionately and said with a cry in his voice, "No! How can you escape from yourself? Your country—your people—are deceived. I watched as they ran from pavilion to pavilion. I saw them exhausted from standing in long lines, wiping their brows, scolding their children because they were hot and impatient. When we boarded the monorail at the end of the day, babies were crying, children were fussing, and parents were drained and bickering. This was their fun?" He went on, "My dear friends, America has exhausted its sense of joy. They have chased after it for so long that when it came in the form they imagined, it was empty." King Solomon was right, "This, too, is meaningless."

What I find disturbing in America is the consuming desire for leisure, convenience, and fun. It seems we, as a nation, have traded God for gadgets. We have traded eternal truth for momentary self-gratification—worshipping false gods of materialism and humanism instead of the Creator of all things. Gone are the days of quiet reflection. Gone are the days of reaping the benefits of a bountiful supper after a back-breaking day in the fields, where laughter filled the family home with joy, and sleep came easily, even when the tin roof leaked raindrops upon little bodies huddled together to keep warm. We have traded hard times, well, for hard times. We have traded sore backs for disillusioned minds; we have exchanged the love of family and home for cyberfriends and living in constant motion that robs the soul from memories—and perhaps from that still, small voice that longs to be heard.

When someone places his own gratification ahead of every-thing else, there are no limits to what a person will do. Ultimately, I believe, even child abuse is a sign of selfishness and disregard for others. This is a tragedy. To injure, ignore, disrespect, and violate the innocence of a child are among the greatest evils known to man.

The press has publicized some of the more shocking and graphic aspects of child abuse—especially the physical abuse that makes sensational headlines—but they have almost entirely ignored the psychological and emotional abuse caused by today's social trends. Today we are experiencing an epidemic of parental neglect, moth-ers and fathers absent from home, children exploited by advertising and mass media, immature sensibilities bombarded by erotic and vulgar programming aimed at vulnerable young minds, and the encouraging of excessive, even pathological, self-interest and self-absorption. Where is the outrage?

THE WORLD OF BIG SPENDERS

There is a serious question of exploitation and abuse in the way media market uses children. At a time when busy, self-absorbed par-ents lubricate their consciences by lavishing expensive electronics and gadgets on their children, clever marketing campaigns take full advantage of the situation. Advertising exploits children, creating the desire for things children can easily blackmail their parents into buying. Entire advertising budgets are built on the strategy that chil-dren determine the buying habits of their parents: "If you love me, buy me this," they demand.

As I suggested earlier, the legacy of the free-thinking sixties has deep roots. The spirit of revolt that blossomed in the 1960s, partly as a result of the Vietnam War, convinced a generation that "turn-ing off and spacing out" was a legitimate lifestyle option. The "yuppies" and the "uppies" of the 1980s and '90s plugged into the cash flow, accumulating possessions and accolades on their way to the top. A pervasive sense of coldness and aloofness infiltrated their mind-set.

Music lyrics and visual imagery continues to grow increasingly erotic, violent, and antisocial. These are the common idiom of youth in the new millennium. The television, iPod, and Internet have trespassed upon the innocence of America's children, while preoccupied mothers and dispassionate fathers stare aghast wondering what went wrong. They don't stop to think of their own contributions to the persuasions influencing their children. After all, where do kids as young as elementary age get money to rent rock videos and the latest rap DVDs? Who takes teens to risqué movies? (I knew Walt Disney many years ago. I don't think he would approve of some of today's programs.) Who allows the television at home to blare prime-time vulgarity posing as comedy? How can children access Internet porn if Mom and Dad are overseeing the home computer? Parents have bought into the world's pastimes chock-full of pop culture, and it is searing the souls of our children. Parents have allowed electronic babysitters to infiltrate their homes and minds; young people's sense of right and wrong is being choked by wild and rank weeds in a moral wasteland.

Even in this darkened veneer, there are signs of a moral groundswell. Christ will always have a presence on earth through His people. Articles and books do emerge from time to time drawing attention back to the Word of God—the only moral authority yesterday, today, and forever.

Dr. James Dobson and Gary Bauer's *Children at Risk* describes America's moral crisis in great depth, calling it a civil war of values. Focus on the Family, the Colorado-based ministry founded by Dobson, regularly targets the exploitation and abuse of children. With coauthor Bauer, a former Reagan administration adviser, Dobson gives a chilling résumé of the rise of anti-Christian secularism and the value-neutral morality being perpetrated on the family. Dr. Dobson offers this assessment:

> Robbed of sexual standards, society will unravel like a ball of twine. That is the lesson of history. That is the legacy of Rome and more than two thousand civilizations that have come and gone on this earth. The family is the basic unit of society on which all human activity rests. If you tamper with the sexual nature of familial relationships, you necessarily threaten the entire super-structure. Indeed, ours is swaying like a drunken sailor from the folly of our cultural engineers.

It is vitally important that preachers, authors, speakers, commentators, and broadcasters—any God-fearing individual with a platform—speak out about destructive behaviors and vividly portray the dangers that confront both young and old in our society. Many parents are like the seven churches in Revelation: blinded to the truth. Many of the churches today are condoning this blindness and conforming to Satan's branding. In contrast, John is sounding the alarm: Wake up! The pressure from the other side is so intense, only a mammoth turning to God can ever hope to counter the trend.

You may wonder, *How do we counter the trend?* The answer is clear. We must saturate our minds, hearts, and souls with God's Word. "Train your*self* to be godly" (1 Timothy 4:7; emphasis added). We must drench ourselves in the living water of His truth. The Bible declares, "Take to heart all the words I have solemnly declared to you this day, so that you may command your children to obey carefully all the words of this law. They are not just idle words for you—they are your life" (Deuteronomy 32:45–47).

Decades of reprogramming by permissive educators and social agencies have perverted and corrupted the foundations of moral discipline in this nation. Can such a culture survive, or has the crisis of deception already taken us much too far toward the Apocalypse?

THE CULT OF SELF-INFLICTED ABUSE

Consider the crises of promiscuity, date rape, drug use, alcoholism, pornography, homosexuality, and sadomasochism even among elementary age children. I recently read about an eleven-year-old boy who was being charged with sexual abuse and sodomy of a four-year-old girl. He learned about such things through a dial-a-porn number given him by a friend in Sunday school.

And what about the health classes taught in today's public schools—even before kids reach high school? The material presented would have been considered pornographic a generation ago. And just because society slips it in under the umbrella of education does not change the fact that all sacredness to personal relationships has been destroyed. No wonder young people today have no shame. They have no idea what a standard of sacred respectability is.

I am told that reliable reports indicate immorality is an epidemic also in our churches. Several years ago, one poll claimed that 40 percent of young people in Bible-believing evangelical churches were sexually active. Furthermore, 60 percent of single adults, including those who attend church regularly and participate in Bible studies, are not only sexually active, but many reported having sex with multiple partners. I'm sure today the number has swelled.

THE CULT OF CRISIS

No wonder the world is in crisis! No wonder teenagers are confused. No wonder there is danger in the streets. No wonder gang violence is at an all-time high. No wonder teen suicide has reached epidemic proportions. No wonder the dropout rate in high schools all over America is astronomical. No wonder young people feel there is nothing to believe in or live for. No wonder the soul of America is in peril. No wonder we fear tomorrow. No wonder the church is watered down, exchanging hymns for hype, preaching for skits, conviction for tolerance, and replacing dedication to God for Satan's deceit. Yes, the deceiver and corrupter is riding roughshod throughout the land. The horses' hooves are beating as loudly as the heavy metal thud blowing out the eardrums of our children.

A news headline recently read: NOISE INDUCED HEARING LOSS— NEXT GENERATION IS GOING DEAF. Many may think that NFD stands for the London-based hybrid heavy metal band: Noise for Destruction (NFD), but the National Foundation for the Deaf (NFD) had the acronym first—more of Satan's clever deception. The NFD reported that Generation Y (also known as the Millennium Generation) is damaging their eardrums. Their Web site warns, "You only get one set of ears to last your whole life so you need to treat them right." It goes on to say, "A devil may care attitude rules many of the 18–25 year olds surveyed . . . who have already experienced symptoms of hearing damage." This devil-may-care attitude is drowning out the hoofbeats . . . and the still, small voice of God.

THE TRENDY WORLD

You cannot watch television or read a newspaper anymore without realizing the dangerous implications of these trends. An editorial that appeared in *USA Today Magazine*, titled "The Decay of Morality," by Gerald F. Kreyche, examined the values perpetrated by the popularizers of immorality. He writes:

> Shacking up; having babies out of wedlock, with the man bearing no fiscal or moral responsibilities; single parenthood—all seem almost *de rigueur*. (A recent news report cited the doubling of births by teens during a two-year period . . . Nationwide, one out of four babies is born to an unwed mother.) Lesbians and gays are unabashed in their relationships. The new head of the National Organization

of Women (NOW) admits to having both a husband and a female "companion." Welfare, instead of being a temporary help to overcome a momentary hardship, has become a generations-old "entitlement," making the American "work ethic" a hollow term. Throughout all of this, we are told by society to be tolerant, understanding, accepting, and above all, nonjudgmental. [May 1992]

Kreyche suggests that any Rip Van Winkle waking up in the last decade of the twentieth century after a long sleep would go into a "value culture shock that would push the needle off the Richter scale." I have to agree. Poll after poll reveals that the majority of U.S. population claims some kind of moral and ethical value system based on a belief in God, yet those values apparently have little or no influence on their lives. Not only have the Christian roots of this nation been banished from the universities, but the Word of God is commonly scorned as misogynous, manipulative, and mythical. Institutions are labeling Christianity by Satan's standard. The Bible predicts this will happen: "The fool speaks folly, his mind is busy with evil: He practices ungodliness and *spreads error concerning the Lord*; the hungry he leaves empty and from the thirsty he withholds water. The scoundrel's methods are wicked, he makes up evil schemes" (Isaiah 32:6–7; emphasis added).

THE CULT OF LIBERATION

Who stands for truth? Does anybody care anymore? At the bitter end of an era of liberation—women's lib, kids' lib, animal lib, and everything-but-ethics lib—America has apparently been liberated from its moral foundations. But for too many, the good life has become a living hell.

I am grieved to see how some churches have compromised on basic principles. In many cases, they have deserted the truths of

Scripture in favor of a lie. But this falling away in our culture and our churches is but another sign that we have entered the "time of troubles" that Jesus foretold. He described the coming storm in the parable of the sower saying that there would be a time when the people would leave the truth and seek after their own lusts. Later, the apostle Paul offered a further glimpse of the Apocalypse in his instructions to young Timothy, when he wrote:

> But know this, that in the last days perilous times will come: For men will be lovers of themselves, lovers of money, boasters, proud, blasphemers, disobedient to parents, unthankful, unholy, un-loving, unforgiving, slanderers, without self-control, brutal, de-spisers of good, traitors, headstrong, haughty, lovers of pleasure rather than lovers of God, having a form of godliness but denying its power. And from such people turn away! For of this sort are those who creep into households and make captives of gullible women loaded down with sins, led away by various lusts, always learning and never able to come to the knowledge of the truth. (2 Timothy 3:1–7 NKJV)

Paul described desperate times in his day that, even fifty years ago, would have seemed impossible; yet, this is the world we live in today. For the benefit of Timothy, his disciple, and the church the young pastor was going to lead, Paul's letter told him to live in obe-dience to the principles he knew to be correct and not to be influenced by the sinful world around him. In his second letter to Timothy, Paul said:

> But you must continue in the things which you have learned and been assured of, knowing from whom you have learned them, and that from childhood you have known the Holy Scriptures, which are able to make you wise for salvation through faith which is in Christ Jesus. (2 Timothy 3:14–15 NKJV)

Hard times had already come to Christians in the Roman Empire. Persecution and death were common. Perhaps for the fainthearted there was greater justification for falling away than there is today, but Paul told Timothy to stand fast. He reminded him that "all Scripture is given by inspiration of God, and is profitable for doctrine, for reproof, for correction, for instruction in righteousness" (2 Timothy 3:16 NKJV). In this statement you will find the central truth of the authority of God's Word that is often disputed in today's world.

American courts of law have been deprived of much of their authority. On the other hand, many judges assault our Constitution by judgments—or misjudgments—they hand down. Today there is little judgment for crime and defiance from the bench for cases to protect religious freedom and parental rights.

By the same token, people from all walks of life have denied the ultimate moral authority—the Bible—in order to condone sin. But much worse, some in the church who should faithfully uphold the authority of Scripture, instead defame and deny it. This, too, is the work of the deceiver. The book of Hebrews warns:

> For it is impossible for those who were once enlightened, and have tasted the heavenly gift, and have become partakers of the Holy Spirit, and have tasted the good word of God and the powers of the age to come, if they fall away, to renew them again to repentance, since they crucify again for themselves the Son of God, and put Him to an open shame. (6:4–6 NKJV)

But we can have new life in Christ, and this is our greatest need as individuals and as a society. Many Christians live defeated as they struggle to discover God's will for their lives, but the Bible plainly tells us, "This is the will of God, your sanctification." Paul wrote, "You should avoid sexual immorality; that each of you should learn to control his own body in a way that is holy and honorable, not in passionate lust like the heathen, who do not know God. . . .

For God did not call us to be impure, but to live a holy life. Therefore, he who rejects this instruction does not reject man but God, who gives you his Holy Spirit" (1 Thessalonians 4:3 NKJV; 3–5, 7–8). The power of the Holy Spirit to defeat the natural inclination to sin within us is available to everyone who will accept Christ as Savior and Lord.

Paul also said:

> Our old man was crucified with Him, that the body of sin might be done away with, that we should no longer be slaves of sin. For he who has died has been freed from sin. Now if we died with Christ, we believe that we shall also live with Him, knowing that Christ, having been raised from the dead, dies no more. Death no longer has dominion over Him. For the death that He died, He died to sin once for all; but the life that He lives, He lives to God. (Romans 6:6–10 NKJV)

So why do we fight against God who loves us? Why do many work so hard for something they can have so freely? What a tragedy that those who follow secular philosophies choose to turn away from the God of heaven to serve false and fallible idols.

THE WORLDLY CHURCH

While the church should open its doors to surrounding communities, the word *community* in today's society has expanded its reach. Phrases associated with this idea of community are "the sharing of common interests," "having similar likes and dislikes," "identifying with specific thoughts and ideas that unify." At first glance, it sounds cozy—perhaps too cozy—especially when applied to the church of the Lord Jesus Christ. Paul said, "[Christ] gave himself for us that he might redeem us from all iniquity, and purify unto himself a peculiar people" (Titus 2:14 KJV). This word *peculiar* is not thought of as favorable anymore, not even by Christians.

I know that young people today enjoy rap music. They say it's great. But I'll tell you something good that has gotten a bad rap, and that is the word *peculiar*. Many words in the English language have multiple meanings. Each generation seems to extract words from the dictionary and slip them into their modern-day vocabulary—giving them a new expressive personality.

In my day, the word *bad* had a negative connotation. Today it means "great," so I'm told. This is the case with the word *peculiar*. When most people hear the word, they cringe. They think of descriptions like "weird" or "odd." But the word describes what Christ expects His church to be—a special people. Another description of the word *peculiar* is "distinctive." Christians should bear distinguishing attributes both within and without. So when the church begins to look like the world, act like the world, and sound like the world, the conclusion is certain. The church is blending into the community by embracing what the world enjoys and, in turn, bringing inside the church the world's ideas and interests. It is not much different on the outside of the church. Seldom do we see a church with a steeple. It is even difficult to find a church bearing the symbol of an empty cross. Again, this is the work of the horseman who deceives. Satan is both a fashion designer and an interior designer. He first appeals to the eye and then shouts, "Gotcha!" Then he goes to work on the "inside job." If you're a Christian, his aim is to keep you defeated so that you will be ineffective for Christ. If you are not a believer in the Lord Jesus, then his goal is to keep you in his armed force.

We are called to distinguish ourselves as Christ followers, not community organizers. We are expected to carry the marks of the Lord Jesus, not adapt to the fashionable counterculture driven by marketing traps. Most of all, we are commanded to "set [our] hearts on things above, where Christ is seated at the right hand of God. Set

[our] minds on things above, not on earthly things" (Colossians 3:1–2). This lifestyle will reflect Christ's church—not community living. Many churches have molded their programs around the community—not the Word of God. This is the work of deceivers and false prophets. It is time we extinguish the worldly influence and conform to the distinguishing marks of the risen Christ. It is time for us to trade in our contemporary leanings and lean on the convictions nailed down in the Word of God.

Satan does not have to build a church and call it the First Church of Satan in order to seduce society. He can do better than that—and he has. He wanted to take charge of our schools and social institutions—and he has. He wanted to infiltrate the thoughts and attitudes of influential leaders—and he has. He wanted to slant the media to call good, evil—and evil, good—and he has. He wanted to taint the policies of our government—and we see his fingerprints on many bills passed in the halls of Congress.

The apostle Paul warned that many will follow false teachers, not realizing that in feeding upon such lies they are drinking the devil's poison. Thousands of people in every walk of life are being deceived today. False teachers use high-sounding words that seem like the height of logic, scholarship, and sophistication. They are intellectually clever and crafty in their sophistry. They are adept at beguiling men and women whose spiritual foundations are weak by appealing to what has become a catchphrase—felt needs. The Lord did not design the church to cater to people's needs—the Lord breathed life into the church to proclaim His truths. When His truths are applied, people will be ministered to the way God intended. The problem is that community dwellers may not like the truthful content.

False teachers have departed from the faith of God revealed in Scripture or never believed in His truth at all. The Bible states plainly that the reason for their turning away is that they gave heed to Satan's lies and deliberately chose to accept the myths of the devil rather than the truth of God. So they themselves became the mouthpieces of Satan.

Writing to Timothy, the apostle Paul warned, "Now the Spirit expressly says that in latter times some will depart from the faith, giving heed to deceiving spirits and doctrines of demons, speaking lies in hypocrisy, having their own conscience seared with a hot iron" (1 Timothy 4:1–2 NKJV).

Paul later wrote to Timothy, "For the time will come when they will not endure sound doctrine, but according to their own desires, because they have itching ears, they will heap up for themselves teachers; and they will turn their ears away from the truth, and be turned aside to fables" (2 Timothy 4:3–4 NKJV). Doesn't this sound familiar today?

This cultural phenomenon has not only taken the world by storm, it has infiltrated many evangelical churches today with thunderbolts. Churches have been swindled by clever marketing firms peddling the concept of capital campaigns to raise funds to make the church campus into a public square. Look at the similarities and ask, *who is following whom?*

- Designer cafés in strip malls—now in church foyers.
- Health clubs in every city—now on church properties.
- Dramas and skits on campus—now replacing church pulpits.
- Heavy metal rock bands in stadiums—now in the sanctuaries.

These observations are not meant to criticize but rather to warn all who represent the church to consider our position in Christ. Satan is a liar, a deceiver, and *the* great imitator. As far back as the Garden of Eden, Satan's purpose was not to make mankind as godly as possible but to make it as god*like* as possible, but without God. Satan's method has often been to imitate God, not in the same sense we are called to be imitators of Jesus. Satan perverts everything good by mimicking and mocking the real thing.

189

In light of the warnings stated in the letters to the seven churches, it may behoove Christians to reconsider how some churches are following worldly trends. When the church begins to entertain the flock and respond to the cult of self—it is diminished to a mere community center. Churches are springing up in communities everywhere and are custom-designing their buildings, their programs, and their sanctuaries based on surveys from community dwellers.

Many churches have their eyes on the culture instead of on Christ. Many Christians run after material goods instead of following the Master. Many pastors preach on *common unity* instead of calling the *community* to repent.

The Scripture says, "For Satan himself transforms himself into an angel of light. Therefore it is no great thing if his ministers also transform themselves into ministers of righteousness, whose end will be according to their works" (2 Corinthians 11:14–15 NKJV).

Satan is still using this form of deception, and often his representatives are being disguised as ministers of righteousness. While propagating that which brings death and darkness to the mind and heart of the sinner, they profess to be representatives of enlightened living. This is satanic deception. By the time the storm of spiritual and moral deception—unleashed by the first horseman—disappears over the horizon, the full power of the antichrist will have come upon the earth, bringing its dreadful curse.

John's account of Jesus breaking each seal one by one indicates that there is no reprieve between the messages of the four horsemen. The action will be like machine-gunfire—rapid and deadly. The Lord reminded the disciples that this would be the precursor to the Great Tribulation, meaning that the sorrow and grief left in the plumes of dust from the horses' hooves would be just a taste of the anguish yet to come. He warned the disciples about this while He was still on earth. He returned in John's vision to sound the last alert with a dramatic demonstration of what had already been predicted. This is the evidence of God's mercy and love to a people who still do not know

Him. Yet in patience He is holding out His arm of salvation. But that day will soon come to an end.

At the appointed time by the Father, the Son will storm out of heaven to stomp out evil and re-create the perfect place of abode for eternity—for a called-out people who have faithfully carried His name to the world. We will someday join those who have gone on before us, even those of ancient times who "admitted that they were aliens and strangers on earth. People who say such things show that they are looking for a country of their own . . . longing for a better country—a heavenly one. Therefore God is not ashamed to be called their God, for he has prepared a city for them" (Hebrews 11:13–16).

Since God has designed an eternal home with us in mind, should we not be happy to conduct our lives on earth by His design? Is God ashamed of our churches today? When people walk into the "hip" church today, do they sense God's presence? When the unbeliever spends time with "churchgoers," do they see a reflection of Christ? The answer, I believe, is found in His letters to the seven churches . . . and the warning the four horsemen carry.

For the older generation, we better put our hearing aids in and turn them up so that we can hear and heed the warnings. For the younger generations, they better set their headphones aside so that they, too, can hear the warnings from heaven. It is time to repent. Our responses will determine which road we'll be on when heaven's clock stops ticking, signifying God's patience is ended.

The apostle John warned us about those who speak for God and those who speak with deception: "They are from the world; therefore they speak from the world, *and the world listens to them*. We are from God. Whoever knows God listens to us; whoever is not from God does not listen to us. By this we know the spirit of truth *and the spirit of error*" (1 John 4:5–6 ESV; emphasis added).

The Lord Jesus Christ does all things well, and the most powerful is victory over His own death and the ultimate blow He will inflict to the great deceiver. Jesus Christ will triumph over the works of Satan and be glorified by all creation as the Conqueror of sin. He empowers us today to triumph over the works of Satan in our lives and in our churches. If your hope is to stand with Him in Glory, you must be willing to stand for Him before the world today.

12

THE RED HORSE RIDES

Then another horse came out, a fiery red one. Its rider was given power
to take peace from the earth . . . To him was given a large sword.
—REVELATION 6:4

There are many distinguishing features of the second horse, but its coat color is the most noticeable. So it isn't surprising to note how John characterized this messenger of fate. He not only identified this second horse as red (the color of war), but further emphasized the intensity of the color—fiery (blazing and burning). The second horseman sits high in the saddle and is given power to take peace from the earth and to make war, represented by the sword. The red horse is dispatched by the authority of God to bring war, but this will not be the ultimate war. The Bible says, "The war horse is a false hope for salvation, and by its great might it cannot rescue" (Psalm 33:17 ESV).

We have already seen that the white horse of Revelation 6 brings a false peace to earth. Now the red horse will snatch peace away as quickly as it came. When Jesus Christ rides the great white stallion to earth to end the war of all wars, He will pronounce victory before the battle begins. He will extinguish the works of this horseman and will bring everlasting peace unlike any man can imagine. What a picture of hope for all who follow Christ.

While as a servant of the Lord Jesus this fills me with great joy, my heart is also overcome with a compulsion to preach Christ only and Him crucified. Only through the shed blood of Christ can the unbelieving heart be redeemed. This is one of the great warnings trumpeted by the horsemen. His swiftness to take peace from the earth is warning enough that the deceiver is an oppressor of the people, not a liberator. I plead with those who don't know Christ—do not ignore this warning. It may sound gruesome, but I can assure you that God, out of the fullness of His love, bids you to listen and obey while there is still time. The Bible says "as long as it is called Today" do not "be hardened by sin's deceitfulness" (Hebrews 3:13).

The warning of the second horseman will spark unprecedented violence and storms of destruction until the final hour when the Messiah Himself will intervene and crush the allies of Satan and the evils of Armageddon. You recall that Jesus told His disciples, "For then there will be great tribulation, such as has not been since the beginning of the world until this time, no, nor ever shall be. And unless those days were shortened, no flesh would be saved; but for the elect's sake those days will be shortened" (Matthew 24:21–22 NKJV).

It would be naive for anyone to ignore the fact that this ominous rider who brings war is, even now, riding relentlessly in our direction. Some said after the Cold War ended that the earth had become a global village—that we were all neighbors. Many contended that the West had won the war. I cautioned that we could not afford to celebrate prematurely; the post–Cold War stockpiles of nuclear weapons would still give mankind the power to destroy the earth seventeen times over, in flames reaching 130 million degrees. No United Nations resolution, no peacekeeping force, no new world order will bring this about. God, Himself, will control the destiny of earth. While we all should work and pray for peace, we know that danger stares us in the face. Are we heeding the warning of the second horseman? Or are we casually looking into an imaginary sawed-off shotgun loaded with mega barrels of gunpowder that will leave massive destruction in the dust of the horse's hind feet?

The number of aggressive Third World nations with such dreams of glory continually grows. There are several military dictators who would think nothing of lobbing a nuclear missile into Tel Aviv or Jerusalem if they had the capacity. So long as men live by the laws of self-sufficiency and expediency, there will be tyrants who can bring calamity upon the world far greater than explosions that have left volcanic ash sprinkled across mountains and plains.

In these tempestuous times, no one can speak of war with confident detachment. Before the final days of World War II, wars were more or less limited to battlefields and sea lanes. Supplies were transported over vast distances. Oceans, mountainous terrain, snow-covered highways, arid deserts, and fast-moving rivers all created natural barriers to limit war and give combatants at least the illusion of distance and safety. Especially for North Americans, wars have been something fought "over there" (overseas).

Then came 9/11. In the aftermath of that monumental, America-changing tragedy, we began to relive the terror that struck Pearl Harbor on December 7, 1941, that brought America to its knees just as it did on September 11, 2001. Those of us who can recall World War II remember the air raids, the rations, the bomb shelters—our country did everything in its power to keep the battle far away from our borders.

Our citizens trembled in fear, then banded together to fight against the evil that threatened not only the way of life in America, but life in many parts of the world beyond our shores.

Then at 8:45 the morning of August 6, 1945, a warning bell rang in the newsroom of the Japanese Broadcasting Corporation, signaling an alert. Some of us can still recall the solemn announcement as the newscaster rushed to a radio microphone to broadcast the emergency bulletin from the Chugoku District Army Headquarters: "Three enemy aircraft have been spotted over the Saijo area," he said.

Suddenly there was a blinding blue flash of light over Hiroshima . . . and a moment of absolute unearthly silence. In the wake of the mind-boggling eruption that followed, an ominous mushroom cloud of boiling gases rose above the incinerated mass where a city once stood. This was to be the symbol of a new era for the decades to follow.

The newsman was vaporized and the entire radio station with him. The consecutive bombings of Hiroshima and Nagasaki had the intended effect. They brought an abrupt end to that terrible war, but they also changed the course of history and taught the entire world the new dangers of warfare.

We sometimes forget, however, that the nuclear bombing of Japan also saved lives. Many Japanese leaders today, even in those two cities, will tell you that the bombs probably saved millions of Japanese as well as Allied lives; for had the war not ended then, and abruptly, the Japanese would certainly have fought to their last breath to protect their homeland.

Historians tell us that the world has seen more than four thousand wars in five thousand years, most of them lasting for years at a time. The Thirty Years' War in Europe lasted for decades and drained the lifeblood and the youth of a dozen nations. We know that more than sixty million people died in the two world wars of the first half of the twentieth century.

Since the harrowing moments of the arms buildup of the 1960s and 1970s—in the anxious days of the East-West nuclear arms confrontation—we understand the potential of political intimidation. Each side imagines the other more powerful than itself, and each demands ever more powerful and inhuman weapons. In the Persian Gulf War we saw the incredible accuracy and destructiveness of modern conventional firepower, its airstrikes powerfully precise.

The fireworks above Iraq, the ancient home of Abraham, is just a foretaste of what an all-out thermonuclear war would unleash. As we have already seen, almost any petty tyrant can become a nuclear or biochemical bully today.

When the first edition of this book was printed, I said, "Even though the total devastation of nuclear war should make such a prospect unthinkable, unpredictable hotheads such as Saddam Hussein or Muammar al-Qaddafi could rock the world with a surprise attack." The change from conventional to nuclear and biochemical weapons has made the task of international diplomacy immensely more complicated.

While we are told to work for peace, we know that true peace will come when Jesus Christ returns to earth. Until that time, the Saddam Husseins will continue to rise up. Some, as he was, will be captured and dealt with, but there will be dictators until the end—irrational leaders who will have the ability to annihilate mankind, using the most inhumane methods. This is the warning of the fiery red horse whose rider charges speedily our way, wielding his big stick—the sword given to him.

THE WARHORSE

No one could have ever imagined that a radically unconventional and ruthless army operating out of desert tents could bring down the world's most prestigious twin towers, turning a sunny day into an outrageous nightmare, leaving plumes of black smoke that will take a lifetime to blow out of our national memory. We must have been slumbering as the enemy slyly put their hideous plan together several years before September 11, 2001. Right under our radar, they took advantage of our benevolent trust and sought training for terrorist pilots to execute an unthinkable attack. While our military forces spanned the globe protecting the harbors and borders of ally nations, terrorism had crept like sea monsters out of the oceans and upon American soil, blending in with the diversity our country had welcomed. Our greatest fear was realized: war had come to the shores of America, the land of the free and the home of the brave. We had been deceived.

Nineteen al-Qaeda hijackers shrewdly boarded four commercial jetliners and masterfully took control of the cockpits, slamming two planes into the World Trade Center's twin towers—skyscrapers that reflected our country's accomplishments of wealth. The third plane blasted into the Pentagon—representing our military power, and the fourth aircraft intended to blast the U.S. Capitol was diverted when a few brave men overtook the terrorist pilots and forced a fatal crash into a rural cornfield in Shanksville, Pennsylvania. These heroic citizens represented for us all our freedom.

Still, such horror paralyzed a nation. I can remember being riveted to the twenty-four-hour news cycle and for long periods of time anchors were silent as footage looped on the screen—over and over we watched people frantically running from the towers that fell into heaps. I am sure we all felt, at any moment, we would wake from the wretched nightmare and life would return to normal—but it never would. We were caught off guard. We woke that September morning to blue skies and sunny thoughts, not knowing that the world we knew was about to be forever changed. The unprecedented attack was of monumental proportion. These are the kinds of storms that drop from the skies when the warning signals are ignored. Osama bin Laden in a videotape months after the 9/11 attack said, "Terrorism against America deserves to be praised because it was in a response to injustice." No one, including bin Laden, can conceive of the devastating blows that will be delivered when Jesus Christ peels open the second seal of the scroll and executes justice to the unjust. Its gruesome message will be delivered with precision by the rider on the fiery red horse. Are we watching? Have we prepared?

I found it interesting to observe how Americans mourned the utter tragedy of 9/11. I thought about the chaos that America's largest city suffered. It brought us to our knees—for a time. Politicians in Congress came together as they stood on the steps of the Capitol and raised their voices—not in political rivalry but in united resolve as they sang, "God Bless America." We saw responders flooding into New York and the nation's capitol. We would not soon forget the sacrifice of so many police officers and firefighters. Memorial services honored the dead.

President George W. Bush asked me to lead the nation in prayer at the National Cathedral in Washington, D.C., days after the attack, while smoke continued to rise through the rubble. Five of the six living presidents attended, with a show of solidarity unlike any other country displays in the face of catastrophe. Churches followed suit as sanctuaries were filled to capacity—but our collective humble spirit as a nation lasted only a handful of Sundays. If only we could *longer* remember the strength our country historically derived from the fact that God had blessed America, our country could possibly be in better standing today. But we are right back to being deceived.

How soon we forget. Most of us remember the fateful day only when watching documentaries on the History Channel—9/11 has been added to the rotation along with wars of the world. In the era of the world wars, airplanes were not transformed into bombs; they dropped the bombs on strategic targets, and then roared higher into the sky, observing MISSION ACCOMPLISHED. Military aircraft—like the B17 bomber—known as the warhorse—flew out of England during World War II. Its crew had a picture of a horse painted on the nose of the plane. It called to mind the fiery red horse that would someday come out of the heavens—its target—the unrepentant world.

Whether unconventional or nuclear armaments, the character of conflict has changed. War is not what it used to be. Author and researcher George Segal wrote, "The fundamental change was that whereas previous wars could be conceived of as useful instruments of policy, a nuclear war would only result in the death of the planet. We would be left with a 'republic of insects.'"

When it became clear that nuclear weapons possessed the capacity to annihilate everything in their killing zone, war strategy had to change. Stealth and craftiness were added. To the world's arsenal of intercontinental ballistic missiles, submarine-launched warheads, silo-based missiles, and even satellite-launched weaponry, we suddenly found nuclear missiles hidden on constantly moving, subterranean railroad cars. With all this motion and commotion, the threat of massive destruction was greatly increased. In fact, most analysts said that total destruction was "assured," and the acronym of the 1970s became MAD, Mutually Assured Destruction.

Around about us today there are wars and rumors of wars. If we add all the nuclear weapons stockpiled by the former Soviet Union, the United States, Great Britain, France, India, Israel, China, and other smaller nations, we then get an idea of the massive destructive potential the nations of the world now possess.

And the rider of the red horse has closed the distance. His hoof-beats bring a deafening sound of war in the clouds above. The storm is not out of sight. We must not put away the warning flags.

Our leaders promise peace, but the best peace has never been more than a restless calm. The world is in such desperate chaos I have to wonder, is peace just an illusion? I often wondered following the fall of Communism and the collapse of the Soviet Union how long we would have a period of peace. Would another storm, perhaps more dreadful, catch us by surprise?

I posed the question, are we in the eye of the hurricane . . . Is a more sinister storm approaching? The answer is found in the Word of God: hoofbeats are approaching.

A DECEITFUL RIDE

For centuries, legislatures and parliaments have attempted to negotiate for peace. In times past, mighty leaders such as the Caesars,

Constantine, Charlemagne, Napoleon, the czars of the East, and the kings of the West each, in turn, promised lasting peace. But they all failed. Today, bold schemes for global unity and brotherhood are being proclaimed in Brussels, New York, Geneva, Tokyo, and Washington, D.C. Leaders, filled with empty notions, claim that peace can be realized if we will give them our votes. There was a popular song in the 1960s that said, "The answer, my friend, is blowing in the wind." The answer from politicians that we will someday attain peace through a new world order is only an empty promise that the wind carries away. For you see, peace will not come until the Peacemaker personally brings His new world order to earth. So the world grows cynical.

For those who belong to Christ, we put our faith not in the State Department but in the promises of the Bible, for they shall all be fulfilled. For this reason, we should not feel hopeless in spite of the troubles we face—but we still must face them, and we can endure with Jesus Christ as Commander in Chief. He may not remove the troubles, but He will see us through them. This is what keeps us humble before Him. He is the Captain of our souls. But He warns us to put on His armor:

> Our struggle is . . . against the spiritual forces of evil in the heavenly realms. Therefore put on the full armor of God, so that when the day of evil comes, you may be able to stand your ground, and after you have done everything, to stand. Stand firm then, with the belt of *truth* buckled around your waist, with the breastplate of *righteousness* in place, and with your feet fitted with the *readiness* that comes from the gospel of peace . . . Take up the shield of faith, with which you can *extinguish* all the flaming arrows of the evil one. Take the helmet of salvation, and the sword of the Spirit, which is the word of God . . . *Be alert* and always *keep on praying*. (Ephesians 6:12–18; emphasis added)

The world is on a deceitful ride, and those following the lead horse are looking over their shoulders wondering who to blame. I have actually heard people blame God for our state of affairs. Political parties blame each other. No one, of course, blames the deceiver himself. Why? Because he cleverly performs his devious acts through mankind—those following his four-legged companion in death. He is the great schemer. He is the illusive manipulator. He prances and dances and drinks in the adulation of his worshippers as he glimmers and shimmers, displaying all that glitters and all that attracts the shallowness of man. Then suddenly the stinging whip wraps them around the waist; they fall to the ground as the stampede executes the deceived followers. The deceiver reins victorious—for the moment—as other followers, aghast and bewildered, blame God for their plight.

This is what is happening in the financial war. The world economy is in serious trouble. Americans had become so complacent that the recession actually took our nation by surprise. We hadn't worried about how to pay our debt; we just shoved a brand-new credit card across the counter—a card we didn't apply for yet happily slid into our wallets. Consider just a few of the consequences of the recent economic downturn:

- America's federal deficit is terrifying with no prospect of ever paying it down.
- Rising debt is a serious problem both for families and corporations.
- Private homes are in foreclosure.
- Bankruptcies are at an all-time high.
- Life savings are going down the bureaucratic drain.
- Crime and violence are overtaking schools and businesses.

Add to the nuclear threat, the financial despair, the moral climate that is disintegrating into cyberspace, and some are beginning to believe that America is living in a post-Christian era. And the sound of hoofbeats causes our hearts to thump.

How does the situation of the world today accord with God's plan for peace on earth? The most important question is not, will we survive a nuclear war, but, where will mankind stand before God when the world finds itself in the center of the greatest trauma the earth and its inhabitants have ever known? We don't grasp the infinitely greater horror of an eternity apart from God. The colossal shock of nuclear war will be transitory as far as eternity is concerned. The horrors that are ahead for all who reject God's offer of mercy, forgiveness, grace, and salvation in Christ are too terrible to imagine.

Remember that moment just before Jesus' betrayal and crucifixion? As Christ was walking away from the temple in Jerusalem, He warned, "You will hear of wars and rumors of wars, but see to it that you are not alarmed. Such things must happen, but the end is still to come" (Matthew 24:6–7).

Even while He was uttering these words, the most hideous and horrendous deed of all time and eternity was about to be carried out: men were about to crucify the Prince of Peace. It is important for us to remember that though Christ warned us there would constantly be wars and rumors of war, it does not follow that we should sit by silently while the peoples of the world destroy each other. We must not allow our silence to give approval to such devastation with weapons of mass destruction. We are commanded to warn the nations of the world that they must repent and turn to God while there is yet time. We must also proclaim that there is forgiveness and peace found only in Jesus Christ as Savior and Lord.

The Scriptures definitely teach that there will be an end to human history as we know it, and most biblical scholars believe that it is coming soon. It will not be the end of the world, but it will be the end of the present world system that has been dominated by evil.

The Bible teaches that Satan is actually "the prince of this world" (John 12:31) and "the ruler of the kingdom of the air, the spirit who is now at work in those who are disobedient" (Ephesians 2:2). As long as he is still roaming the earth, in constant conflict with God and pursuing his deadly plan, be assured that wars will continue and death and disaster will multiply. Without God there will be no hope for humanity.

Scripture also shows that a number of easily discernible signs will occur as we approach the end of the age. These signs seem to be coming into focus even now. Jesus said in Matthew 24 that there would be famines, pestilences, and earthquakes, but He also said that these would only be the beginning. Jesus said that people "will betray and hate each other, and many false prophets will appear and deceive many people. Because of the increase of wickedness, the love of most will grow cold" (Matthew 24:10–12). But He added, "This gospel of the kingdom will be preached in the whole world as a testimony to all nations, and then the end will come" (Matthew 24:14). In this sign alone we see the possibility of reaching the entire world with the Gospel through revolutionary new technologies. This is an unprecedented opportunity that could never have come about before the communication and technology boom.

During our London Crusade in 1989, we were able to reach 230 cities throughout Britain and thirty-three African nations by live satellite during prime-time viewing hours. In 1993, during our all-European crusade from Essen, Germany, a satellite system enabled us to have a far reach across the continent and into others. In 1995 from San Juan, Puerto Rico, technology made it possible for us to beam the crusade to 185 countries and territories. And in the twenty-first century, the Billy Graham Evangelistic Association is taking the Gospel into living rooms and storefronts around the world through our television program *My Hope*.

While no one evangelist or ministry can evangelize the whole world, we certainly want to do our part to reach as many people for Christ before the warnings of the horsemen are loosed. Only God knows when the alarm will sound, ending the work and ministry of evangelism as we have known it since the time of Christ.

THE HORSE OF FURY

Jesus indicated that there would be many wars, perhaps thousands, before the last great war and before His return. In the context of the increasing intensity of warfare, He said, "See that you are not troubled; for all these things must come to pass, but the end is not yet" (Matthew 24:6 NKJV). For nearly two thousand years since He spoke those words there have been alternating cycles of war and peace—wars big and small, domestic and foreign. But modern technology has dramatically changed the rules of the game. The war to come will likely be a single world war in which the triple terror of nuclear, biological, and chemical weapons will be used in the destruction of the world.

These are quite possibly the weapons of the second horseman of Revelation 6. In verse 4, we see that he has the power to take peace from the earth. This surely means world war, not just civil wars or conventional conflicts.

John's heavenly vision is God's way of showing us our folly and warning us of its consequences. Jesus indicated that when such a war does come to pass, "if those days had not been cut short, no one would survive" (Matthew 24:22). This means total war, with the annihilation of all humanity as a probable outcome, barring divine intervention. Never before has total cosmocide—the destruction of the entire planet—been at our fingertips. There are no precedents in political science or human history to guide the people who command such power. The world has been at war since the time of Adam, but never on the scale that Jesus predicted in Matthew 24 and Revelation 6. Never before has the world had the potential to obliterate the entire human race.

Listen! The distant sounds of those same hoofbeats can be heard closing in on the place you now sit reading. Above the clatter of the horses' hooves arise other sounds—the metallic thud of machine guns, the whistle of flamethrowers and mortar rounds, the crackle of burning schools, homes, and churches, the high-pitched shriek of missiles zeroing in with their nuclear warheads, the explosion of megaton bombs over our cities.

Power blocs in Europe, Asia, and North America are already being formed that could eventually clash over economic and trade issues, over immigration and population, or in some other scenario that might lead to the most devastating war in human history. Whatever the provocation, and whoever the participants may be, it will be a war so intense and destructive that, without God's intervention, all of humanity would die.

Albert Einstein predicted that a full-scale nuclear exchange would incinerate at least a third of the world's population. This is the same proportion the Bible indicates: "One-third of you shall die of the pestilence, and be consumed with famine in your midst; and one-third shall fall by the sword all around you; and I will scatter another third to all the winds, and I will draw out a sword after them" (Ezekiel 5:12 NKJV).

If the human race would turn from its evil ways and return to God, putting behind its sins of disobedience, idolatry, pride, greed, and belligerence, and all the various aberrations that lead to war, the possibility of peace exists. But when we see society as it is, with anger and violence around us, who can anticipate such a transformation? To turn away from its habits of vice and animosity, the world would need to come to God through humility and repentance, on a global scale.

A FEARFUL RIDE

I was interviewed in 1986 by a very agitated reporter for the French newspaper, *Le Figaro*. He was confused by my use of the terms *Revelation* and *Apocalypse* interchangeably in my sermons. I tried to clarify that, while one is an English word and the other is Greek, both words mean the same thing. He couldn't grasp that fact but asked, "Do you think it is a useful and Christian thing to frighten the people with such things?" I replied, "Have you read the front page of *Le Figaro* lately? Every day your own headlines frighten the people with news of murder, disease, scandal, and corruption. Most of the world lives in a constant state of fear." The reporter interrupted me and said, "But those are daily things. Apocalypse is not a daily thing! I think you just want to frighten the people."

I understood what this man was saying, but it was obvious that to him the teachings of the book of Revelation were only myths and fairy tales. He did not consider them the revelations of God concerning a very real and imminent end of civilization—a culmination far greater than all the world's stunning headlines together. So I said to him, "Sometimes it is my responsibility and my duty as a minister of the Gospel to frighten people. I always warned my children when they were small, 'Be careful when you cross the street; you could be hit by a car.' That is a legitimate fear. It is not unusual to see poisonous snakes in the mountains of North Carolina where my wife and I raised our children. We would tell them, 'Be careful where you walk; watch out for snakes!' That is also a legitimate fear. We have been told by God that, if we sin against Him and break His commandments, He will bring judgment upon the world. That is also a legitimate fear, and if we don't listen to those warnings, we are living in great danger.

The Bible says, "The fear of the LORD is the beginning of wisdom" (Psalm 111:10). We don't fear Him as a tyrant but we are to reverence Him as a loving and just Father who leads us in wisdom and truth to do what is good for us, what will prolong and preserve our lives. But since God is a just Father, we know He will discipline and punish us when we defy Him and break His rules. That is the message I must deliver.

As the book of Exodus records, God sent plague after plague upon Pharaoh and the ancient Egyptians so His people would be freed from the slavery they had suffered for four hundred years. After a plague, Pharaoh would make promises that he did not keep. The Bible says, "Pharaoh's heart grew hard, and he did not heed them, just as the LORD had said" (Exodus 8:19 NKJV).

In Revelation, we see a parallel situation when God warns His people to obey and put away their idolatry, but they will not keep their promises. John wrote, "But the rest of mankind, who were not killed by these plagues, did not repent of the works of their hands, that they should not worship demons, and idols of gold, silver, brass, stone, and wood, which can neither see nor hear nor walk. And they did not repent of their murders or their sorceries or their sexual immorality or their thefts" (Revelation 9:20–21 NKJV).

The grace, mercy, and goodness of God did not lead the people to repentance. They presumed upon His long-suffering. In both stories, however, the result is swift. Today, our promises of faithfulness to God's commandments have not led the nations to repentance. I have been preaching repentance for seventy years; there are thousands of ministers of the Gospel all over this planet preaching repentance this very hour; for two thousand years prophets, preachers, pastors, evangelists, and followers of Jesus Christ have been calling the world back to the righteousness of God, and most of the time the world has laughed in the face of the King of kings. Today, men and women are still trying to ignore the very clear warnings of the approaching storm.

RIDING THE CLOUDS

Apart from God, our hearts grow cold and unrepentant. The second horseman of the Apocalypse will teach humanity its responsibility before God through the horror of a dreadful global war.

This brings us back to the question: is there anything that we can do about war? Yes, as Christians we have a responsibility to seek peace and to make peace whenever and wherever we can. Jesus said, "Blessed are the peacemakers, for they shall be called sons of God" (Matthew 5:9 NKJV). We have been commanded by our Lord and Savior to work for a just peace on this earth. When the angels announced the birth of Jesus, they proclaimed, "'Glory to God in the highest, and on earth peace, goodwill toward men!'" (Luke 2:14 NKJV).

Christ came in the form of a baby to save humanity from self-destruction. He promised peace on earth, and someday when He splits the sky open, He will return, reclaim His territory, judge those who rejected Him, and bring lasting peace to all those who heeded the terrifying sound of hoofbeats.

Peace *with* God and the peace *of* God are possible if we repent of our sins, believe in Him, and follow Him by obeying His commands. As servants, followers, brothers, and sisters of the Savior, we are commanded to be His allies in the cause of the true and lasting peace that He can bring. Nowhere does He promise that we will succeed apart from Him, but He calls us to live for Him even in the face of insurmountable odds. We are to expect the coming of Christ at any time, but we are to work as if He were not to come for a thousand years.

Understanding the consequence of sin and arrogance should motivate every Christian to pray for repentance and revival.

I am thankful that in 1992, God moved in the hearts of Shirley Dobson and Vonette Bright to organize the National Day of Prayer. More than twenty-five hundred communities all across America held prayer vigils on the steps of their city and town hall buildings. Some five hundred diplomats and Christian leaders met in Washington, D.C., to pray for America and for a revival of Christian values.

This special day of prayer, decreed by President George H. W. Bush, was a wonderful outpouring of God's Spirit.

Unless we succeed in prevailing upon the mercies of God and gaining His clemency, I fear that the destiny of our civilization is already sealed. I believe this is the kind of commitment we must make in order to slow the horses' dissension, so that we may continue to preach and proclaim the saving grace of Jesus Christ.

The second horseman of the Apocalypse will come brandishing the sword of destruction in ever-widening arcs. Only God can intervene on our behalf. We must pray for peace, because prayer is the most powerful weapon we have in our spiritual arsenal to stand against the world's greatest enemy, the one who presents himself as an angel of light (2 Corinthians 11:14).

You may ask, if Scripture says that peace will not come until Christ returns, why work for peace? The answer for the follower of Jesus Christ is that we are to pray for God to empower His message, through the Holy Spirit to His people, leading lost souls to repentance. It is only through salvation that mankind will truly know peace.

The Prince of Peace commands that we face the reality of sin in our world. Selfishness, promiscuity, hatred, and hundreds of other factors raging out of control are proof that we are helpless without Him. His judgment echoes the sound of hoofbeats, but His love quietly convicts. We are commanded to respond, and no response is the final decision.

God spared the great city of Nineveh from destruction when the people of that ancient land repented under the preaching of Jonah. When sin flourished the following 150 years, God brought final judgment and destroyed the city and its people. Why should we think He will always contend with those who disobey His command to repent? The Bible says: "The LORD reserves wrath for His enemies; the LORD is slow to anger and great in power, and will not at all acquit the wicked. The LORD has His way in the whirlwind and in the storm, and *the clouds are the dust of His feet* (Nahum 1:2–3 NKJV; emphasis added).

My wife wrote a wonderful poem years ago taken from this scripture and later entitled a book, *Clouds Are the Dust of His Feet.*

> *Clouds are the dust of His Feet*
> *and watching the evening sky*
> *I chuckled to think, "How neat.*
> *God just passed by."*

My friends, God will not only pass by, but He is coming back to this earth mounted on a warhorse. Where will you be on that day? Will you be playing, daring Him to intrude into your life of sin, thinking that you can overcome His lasting judgment? He longs to give you peace and joy. He longs to save you from choking on the dust that will swell the skies when the hoofbeats ride high.

13

THE BLACK HORSE
THUNDERS

I looked, and there before me was a black horse!
Its rider was holding a pair of scales in his hand.
—REVELATION 6:5–6

The first mention of horses in the Bible is found in the book of beginnings—the creation book—Genesis. This is where the horse is connected to one of the great famines of all time. "Now there was no bread in all the land; for the famine was very severe, so that the land of Egypt and the land of Canaan languished because of the famine" (Genesis 47:13 NKJV).

To put this story in its proper setting, after Joseph was sold into slavery by his wicked brothers and found himself in the service of the Egyptian kingdom, he was called on by the Pharaoh to interpret a troubling dream. Joseph told him that he could not interpret the dream but through him "God will give Pharaoh the answer" (Genesis

41:16). "Seven years of plenty will come throughout all the land of Egypt," Joseph told him, "but after them seven years of famine will arise, and all the plenty will be forgotten . . . and famine will deplete the land . . . it will be very severe" (Genesis 41:29–31 NKJV). Joseph told the Pharaoh that the seven years of plenty should be reserved for the seven years of famine ahead. Pharaoh said, "Inasmuch as God has shown you all this, there is no one as discerning and wise as you" (Genesis 41:39 NKJV). Not only did Pharaoh acknowledge the God of Joseph, but he heeded the warning of the approaching storm and took immediate action. He elevated Joseph as second in command to implement the plan that God had revealed.

When the famine began to weigh heavy on the people, they complained to Joseph, "Give us bread . . . for the money has failed" (Genesis 47:15 NKJV). Joseph said, 'Give your livestock, and I will give you bread' . . . Joseph gave them bread in exchange for the *horses* . . . flocks . . . cattle" (Genesis 47:16–17 NKJV; emphasis added).

This first mention of famine could be seen as perhaps the earliest foreshadowing of things to come in the end times. Throughout Scripture we read of warnings preceding disaster. Such alerts from God are part of His grace and provision, yet so many complain. His love for mankind is evident in the caution signs He posts along life's highway. In spite of their disobedience, the children of Israel continued to hear from the Lord. He said in Old Testament times, "Set up road signs; put up guideposts. Take note of the highway, the road that you take" (Jeremiah 31:21).

Jesus is still among men graciously warning: "There will be famines, pestilences . . . in various places" (Matthew 24:7 NKJV). Men will beg for food for their families; mothers will cry out for their children.

The images are stark but all too familiar: Here they come: the stick children with the flat, unseeing stares. Their knee sockets are so large, and their calves are so thin that we wonder how they manage to walk. They are too weak to sweep away the flies that have settled on their mouths and nostrils. They can only hold their bowls out toward the television cameras. The scene being described is not from Bangladesh in the 1970s or Ethiopia in the 1980s, but from East Africa today. War often leads to famine, so the order in which the horsemen are sent out is remarkable.

The third horse—black as tar—appears before John. I can just imagine such a horse, hooves pounding, flanks heaving, eyes flashing. While the animal stomps and snorts—ready for his destructive journey—the rider holds a balance scale in his hand. John hears a voice cry out, "A quart of wheat for a day's wages, and three quarts of barley for a day's wages." (Revelation 6:6).

In John's time, a denarius was a day's wages. It amounted to perhaps twenty cents in our currency today, and it would buy a quart of wheat or corn, from which a worker and his family could make a single meal. In those days barley was a cheaper grain, generally used for horses and cattle, but in times of famine it would be used for food. Three quarts of barley would be enough for a full day's meals. In the time of Christ, a denarius would purchase about twenty-four quarts of barley, but in John's vision the same amount buys only three quarts.

So when John hears the second cry, "three quarts of barley for a denarius," he realizes that the speaker is describing the hyperinflation that would naturally accompany a crippling famine. The value of money would be one-eighth, or just 12 percent of its former value. In today's terms, that would be like a worker's wage of $20,000 shrinking to $2,400. The loss would be shocking.

A news story from famine-ridden Mozambique included this comment: "The problem is that money has no value here anymore." The reporter goes on to say that if a person's wages were double what he had made twelve years earlier, he still couldn't provide the basic needs of his family. The time will come when the money man puts all of his confidence in will be less valuable—less desired—than food for the stomach.

Holding up his scale to weigh the tiny amount of grain available to the average worker, the rider on the black horse is a symbol of just such a desperate plight in the world. So the stallion thunders in our direction with famine, disease, and starvation on his back. As we have already seen, Scripture indicates that deception, false religions, and apostasy lead to war, and that war in turn leads to famine and pestilence. Following the destruction wrought by the riders of the white and red horses, famine will engulf the earth. Millions will die of hunger, and millions more will suffer malnutrition. With malnutrition come diseases, mental and emotional deterioration, despair, and death. The black horse and its rider represent God's warning of the human suffering that lies ahead because of humanity's refusal to obey His commandments.

THUNDERING CRIES OF HUNGER

The voice that had cried out with the appearance of the third horseman gave another command: "Do not damage the oil and the wine!" (Revelation 6:6). Since ancient times, oil and wine were associated with wealth and plenty, and perhaps this is a picture of famine coexisting with luxury. Jesus told Peter, Andrew, James, and John that prior to His return, famine would stalk the earth and starve whole nations in various parts of the world (Matthew 24:7; Mark 13:8; Luke 21:11). But He also characterized those with power as eating and drinking, apparently to great excess. John later prophesied that there would be societies in the last times living in Babylonian splendor, living out the lifestyle of the rich and famous. Many societies today reflect the "feast or famine" syndrome. In many countries, there are the affluent and the afflicted—the rich and the poor.

The reports of the famine in Africa and Asia contrast starkly with the image of overfed North Americans and Europeans who are, almost without exception, living in luxury while the world starves. It was reported that from 1994 to 2004 Americans gained more than a billion pounds, characterizing the self-indulgence around us. In 2004, Americans spent about $46 billion to lose weight and $22 billion on cosmetics. Those expenditures alone would make the difference between life and death for the people of the world who are dying of starvation.

Many articles and television reports concerning the famine in Africa comment on the lack of public response. Some reporters in national news insist that the world is weary of hearing about starving Africans. They say, "Don't show us any more pictures of starving children. We don't want to know." But there is something terribly wrong when those who have so much are indifferent to those who have so little. This is a sign that Western society is hastening to its ruin, and this is yet another message of the rider on the black horse.

One of the great problems today is that there is scarcity in the midst of plenty throughout the world. This is a crisis that will increase drastically as we approach the end of the age. It is a social maladjustment, a monstrous inequity on a worldwide scale. If the nations do not turn to God, the black horse and its rider will complete this work sooner. The storm of God's outrage will descend upon us, and the whole human race will suffer the consequences.

The world community is also wrestling with crop failures and food shortages. It is not simply a matter of the total quantity of food, but a problem of distribution in most places. Dishonesty among some relief organizations, government officials, and even the victims themselves complicates the problem of getting help to those who desperately need it.

Only a few countries in the world—the United States, Canada, and Australia—annually produce more wheat than they consume. Some of the member nations of the former Soviet Union have the potential to produce more than any other nation. Because of adverse weather, inefficiency, and difficulties, other farm regions such as the Ukraine and others may be lucky to get one good crop every four or five years.

Ironically, I remember hearing someone boast that modern methods of agriculture had solved famine, claiming that any amount of grain can be produced. The Scriptures teach that famine and pestilence will continue and intensify until Christ returns as Prince of Peace and Ruler of the world.

THE BLACKNESS OF DISEASE

No one really knows how many people die of starvation each year. Many underdeveloped countries keep irregular and often unreliable statistics, particularly concerning the deaths of infants and children. In regions where famine exists, people frequently die not from starvation directly but from indirect causes, such as illnesses and acute physical conditions that overcome people whose resistance has been lowered by malnutrition. Such deaths are not always reported by family members.

Furthermore, there is a sociological and psychological component to reports on famine and disease. Bureaucrats and officials of many small governments simply do not report such disasters for fear that news of widespread deaths will damage business, trade, tourism, confidence, and other factors. In reality, the death toll from such crises as famine, pestilence, disease, and epidemics of any kind is almost always greater than the numbers reported.

Millions of infants die due to the effects of malnutrition every year in the developing countries. Millions of children go to bed hungry every night.

THE THUNDERING RAGE

The population of the earth continues to grow at a staggering rate. In an address on the campus of Indiana University at South Bend,

Michael Marien, editor of *Future Survey*, reviewed the population dilemma facing the world. In 1930, he reported, there were approximately two billion people on this planet; by 1975, the number had doubled to four billion. At that rate, based on his calculations, we will pass the eight billion mark by 2019. The bulk of this population growth will be in the Third World countries—the nations that are least able to meet the demand for food such growth would entail.

By 2020, Marien estimated, there will be 50 percent more people on this planet. In his remarks, the futurist ominously observed that these extrapolated numbers would only be lowered by war, famine, AIDS, or some kind of breakthrough in birth control technology. "Unfortunately," he added, "war, famine, and millions of deaths from AIDS are likely; major birth control advances are not."

Obviously, in East Africa these potential problems have already become a dreadful reality. This disastrous cycle rages across the land, complicated by an uncontrollable and escalating AIDS epidemic.

From Somalia and Ethiopia, in the horn of Africa, to the Cape of Good Hope in the south, the entire east coast of the African continent has been devastated. The disaster surpassed the Ethiopian famine of the 1980s that left so many gruesome images in our minds. Relief workers estimate that, short of a miracle, twenty million people will starve to death in a lifetime.

Violence is a major secondary problem growing out of short supplies, hunger, and mounting anger. Lagos, Nigeria, on the west coast of Africa was turned into an armed camp, reporting uncontrollable rioting and looting. Mozambique, also hit by famine, suffered more than a million violent deaths.

Of the forty lesser-developed countries (LDCs) in the world, twenty-eight are in Africa. The complexity of the social and political problems in these countries has led to a situation that may be too big to solve under current conditions. International affairs specialist George Segal says, "With all the good-will in the world, the root of

the food problem lies beyond the reach of international agencies."
Lagging food production, ineffective communications, plus the
need for trade stimulation, revitalized market strategies, and land
reform have made the mounting problems in the poor nations a
pernicious and seemingly insoluble enigma.

Perhaps the classic example of effective foreign aid was the United
States' Marshall Plan, which pumped $14 billion into Europe four
years following World War II. By 1956, European productivity was
38 percent higher than in 1938 when the first signs of war appeared.
Such an effort might indeed make a difference on the continent of
Africa, but the $220 million appropriated a few years ago by the U.S.
Congress for disaster relief in East Africa hardly made a dent.

Compounding the disaster, many are reluctant to send money or
food. The news reports call this a serious problem of "donor reluc-
tance" or "donor fatigue," not only because of the uncontrolled
violence, but also widespread corruption among the so-called
Crocodile Rulers and bureaucrats. Money is consumed voraciously,
especially in Mozambique, where the government levied a surcharge
of $150 per ton of food transported to its remote villages.

New York Times foreign affairs correspondent Leslie Gelb reported
in May 1992 that poor countries annually spend twice as much on
arms and soldiers as they receive in aid from all sources. The combined total surpasses $175 billion per year. Unstable conditions have
made most LDCs such bad credit risks that the World Bank, the
International Monetary Fund, and other traditional lenders will not
extend loans to them. Gelb says that their only source of capital for
arms and military budgets is increased taxation and withholding wages
and benefits from its own citizens.

It is clear how such policies would intensify the health and welfare problems of these countries. The operations director of the
World Food Program once stated, "I'm afraid I foresee deaths in very
large numbers." He added, "We can't reach large numbers of the
population. If we can provide for half of these people, we will be

doing very well." Many are already forced to subsist on roots and tubers. One elderly farmer told a reporter, "When the donors come, they don't understand why we are still alive."

These are horrifying stories, but the problem of hunger and malnutrition is not limited to developing countries. The Congressional Office of the Budget announced some time ago that many of America's children also suffer from malnutrition. Millions in North America live below the poverty line. Of course, the poverty line here is very high compared to the developing nations. What would be considered poor in America would be considered wealthy in many countries of the Third World. If you have a pair of shoes, fresh water, and food, you would be considered rich in many places in the world today.

Remember the Scripture passage when Jesus interrupted an important discussion with His disciples? Perhaps the neighborhood children of Capernaum had interrupted Jesus. Perhaps they were playing nearby when a ball landed at Jesus' feet and the children burst in to retrieve it. Whatever happened, we're told that Jesus called one of the children to Him, and said to the assembled throng, "If anyone causes one of these little ones who believe in me to sin, it would be better for him to have a large millstone hung around his neck and to be drowned in the depths of the sea" (Matthew 18:6). While we know that "little ones" mentioned in Scripture often refers to believers—Christ's children—there is no doubt that Jesus elevated the worth of a child by holding him up as an example.

Just preceding that account is another deeply moving story that illustrates Jesus' compassion for children. A distressed father rushed into Jesus' presence, begging Him to heal his mentally ill son. "I brought him to your disciples," he cried, "but they could not heal him" (Matthew 17:16). I imagine Jesus' eyes flashed as He turned to His disciples and said, "O unbelieving and perverse generation, how long shall I stay with you? How long shall I put up with you? Bring the boy here to me" (Matthew 17:17). Jesus cast out the demon, and the child was healed.

Distressed parents hold up the bodies of their dying infants to us who are believers in Christ. Jesus turns to us and says, "O unbelieving and perverse generation, how long shall I put up with you?" While Christians have always been a generous people, we can do more. Jesus asks that we give abundantly because all we have is His. This, too, is the message of the rider on the black horse who brings famine and pestilence. We can't do it all, but we can do something! Both by His actions and by His command, Christ calls us to do all we can to heal the sick, feed the hungry, and help those who are suffering. Christ's great mission was to bring redemption to humanity through His death on the cross, and when He faced the cross He could say that He had finished the work His Father had given Him to do (John 17:4). But that did not mean He neglected those around Him who were suffering and hungry. This is His example that we are to follow.

THE DARKENED WATERS

It is difficult to imagine the vast difference between health care in Western nations and in the least developed countries. Some years ago, I was given statistics stating that in Europe and North America there is one doctor for every 572 people, in East Asia one doctor for every 2,106 people, in Southeast Asia one doctor for every 14,956 people, and in East Africa, where such great suffering is found, there is only one doctor for every 17,480 people! The shortage of nurses and midwives is similarly grim.

Prevention of illness is also lacking in most of the world. If this could be addressed more effectively, the necessity of curing disease would lessen. Preventative health care is nearly nonexistent. One child in three (of those who survive birth) in poor countries is unhealthy because of inadequate nutrition. Every time we eat a balanced meal we should pause, not only to thank God for the food before us but to pray for those starving children and to ask Him to show us how we can best exhibit His love and compassion to those who lack the basics. More important, pray that the door of opportunity will open to share with the hungry that Christ can meet their needs.

I have often counseled those who are young, and looking for a purpose in life, to consider the world's children. Even to those who are older and looking for ways to spend retirement years, why not reach out to those who will never know retirement because they have never known the satisfaction of comfort. Pray for guidance—seek the Lord—and ask Him to use your talents and abilities to help others in His Name.

Many years ago after traveling through the Third World, the Lord impressed on my heart to always be on the cutting edge of helping those less fortunate. I felt led to establish the World Emergency Fund under the umbrella of our organization. Through this fund, many thousands have been helped in time of famine. We have also been able to respond within hours to victims of earthquakes, hurricanes, tsunamis, and other shattering storms that have battered villages, cities, and nations.

My son Franklin, who now serves as president and CEO of the Billy Graham Evangelistic Association (BGEA), also leads one of the largest relief and evangelism organizations in the world called Samaritan's Purse. The BGEA World Emergency Fund has partnered many times with Samaritan's Purse in providing relief supplies and chaplains to those who find themselves in despair because of natural disasters that have washed their futures away as storms recede.

We have seen an outpouring of response to the earthquake that rocked Haiti in January 2010. Battalions of God's people reached out through our organizations to provide not only tangible help but beacons of hope to the suffering in Christ's name. If you have a desire to help in this way or would like to learn more, please write to me:

Billy Graham
1 Billy Graham Parkway
Charlotte, North Carolina 28201

On a visit to the central highlands of Guatemala a few years back, Franklin encountered a family that had walked several days through thick jungles to government-controlled territory in order to escape from an area overrun by guerrillas. Their children were so malnourished that they could not even sit up by themselves. Franklin said that when he looked at the children, it was almost like looking at skeletons covered by a layer of skin. He said that the children quietly sobbed—there was no expression of joy—just a constant low moan. The doctor who examined them doubted they would survive. As with the eating disorder known as anorexia nervosa, there is a point in starvation where a person's vital organs begin to break down, and the damage that has been done cannot be repaired.

There is serious concern over water and sanitation in the world's least developed countries. Four children out of every five in the rural areas of the world do not have save drinking water or sanitation. In Africa, ninety out of every hundred people have no piped water, and worse yet, the great rivers of Africa carry dangerous germs, liver flukes, amoebic dysentery, and other infections. One African authority calls the waterways of the continent "the waters of misfortune." If people in Africa are to survive, they must have pure water and delivery systems comparable to those we take for granted in this country. The watering hole is spreading disease to an unprecedented number of people.

I once saw a young girl in India with an empty five-gallon water drum on her head. She was walking from her home village to a dirty water hole several kilometers away. I have seen older women from tribal villages return to their huts bent under the strain of heavy loads of filthy water. Like the woman at the well at Sychar in Samaria to whom Jesus ministered, these young girls and women also needed the water of life, both physically and spiritually.

To touch the hearts of a hurting world, we must also touch their need for the basics: food and shelter. My wife often said, "Needs consist of bread, water, and a place to sleep." Surely the Christian community around the world will always be a resource for those in need. Our desire to see people come to saving faith in Christ must also accompany tangible evidence of our love and care for them in the name of Jesus. We are called by God to bring the water of life to both soul and body. God created them both, and His purpose is to redeem them both. The death of Jesus Christ on the cross demonstrates God's concern for the eternal salvation of man's soul. The resurrection of Jesus Christ from the dead—and the promise that we will someday share in His glorious resurrection—demonstrates God's concern for our physical being.

We are created in the image of God and even though that image is scarred and torn by sin, we are still His creation. Since Christ expresses His great care for even a sparrow, how can we doubt His abounding love for us? He has equipped us to be His hands and feet on earth. Must we disappoint Him by turning our eyes away from the hurting and fix them on satisfying our own pleasure?

The causes of trauma in our world—from starvation and famine, to diseases as different as diphtheria and AIDS—effect all victims crying out for compassion and care. God is concerned about those who suffer, no matter who they are, where they are found, or why they hurt. He also cares about how we respond to the hurting. Christ told us to pray for those who are lost, to serve even "the least of these," to feed the hungry, and to clothe the naked. This is our Christian duty. Even in cases where famine or disease may possibly be seen as the judgment of God, Christians are to demonstrate the love of God and show compassion. Let's remember the parable Jesus told of the good Samaritan (Luke 10). Let's not pass by with blinders on but rather stoop down in order to lift up the fallen along the highway of life.

Several years ago, the late Dr. Ernie Steury, a surgeon at Tenwek Hospital in Kenya, East Africa, told of an expectant mother from the bush country who had been in labor for two days. The family had sent for the witch doctors, but of course the witch doctors could not help her. In desperation, the family took her to the mission hospital in Tenwek. They carried her several hours down a narrow jungle trail. Once they reached the road, several hours passed before a bus arrived.

They had one delay after another but finally got to the hospital in late evening. The nurse sent for Dr. Steury. When he came and examined the woman, he discovered that she was already dead.

Dr. Steury met the woman's anxiously awaiting husband in the corridor and gave him the grim news: it was too late. The man cried out, "Oh, but please sir, isn't there anything you can do? Isn't there anything at all you can do?" Dr. Steury sadly shook his head no.

As the doctor told the story, he said, "What crushed me more than the loss of life was that she died never once having heard the Gospel message of life everlasting. Thousands of people die every day without contemplating life after death or knowing that Jesus freely offers eternal salvation. This is what compels me to remain in the African jungle," Dr. Steury said, "serving the people as a volunteer missionary doctor. This is what drives me to keep on. Last year we had more than eight thousand inpatients. While I cannot claim that each one repented of sin and was saved by the Lord Jesus, I can confirm that each patient heard the Gospel and we believe that at least five thousand accepted Jesus Christ as their Lord and Savior. We can't reach them all, but we can reach some. I sensed the call of God upon my heart to serve Him through medicine and this is how I have spent my life, spreading the Gospel message into this part of the world, and it is humbling to do so, in His name."

Each time I heard the testimony of this dear servant of God, my heart was stirred. He is now in the presence of the Lord, and I thank God for the example he has left behind, for many are following his steps. I believe this is the level of compassion and commitment that must motivate us to serve the afflicted.

THE RED AND THE BLACK

While famine and disease stalk much of the Third World, nearly all countries, even the smallest, are stockpiling armaments. This is one of the most pathetic developments of our time, illustrating the contemporary relevance of ancient biblical truth.

Our world is obsessed with war, violence, and death. The trillion or more dollars spent annually in the arms race would feed, clothe, and provide shelter for the billion or more people living below the subsistence level.

In 1982, former prime minister Malcolm Fraser of Australia hosted world leaders in a North-South Dialogue. In a part of the Melbourne Declaration, as it has come to be known, it was stated that "the protracted assault on human dignity and the deprivation from which many millions in developing countries suffer must inevitably lead to political turmoil. Such turmoil would be used to extend the realm of dictatorship in the world."

Many at that conference felt that only a new political order or a new economic order could hope to solve such problems. I must say that they are right—only a world government can solve it. The only lasting "new world order," however, that will succeed in solving the problems of this world will be the dynamic spiritual leadership established by Jesus Christ when He comes to establish His kingdom on earth and rule as King Jesus.

So while we wait for Christ's return, and care for the needy and seek peace with our enemies, the world marches on. As we anticipated the turn of the century and waited with bated breath to see if Y2K, called the millennium bug, would bring world communications to a deadening halt, we breathed a prolonged sigh of relief as each nation's clock passed midnight—without calamity. The sky canvassing the world lit up the darkness on January 1, 2000, and a new day, a new month, a new year, a new decade, a new century, and a new millennium blasted off without a glitch—not even a malfunction in fireworks. When the world woke up that winter morning, accusations floated through the airwaves that Y2K had been a hoax—perhaps even a government tactic to scare the public into spending money for new computers, canned goods, and stockpiles of water. The Y2K warning caused a spike in technology stocks, skewing the market for the first decade of the new century. While we were preoccupied with spending money on the latest computer advancements and assuring our stockpile of food, master terrorists slipped in the back door of our country and prepared plans to bomb America, leaving an indelible mark on us. The twenty-first century has seen only further decline.

The world's situation may have reached a point of no return, and Christians and secular analysts alike believe the dangers will continue to worsen until we reach some sort of tragic climax. The Bible laid out the details of that climax in both the Old and New Testaments. But it is not enough for Christians to stand glibly by and applaud the impending Apocalypse—in fact, it would be wrong. It is up to us to pray and work. Even if we feel small and helpless before such unwieldy problems, we should remember the words of the man who said, "I only have one bucket of water to throw on the fire, but I am going to throw it with all my might, asking God to use it as He did the five loaves and two fishes."

THE COMING THUNDER

The thundering storm clouds are bringing the black horse and its rider ever closer. Biblical prophecy is being fulfilled before our eyes. All around us we see the human tragedy of destitution and disease. Starving people rummage through garbage heaps and ditches for a few paltry crumbs to deaden their chronic hunger pangs. How should we respond? By my reading of Scripture, I am convinced that we are called to action, not apathy; and to involvement, not detachment.

One of the great judgments of Scripture was when God rained upon Sodom, and one of the great sins was their neglect of the poor and needy: "Now this was the sin of your sister Sodom: She and her daughters were arrogant, overfed and unconcerned; they did not help the poor and needy" (Ezekiel 16:49).

Jesus outlined our responsibilities in Matthew 25:35–36: "For I was hungry and you gave me something to eat, I was thirsty and you gave me something to drink, I was a stranger and you invited me in, I needed clothes and you clothed me, I was sick and you looked after me, I was in prison and you came to visit me." This is one of many biblical passages that teach the importance of serving others, showing hospitality, reaching out to meet the needs of those around us—and most important—doing it in the name of Jesus and exemplifying His nature. This is Christ living through us.

Some say that the Bible contradicts itself. Thorough study of God's Word reveals nothing of the sort. While we are called to work toward world peace, the Bible promises only lasting peace in Christ. While Jesus left an example that we should care for the poor and needy, He did not tell us that in doing so the world would someday overcome poverty, but rather poverty would only be conquered when Christ—the only One who can give abundant life—reclaims the earth for Himself. Jesus clearly stated, "The poor you will always have with you" (Matthew 26:11).

So we are commanded in Scripture to reach out to the suffering. Why? I believe one reason that God allows poverty and suffering is so that His followers may demonstrate Christ's love, mercy, and comfort to them. For this reason alone, we should be about the Father's business by pouring His compassionate love into aching and parched souls that have nowhere to turn, no one to love, and no one to care. Let them see Jesus in us. That is a living testimony that can soothe someone's broken heart with the salve of godly love.

Another opportunity we have to demonstrate God's love to the hurting is to show compassion instead of cast blame. Many believe that a criminal, for example, is only a victim of his environment. Yet the first crime on earth was committed in a perfect environment. Today, statistics prove that many of our crimes are committed in upper-middle-class or affluent environments. There is a program on TruTV called *Power, Privilege and Justice* that documents true stories of the rich and famous who steal from their own families and murder their blood relatives—all because of greed. Poverty is no excuse for crime any more than the girl from a socially prominent family could be excused for murder because she had too much of everything. The fact is that God created us with the power to choose. Each of us will ultimately be held accountable for the choices we make on earth.

Another point that calls for clarification is the commandment, "Do not follow the crowd in doing wrong. When you give testimony in a lawsuit, do not pervert justice by siding with the crowd, and do not show favoritism to a poor man in his lawsuit" (Exodus 23:2–3). Leviticus 19:15 says, "Do not pervert justice; do not show partiality to the poor or favoritism to the great, but judge your neighbor fairly." Too often, I fear, some people compromise justice by overemphasizing the plight of the "disadvantaged." That is clearly wrong. But I am persuaded that the very threat of the four horsemen of the Apocalypse is not just to warn or judge, but to awaken. They come not merely to move us emotionally, but to motivate us to do something—to point men and women of the world in the direction that God would have them go. God calls us to action; the results are in His hands.

THE PLAGUE OF HOMELESSNESS

America has never seen such a plague of homelessness as we have today. We have an epidemic of impoverished families and individuals who have lost their ability to make ends meet. To compound the problem, we have recently seen two-income families in which husbands and wives made large incomes but lived beyond their means—buying their children's happiness with things instead of giving them their time. Large estates are being abandoned because mortgages can no longer be paid whether from insurmountable credit card debt or losing life savings in the stock market.

For those living more simple lives, they, too, have come into hard times where job loss is at an all-time high, yet cost of living skyrockets. It leads to broken homes, emotional problems, and what some call "the walking wounded." Tens of thousands of Americans live in night shelters, missions, or on the streets in the twenty-first century. America "lived it up" on credit in the last part of the twentieth century and now, in the new millennium the banks are foreclosing and calling in the chips. Now we can't pay the price for the pleasures we enjoyed for a moment in time.

The problem is not limited to America. The same is happening in other Western nations and even in the already poor countries oppressed by evil empires.

How can anyone deal with such stirring problems of such enormous dimensions? Many local churches have established programs to help the needy. This allows Christians the opportunity to meet practical needs and, in the process, perhaps they will be given an opportunity to tell others about the One who cares for them. This is an open door for the Gospel.

"What else can we do?" some may ask. Prayer is a key to God's provision. Families within the church will be blessed as they petition heaven for the sake of others. We are called to be intercessors, just as Christ intercedes for us. We cannot count on world governments to meet the need. Nor can we feed the world. But God in His sovereignty can touch the hearts of people everywhere to do what He calls them to do. Are we listening for His solutions? Or are we just content to hear the hoofbeats of the black horse? Prayer is central to the problems of privation and human hunger, but prayer also goes hand in hand with action.

We can easily get discouraged if we keep our eyes on the overwhelming need, but many times the most effective way to make a difference is to partner with those who have the outlets and know-how to cut through bureaucracy that is present in every community and nation in order to make a difference.

I mentioned earlier that along with many effective groups, the Lord has enabled BGEA and Samaritan's Purse to give effective leadership in responding to crises here in America and around the world. The local church is doing the same. Christ called us to care for the widows and the orphans. In no uncertain terms, He commanded us to feed the hungry and to clothe the naked. We don't have to carry this burden alone. The Bible says, "[Cast] all your care upon Him, for He cares for you" (1 Peter 5:7 NKJV).

THE BLACK CLOUDS OF WAR

During the 1950s, it was my privilege to be a friend to Dwight D. Eisenhower both before and after he served as president of the United States. He had a strong impact on my thinking, and I hope that I had some influence on him for the Lord. He made a statement to the American Society of Newspaper Editors in April 1953. While it was written more than a half century ago, it still stirs my heart. He said:

> Every gun that is made, every warship launched, every rocket fired signifies—in the final sense—a theft from those who hunger and are not fed, those who are cold and are not clothed. This world in arms is not spending money alone. It is spending the sweat of its laborers, the genius of its scientists, the hopes of its children. . . . This is not a way of life at all, in any true sense. Under the cloud of war, it is humanity hanging on a cross of iron.

President Eisenhower's words, in part, prompted me and some of my colleagues in 1956 to make our first tour of the developing countries. Before that time I had seen few people dying from starvation, and I had never experienced firsthand the horror of an almost entirely poverty-stricken nation gripped by hunger. Destitute people wearing tattered clothing or next to nothing were everywhere we went. In some places, beggars were so common we could not make our way through the streets.

Such conditions would leave the most insensitive sickened and horrified. When I returned to the United States after that tour, it seemed that everyone looked as affluent as the rich man in Jesus' story in Luke 16:19. I went directly to the White House and shared my feelings with the President. He listened intently, and then he asked me to share my impressions with Secretary of State John Foster Dulles. Dulles was a churchman. Mr. Dulles was very cordial and asked that I come to his home for a visit rather than meet him in his state department office. We talked at length about the hungry people I had seen. He graciously allowed me to make some suggestions that might go a long way in meeting some of the needs.

I believe that when God opens doors to us, His purpose is to advance the Gospel, and one of the elements of the Gospel is to reach out to others in their time of need.

Until my first tour overseas, I was not aware that millions of people throughout the world live on the edge of starvation. Today these problems are much easier to identify. As I traveled the world and studied the Bible on these issues, my convictions regarding our responsibility as Christians has deepened.

CHRIST SHINES THROUGH
THE BLACKNESS OF DESPAIR

Over a period of years, my son Franklin and his associates at Samaritan's Purse have done tremendous work on nearly every continent. They have worked with Christians throughout Eastern Europe, Asia, South America, and the Middle East. This has been a mission designed to meet basic human needs, given freely in the hope that their acts of Christian charity will make a difference in the lives of those who need the Savior—and it has.

Many Christians working around the world are earning the right to be heard. They are backing their message with compassion. Of course it isn't a new idea. Missionaries, lay men and women, and clergy have been in the field for generations, earning the right to be heard.

Jesus had compassion on all those He met who were in need. This is our example. God has given each of us different gifts, talents, and abilities. We are different parts of the same body. Today engineers, architects, weekend volunteers, teachers, pastors, and evangelists alike should all stand shoulder to shoulder to help slow the work of the black horse of famine and accomplish the work of the kingdom while there is still light.

Does that mean we are all called to give away everything we have? No, not necessarily. There is nothing wrong or immoral in having wealth. Some may be called by God to make great sacrifices, but God desires that we respond to His call in each of our lives. For those who have little, they can pray for those who are willing to serve on a foreign field, and the wealthy can help out of their abundance to support those who have walked away from lucrative jobs to serve those less fortunate. This is the body of Christ working as one, and it pleases the Lord. Paul wrote to the Romans, "So then each of us shall give account of himself to God" (Romans 14:12 NKJV). We each have different talents and opportunities. The real question is, are we using what we have for the glory of God? Are we loving our neighbors as we love ourselves? Are we using our gifts for the physical and spiritual betterment of the world?

We are only stewards of the world's resources. They are not ours; they are God's. When we find our security in Him, we can then give generously from what He has entrusted to us. This is our Christian duty.

But in meeting the practical needs of others, we are never instructed to be preoccupied by our works that we neglect feeding our souls. The Bible teaches that there will be a famine of the Word of God in the last days: "'The days are coming,' declares the Sovereign LORD, 'when I will send a famine through the land—not a famine of food or a thirst for water, but a famine of hearing the words of the LORD'" (Amos 8:11). This, also, is a warning carried by the black horse. Spiritual starvation leads to spiritual death.

As a society, we allow the cares of this world to choke out the greater need for feasting on God's Word. Oh that we would hunger to be filled with the Word of God; for there is no greater armor, no greater strength, no greater assurance that He is with us, and in us, when we go forth in battle equipped and nourished by His instruction and determined to stand firm on His promises.

My prayer is that followers of Jesus Christ will overcome the famine that is destroying our Christian testimony and influence, and that we will do as the apostle John was commanded in Revelation: "Take and eat it [the Word of God] . . . It will be as sweet as honey in your mouth" (Revelation 10:9 NKJV). Just as Jesus commanded the apostle Peter to feed His sheep, we are commanded to feed upon the Word of God, for it is the only preventive action we can take to avert spiritual famine.

14

Death Mounts the Pale Horse

I looked, and there before me was a pale horse! Its rider
was named Death, and Hades was following close behind him.
—Revelation 6:8

John must have recoiled at the sickly sight of the ashen coat that identified the mission of the fourth horse. The corpselike hide reflected the fate of his victims—his tenacious stature matched the power of the executioner upon his back—its rider's name—Death! The apostle's description included a postscript: "and Hades was following close behind." In that awful moment, John reported, "they were given power over a fourth of the earth to kill by sword, famine and plague, and by the wild beasts of the earth" (Revelation 6:8).

Death casts its shadow over the land. On every continent, in every nation, and through every city, town, and village, death rides unfettered. It brings hardship, suffering and sorrow wherever it goes.

The specter of the Apocalypse is nowhere more visible than in the dreadful work of this grim reaper. David, the great warrior king, wrote about the "valley of the shadow of death" (Psalm 23:4). It speaks of a foreboding environment. This pale horse was making ready to enter such a place. With combustible energy, tail lashing, and ears pinned back with resolve, it was prepared to stomp everything in its path with Death choking the reins.

Death is an accomplished master of destruction, and his credentials precede him: abortion, abuse, addiction, adultery, brutality, conflict, crime, disease, drugs, hatred, idolatry, irreverence, jealousy, lies, lust, murder, neglect, pestilence, racial conflict, rape, rebellion, revenge, starvation, stealing, suicide, violence, and war. These are Satan's calling cards, and his record of achievement swells with each passing year. All of these are victims of the dread stalker.

PALE HORSE, PALE RIDER

In the Victoria and Albert Museum in London, there is a painted reproduction of a series of seven tapestries woven in the fourteenth century. Some 472 feet long, it depicts John's vision of the Apocalypse. Six hundred years ago, the artist-weavers read the sixth chapter of Revelation and artistically interpreted the rider as a skull wrapped in grave clothes sitting upon a pale horse and carrying a Roman broadsword in preparation for the carnage he would inflict.

In the fifteenth century, Albrecht Dürer depicted John's vision in fifteen large, carefully cut woodblocks. These are perhaps the most famous illustrations of the horsemen. Death rides the pale horse in the more traditional form of Father Time, an emaciated, bearded harbinger of judgment carrying a three-pronged spear and riding at full gallop toward men whose faces are upturned in defenseless horror. For centuries artists have tried to portray this grisly scene, but nothing captures the horror of the reality.

THE VISION THAT WILL NOT PALE

When John saw this image of Death and Hades, he used the mysterious phrase, "They were given power . . ." It is important to realize that the horrors unleashed by the four horsemen have a compounding effect. The four horses and horsemen are sent out one after another. The first is joined by the second, then by the third, and then the fourth. The rider who brings pestilence and death is accompanied by each of the others we have already observed. The combined effect of the four horsemen is the climax of everything disastrous. The white horse brings false peace and deception, the red horse unleashes war, the black horse wipes out food supply and spreads disease, and now the pale horse completes the herd by adding the gruesome blow of death.

Death is given permission to kill hordes of humans, a holocaustic one-quarter of the population of the earth.

Predictions were made that by the end of the twentieth century, the population of the world would surpass 6 billion. If this forerunner of judgment were given divine permission to kill one-fourth of the world's population at that time, 1.5 billion people would be slain. That would represent the population in Europe, South America, and North America combined.

Why would God allow such suffering to take place? John's vision is consistent with ancient biblical pictures describing what happens when God sends His wrath upon those who disobey Him. William Barclay warned, "At the back of it all there is the permanent truth that no man and no nation can escape the consequences of their sin." Lynn Harold Hough explains that Death, here, does not bring meaningless destruction, "but destruction which serves the purposes of the justice of God. [Death] is a part of the divine administration. A fourth of the earth feels his power that the rest may see and have the opportunity to repent."

The world was horrified by the Holocaust, in which Hitler cold-bloodedly sent some six million Jews (as well as millions of Poles and other non-Jews) to the gas chambers. But no one was more grieved than God. It is not God's intent that any should perish, but when people defiantly refuse God's plan, the consequence of this disobedience is death. The rider on the pale horse is only fulfilling his assignment.

VICTORIOUS OVER DEATH

Even in the darkest moment, before death snatches man's last breath, God is willing to save a lost soul. This evidence of love is seen in the warning of the fourth horseman. Until the horsemen complete their lethal task, the Holy Spirit of God is calling out to all, willing that none should perish. His great love was demonstrated when He sent His Son to die the most horrible death on the cross.

We should not be horrified at what God is doing. The Bible records death tolls and predicts more to come—it is part of the cycle of life. What if Adolf Hitler or Joseph Stalin were still alive? This world would be a living hell had they lived forever. But people not only die physically; they are spiritually dead while they are physically alive until they find new life in Christ. The Bible speaks of the second death, or eternal death. This refers to hell. Billions will be there who have, by their own rejection of Christ, chosen death over life.

Just as there is physical starvation that causes death of the body, there is a spiritual starvation that leads to death of the soul, as we have seen. This is why the warning of the pale horse is the last hope for earth dwellers. The Amplified Bible translates Deuteronomy 28:15, 22, 27–28 this way:

> If you will not obey the voice of the Lord your God . . . the Lord will smite you with consumption [wasting, degenerative diseases?], with fever and inflammation [communicable diseases?], and the tumors [cancer?], the scurvy [deficiency diseases?] and the

itch, from which you cannot be healed [such as genital herpes, syphilis, and AIDS?]. The Lord will smite you with madness [mental illness?] and blindness [birth defects?] and dismay of [mind and] heart [emotional traumas?].

The bracketed questions in the above passage are inserted to stimulate your own thoughts. This is only a short list of what pestilences will inflict on the population when the rider on the pale horse traverses the earth.

Also to be considered are those slain by wild beasts. Moses, Ezekiel, and John lived in a world where wild beasts frequently stalked wayfarers as they trudged primitive roads. Predators terrorized and dismembered inhabitants. Today we try to tame the animal kingdom. When we fail, we cage them and put them on display in zoos for our entertainment. I have always had pets—beautiful dogs that would protect me by sacrificing their own lives, if necessary. But humanity is still threatened by nature's beastly power. We watched in horror as an experienced female trainer was killed by a "friendly" whale in front of a live audience at Sea World. Man may think he can tame the power of nature—but we cannot. Nor can we tame man-made beasts.

Like the evolution from sword to nuclear missile, wild beasts have evolved into modern killers that stalk us everywhere we go. Oh, there is still the very real threat of actual wild beasts raiding cities in search of food and water, like the coyotes of Southern California, or the herds of wild boar that occasionally invade a Third World village. But there are other wild beasts among us, and this may also be what the Scripture suggests.

THE RACIAL CONFLICT THAT WILL NOT DIE

It's interesting to note that when God selected horses as the collective precursor to the Apocalypse, He chose a variety of colors: white, red, black, and pale. The world continues to be bombarded by stalkers of every kind. We continue to hear about the horror of ethnic and racial violence. This ancient beast refuses to die. Seventy years after Auschwitz, Bergen Belsen, Buchenwald, and Dachau, armed bands once again persecuted minorities in Germany. In the first ten months of 1991, there were more than fifteen hundred reported attacks on immigrants in both the eastern and western sectors of this once-divided nation. Neo-Nazi skinheads were the main offenders, but not only did law-abiding citizens not protest their acts; in many cases crowds stood by and applauded the beatings, verbal abuse, and other forms of brutality.

But the shadow of rage, hatred, and death all over the world is never far from sight today. Racism has become an issue in France, Britain, Italy, and Scandinavia as well. The fourth horseman foreshadows this stormy demise.

The evidence of brutality is everywhere. What was once called fantasy has become the very shadow of death. We no longer have to buy the latest horror novel to get a taste of the underworld. The suspense of a science-fiction movie no longer bids us to stand in long lines at the theater. We can simply turn on our latest gadget of technology and follow the ghastly true-to-life crimes where the perpetrators often become infamous on twenty-four-hour news. The villains do not wear masks; they are real and they are in our midst to ravage, conquer, and destroy.

Simply scan the morning headlines, listen to talk radio as you drive along the freeway, or log on to any number of websites to get the moment-by-moment breaking news. We live in such a saturated news-hungry world that the major cable network news channels keep a runner at the bottom of the screen in constant motion: NEWS ALERT . . . NEWS ALERT . . . signifying to stay tuned because something is bound to happen at any moment. Do they by chance have a reporter's ear to the ground . . . could they possibly hear the rumble of horses?

Violence terrorized Yugoslavia and escalated ancient ethnic hatred in that divided country. More than two million people were forced from their homes, creating one of the largest refugee catastrophes in history. The war was another stark example of racial violence, with more than a million Arab and Muslim families expelled from Serbia and Bosnia-Herzegovina. Local officials called the atrocities carried out by the Belgrade-based Serbian Army a "cleansing" of ethnically undesirable peoples. In its most sinister forms, the violence, extending from Slovenia to Macedonia, gave that ancient land, where the first shots of World War I were fired, the atmosphere of Nazi Germany. Grim scenes glaring with evil revealed inhumane atrocities and proved again the truth of God's Word: "There is deceit in the hearts of those who plot evil" (Proverbs 12:20). And the pale horse rides.

The body count of the slain by the symbolic sword just in recent years causes us to gasp!

Pipe bombs and machine-gunfire in Belfast, continual massacres in Africa, and shootings in America's schools are no longer just occasional crimes; they are everyday occurrences. Terrorist attacks in London and bombings in Beirut were precursors to the fateful day the world will not soon forget—9/11. Death exploded in the city that never sleeps. Lives were snuffed out as a plane plummeted into the quiet fields of our eastern farmlands. Will evil never cease to lurk? The answer, my friend, is found in the Bible, and the ancient words may surprise you, for they ring of hope: "There will be no more death or mourning or crying or pain, for the old order of things has passed away" (Revelation 21:4). This promise rings with hope, and every Christian should cling to it and share it with those who have none at all.

THE EARTH IS DYING?

The debate about global warming has gathered like a thunderstorm. There is no question that the depletion of natural resources and the destruction of the environment have loomed as ever larger issues on the political agenda. The first widespread public visibility of such issues at times focused on blocking economic development and returning the earth to some sort of preindustrial paradise. In more recent years, the focus has been on finding appropriate ways to dispose of society's waste products, of stopping manufacturing industries from releasing hazardous chlorofluorocarbons that damage the ozone layer, stopping the spread of deforestation and desertification in Third World countries, and legislating a global program for "biodiversity"— the movement to preserve endangered species.

As with any movement of this kind, many special interests and many kinds of activists, including some extremists, have attached themselves to this cause. Some readily grant higher status to insects and mollusks than to human life. It began as a small fringe element, but academic credentials and scientific research have elevated its profile and raised its influence with voters. Some entrepreneurs and bureaucrats have aligned themselves with this cause, gaining recognition and profit. Still others are public-spirited citizens sensitized by the media who want to see a healthy and productive balance between the various components of the ecosystem.

There is no doubt the earth is in trouble. Garbage dumps are bulging, sewage treatment is unmanageable, consumerism has created mountains of virtually indestructible waste, rivers are drying up or being polluted, the seas are being endangered by illegal dumping, and nuclear contaminants and other hazardous materials are being stored in unsafe places and, in some cases, seeping into the water table to become carcinogens and sources of contagion for the next generation. Compounding the tragedy, the earth's tropical rain forests are disappearing, being leveled at a pace of up to twenty thousand acres a day by timber or agricultural operations. These are genuine problems, but there must be some sense of priority in addressing them.

One troubling aspect of the environmental debate is the pseudo-religious tone it has sometimes taken on. The language of ecology is apocalyptic and evangelical at the same time. *Newsweek* magazine began its coverage of the 1992 Earth Summit in Rio de Janeiro with an allusion to the fall of Adam in the Garden of Eden and featured a global survey of nations to determine if "apocalypse soon" was a reasonable threat. Supporters of the movement calling for "environmental stewardship" often appear to worship not the God of heaven, but the god of nature. This is a dangerous form of idolatry in itself. Furthermore, any time animal life becomes more sacred in our view than human life, we have lost sight of our proper priorities.

The possible death of our planet by some type of ecological suicide is not God's will. Nor will the earth be saved by legislation. The Bible says, "The earth is the LORD's, and everything in it; the world, and all who live in it" (Psalm 24:1). So we must be responsible stewards of the resources we have been given by God.

The Bible reminds us that God gave man rule over all the earth—we are simply the caretakers, not the landowners. We should take seriously our responsibility to care for the earth; it is our home—for now. We are to till the soil and work the land—not worship it. Our worship must be directed to the One who holds the world in His hands. Only God knows the hour that He will loose the reins of the horsemen and send them charging down through His galaxies to trample all those who refuse to acknowledge Him as earth's rightful landowner—He alone holds the title deed and He is the One holding the scroll and breaking the fourth seal.

The Bible is clear. God said, "I give you every seed-bearing plant . . . and everything that has the breath of life in it" (Genesis 1:29–30). This leaves no doubt that God is the Creator of life. He is also the Sustainer of life. He has given the "seed" of life that produces what we need to exist. We have been entrusted with the seed of life and the breath of life, and our responsibility is to protect these sacred gifts given by the Father in heaven. This is why the hot button of abortion reaches the height of holocaust. Man has no right to steal from Creator God or destroy what belongs to Him.

DEATH BEFORE BIRTH

Few issues have polarized our society as much as the debate over abortion. It is not my purpose to get involved in the complex legal and political issues that swirl around this difficult question. There admittedly are isolated cases where abortion is the lesser of two evils, such as when the mother's life is clearly at risk. However, for many people today abortion has become little more than another means of birth control, practiced for mere personal convenience with no regard for the fate of the infant growing in the womb—and from the Bible's declaration, that self-centered approach is sin. All too often the right to life of the unborn child has been tragically lost in a tidal wave of cries for the "right" to choose.

Scripture makes it clear that God sees the unborn infant not as a piece of superfluous biological tissue but as a person created by Him for life. The psalmist said, "For you created my inmost being; you knit me together in my mother's womb . . . My frame was not hidden from you when I was made in the secret place. When I was woven together in the depths of the earth, your eyes saw my unformed body. All the days ordained for me were written in your book before one of them came to be" (Psalm 139:13, 15–16). God expressed a similar truth to the prophet Jeremiah: "Before I formed you in the womb I knew you, before you were born I set you apart; I appointed you as a prophet to the nations" (Jeremiah 1:5).

When Mary, the virgin mother of Jesus, visited her cousin Elizabeth, who was pregnant with John the Baptist, we are told that Elizabeth declared to Mary, "As soon as the sound of your greeting reached my ears, the baby in my womb leaped for joy" (Luke 1:44). This is a clear indication that that unborn infant was a person, not just a piece of tissue.

From these and other passages, I cannot escape the conclusion that the unborn child is worthy of our concern and protection just as much as a newborn infant or an adult. The liberated practice of abortion on demand is just another grim sign of the clapping hoof-beats of the rider on the pale horse.

In 1960, there were fewer than 100,000 abortions in this country annually; in 1972, there were nearly six times that number; in 1978, with the legalization of *Roe* plus the backing of pro-abortion and feminist groups, more than 1.4 million abortions were carried out. Two decades later, as the twentieth century drew to a close, the annual average rose to an estimated 1.6 million abortions in the United States alone. Since the explosive Supreme Court case *Roe v. Wade* in 1973, there have been well over thirty million babies cut off from life while still in their mothers' wombs. As the staggering death toll rises, so does the sound of hoofbeats.

While we fret about which world powers have access to the nuclear button, there are judges that have already applied their collective fingertip to the button of death. They are called "supreme justices," but their act is not "just" in the sight of the Giver of life—the Just God. It does not matter what politicians say or how the court rules concerning when life begins—they did not give the seed life, and they cannot give life its breath. Their high-minded authority is trumped by the authority of the Life Giver. He will demand retribution, and it will come in the form of a pale horse. Innumerable faces will *pale* when this rider passes through their ranks.

The Bible says, "For the life of the flesh is in the blood, and I have given it to you" (Leviticus 17:11 NKJV). Babies are living souls before their physical birth. Their tiny veins are flowing with blood and their developing lungs are pumped with the breath of life by the Creator Himself.

Easy morals and promiscuity lead inevitably to disappointment, despair, and death. Sexual promiscuity is another of the major pandemics. In 1988, one of every four births in this country was to an unwed mother. Even history declares the tragic legacy of promiscuous societies—from Carthage and Rome to Renaissance France. The Bible declares repeatedly that this lack of sacred respect for the sanctity of life will not escape the wrath of God on those who persist in such sin.

As we look back on the twentieth century, how can our hearts not ache for millions of men and women all over the world that have turned away from God and indulged in hedonism and the idolatry of self? In their search for absolute freedom from moral restraint or personal responsibility, many believed—and still do—that they could pay for their sins with cash. When pregnancy is the problem, or when the love and nurture of a child is not in their plans, they simply pay a specialist to cut the problem out, not even wincing that the "problem" is the beating of new life.

This libertine mentality of playing now and dealing with the consequences later has blinded many young mothers. Only later do they discover that they must deal with the physical and emotional scars forever. Many will lose heart when they are finally confronted with the result of their selfishness . . . many a mother will cry herself to sleep, wishing she could draw her child close and feel the tiny heartbeat. Instead . . . mothers will hear hoofbeats.

I have heard some people say, "Well, I'm against abortion, but with the population crisis and all the unwanted children in the world, especially among the poor, abortion is probably for the best." Let me be quick to say that this kind of reasoning is false and dangerous. Robbing another's life—especially when an innocent child cannot defend his or her rights—is not the way to solve the population crisis. Don't fall prey to the world's viewpoint of personal preference. Taking a human life is against God's command. I encourage all who are given the opportunity to counsel women during this precarious time to share God's truth with them—that He loves them and has a plan for their lives. Take them to God's Word and show them what He says concerning the sacred gift of life that He gives. Let them read about the rich promises from the Life Giver Himself. Pray that He will give them a change of heart—new life in Christ—just as He plans to give the miracle of birth through the life they carry.

We don't have to be teachers or pastors to direct others to the Bible. As Christians we have an obligation to show them what God says to us about living self-controlled lives and being responsible for our moral actions, as He defines them. This is how we can demonstrate God's love. But we must never think that we can solve one moral crisis by condoning another, especially the crime of murder, for unrestrained abortion is nothing less than that. In this issue alone, we can see all the evidence of the four horsemen:

- The first horseman who deceives (it's just tissue)
- The second who brings strife (ignore the consequences)
- The third who brings famine (cutting off a baby's development)
- The fourth who brings death (robbing a baby's first breath)

All life is sacred, created in the image of God. The horsemen bring warning. Will we turn our eyes away, or will we swiftly confront the sin that envelops our lives and accept God's forgiveness? We must decide, because once the horses are released they will beat the air with swiftness.

BLOOD TRANSFUSION

On the heels of legalizing abortion, newscasters began reporting other sensitive issues—AIDS and STDs (sexually transmitted diseases). These are reaching epidemic proportions in the United States and around the world. Research suggests that the majority of all STD infections affect people under the age of twenty-five.

We cannot turn our eyes away from either. The mysterious disease known as acquired immune deficiency syndrome (AIDS) has burst forth much like the plagues recorded in the Old Testament. HIV/AIDS has become a fatal disease afflicting the world. Already it has left a staggering trail of death and destruction.

The *Journal of the American Medical Association* reported in June 1991 on the incidence of AIDS since the first cases appeared in 1981. In that year, a total of 189 cases were reported to the Center for Disease Control (CDC) from fifteen states and the District of Columbia. The large majority—more than 76 percent—were from New York and California. Of all known cases, 97 percent were among men, 79 percent of whom were homosexual/bisexual men. There were no known cases in that early period among children.

By 1990, however, the picture had changed dramatically. In that year, forty-three thousand cases were reported from all states, the District of Columbia, and the U.S. territories. Two-thirds of the cases were from outside New York and California; 11 percent of all cases reported among adolescents and adults were among women; and nearly eight hundred cases were reported in children under the age of thirteen.

By any standard, such a rapid spread of a disease would be seen as epidemic in nature. AIDS has become a leading cause of death in both men and women under the age of forty-five and in children between the ages of one and five in the United States.

From the total estimated number of 1.5 million cases in 1992, the toll predicted by the turn of the century was expected to exceed 15 to 18 million. Since many of the cases take place in impoverished countries where statistics are at best imprecise, the numbers no doubt are much greater than the reported statistics reveal. Estimates from 1990 to 2007 report that 2 million people have died from AIDS, with 33 million adults and children living with HIV/AIDS.

AIDS is the most dreadful epidemic of our generation and may yet be the most fearful killer of all time. Yet reporting on this epidemic is nearly impossible since the WHO suspects that less than 10 percent of the actual occurrences of the disease are ever reported.

Prostitutes are the largest source of contagion in some areas. In countries like Thailand, it is estimated that 75 percent of the male population has visited prostitutes, many of whom, it is now clear, are infected with the AIDS virus. Already Brazil has the largest number of AIDS cases in Latin America and the fourth largest in the world.

In France, both AIDS and hepatitis are on the rampage due to distribution of AIDS-infected blood supplies by the public health service.

One of the most frightening aspects of HIV/AIDS is its ability to mutate rapidly. It literally hides from antibiotics and virus medications. Only twelve years after the first reported cases, AIDS activist Larry Kramer stated in a May 1992 article in *USA Today Magazine* that the war against AIDS had already been lost. Despite the expenditure of more than a billion dollars on research into AIDS and HIV, no cure or even promising therapies have been discovered, and the disease continues to escalate at an alarming rate. "When I first started hearing about and fighting against what was to be called AIDS," wrote Kramer, "there were only forty-one cases. When I first started getting really scared and vocal, there were one thousand. America rapidly is approaching two-hundred thousand cases of full-blown AIDS, with up to ten million people infected with the HIV virus worldwide. No one knows how many there really are. No one knows how to count them."

How do we respond to these souls ravaged by such a stalking killer? Whether sufferers have been infected through immoral lifestyles, patients poisoned by contaminated blood transfusions or needles, or men and women tainted by unfaithful spouses, I believe God blesses those who reach out to the sick and weary with godly compassion that demonstrates the love of Christ. While we cannot bring healing to their bodies, we can bring comfort through the Word of God—and we must. This, in one sense, is a brand-new kind of mission field. It is overpopulated with carriers of diseased blood that will run through the veins and organs of countless bodies that are experiencing something even worse: breaking hearts—hearts that slowly continue to pump the treacherous blood through their systems, with no hope for cleansing. Except for the healing touch of the Great Physician.

As we contemplate the monumental scope of this horrific eruption, we gasp at the realization of watching this rampant disease evolve and spread like wildfire in just one generation. We must realize that there is a greater toxin that makes HIV/AIDS pale in comparison, even as the fourth horse rears and snorts with determination to storm ahead. That is the disease that has infected the world since the beginning of time. It is called sin.

Psychologists have no solutions or answers.

Doctors have no cures.

Scientists have no remedies.

But God does have the answer—redemption.

Christ has the cure—forgiveness.

The Holy Spirit has the remedy—the truth.

The triune God bears witness: "For there are three that bear witness in heaven: the Father [God], the Word [Jesus], and the Holy Spirit [the Truth]" (1 John 5:6–7 NKJV).

After the resurrection of the Lord Jesus and before His ascension, He told His disciples that He was leaving two important things with His followers: His presence through the Third Person of the Trinity, the Holy Spirit; and His command to go into the world with His message of salvation.

What is the message? The Bible says, "This is the message we have heard from [God] and declare to you . . . 'The blood of Jesus, [God's] Son, purifies us from all sin. If we claim to be without sin, we deceive ourselves and the truth is not in us. If we confess our sins, he is faithful and just and will forgive us our sins and purify us from all unrighteousness," (1 John 1:5, 7–9).

We are to give God's Spirit a dwelling place and make the work He has entrusted to us our calling—to tell the world about His Son. Will we be found faithful? We are the carriers of the only life-giving message that can relieve such excruciating anguish—it is the crimson blood shed by the Lord Jesus Christ for each sinner. It is His precious blood that cleanses the disease of the soul that infects the whole world. Christ, the King of glory, died and was raised from the grave to give every man, woman, and child a heavenly blood transfusion. Only He can replace the tainted blood of man's sin with His royal blood that will thoroughly cleanse.

The church has come under attack by outspoken advocates of those who suffer from HIV/AIDS. They point the finger of ridicule at the church for the lack of Christian compassion. Perhaps the church was slow in responding, but when believers began to grasp the facts and understand that this was an opportunity for the Gospel, we did ask, "What Would Jesus Do?"

Believers in Jesus Christ, around the world, were among the first to respond to this epidemic. I have seen compassion extended from the pocketbooks of Christians, especially in Western nations. Generous donations have been given to churches and mission organizations with armies of God's servants willing to go as good Samaritans to care for those who have been given their death sentence. The question is: do they know their destiny?

Perhaps many of these people have never contemplated the reality of God. They are frightened and perplexed, desperate and lonely. Most are rejected and ridiculed, ashamed and dejected.

Like so many of us, it often takes a tragedy to open our hearts, minds, and wills to the truth of God's Word. Some are listening to Him for the first time in their lives. Likewise, many Christians are demonstrating God's compassion to the dying and testifying to the only cure that offers hope—even in the death watch. May we all storm the gates of heaven for the souls of the anguished, that in their greatest time of need they will hear the gentle voice of God's Spirit calling them to the same repentance every believer has realized, that "all have sinned and fall short of the glory of God" (Romans 3:23). Through confession of sin and acceptance of Jesus as Lord, He will meet them in their hour of decision and gloriously save them.

Let's be intercessors. Perhaps God in His mercy will bless the faithfulness of our prayers on behalf of the dying and will slow the hoofbeats of the pale horse on his hellish ride.

15

SEALED FROM
THE STORM

When he opened the fifth seal, I saw . . .
the souls of those who had been slain.
—REVELATION 6:9

As we approach the opening of these last seals, there is a sense of bittersweet for all who follow the Lord Jesus. While these revelations stir the heart with fear and trembling for the fate of unbelievers, they fill the soul of the Christian with great expectancy. We will stand in the presence of the glory of the Lord—after we spend considerable time worshipping at His feet. I don't know what our first descriptions will be in that moment, but my thoughts greatly wonder how magnificent must have been the vision of John. Certainly at the opening of the fifth seal, the apostle must have been overcome with unspeakable questions.

THE FIFTH SEAL

There is a dramatic shift in John's vision at this point. Perhaps the dusty clouds kicked up by the four horsemen veiled John's eyes momentarily. But when he fastened his eyes upon the mighty hand that severed the fifth seal, the sound of countless voices was heard. John must have gasped at the sight God revealed to him. And his memory surely recalled the words of Jesus years before: "If anyone would come after me, he must deny himself and take up his cross and follow me. For whoever wants to save his life will lose it, but whoever loses his life for me and for the gospel will save it" (Mark 8:34–35).

John's attention was focused.

> I saw under the altar the souls of those who had been slain for the word of God and for the testimony which they held. And they cried with a loud voice, saying, 'How long, O Lord, holy and true, until You judge and avenge our blood on those who dwell on the earth?' Then a white robe was given to each of them; and it was said to them that *they should rest a little while longer*, until both the number of their fellow servants and their brethren, who would be killed as they were, was completed. (Revelation 6:9–11 NKJV; emphasis added)

These were the souls of the martyrs from ages past, no doubt among them the first martyr, Stephen. Did John, at that moment, recall the day Stephen was stoned for his unshakable faith in Christ? This man, "full of the Holy Spirit, looked up to heaven and saw the glory of God, and Jesus standing at the right hand of God. 'Look,' he said, 'I see heaven open and the Son of Man standing at the right hand of God,'" (Acts 7:55–56). Stephen's accusers covered their ears and yelled in defiance at what Stephen's eyes were beholding. They took him and dragged him out of the city to stone him. And the Scripture says that "the witnesses laid their clothes at the feet of a young man named Saul" (Acts 7:57–58), the very man who was transformed later by Christ and became the apostle Paul. This account is chilling. It is also thrilling.

Now as John stands before Jesus and hears these voices from the altar he, too, must have been breathless. What must have come over the saints in that awful pause when their questions hung in the air awaiting answers? We hear the gut-wrenching plea of the martyrs. But do we hear the calm Voice of assurance in response? They were not given the answer they asked for—they were given what they needed: comfort and assurance that their answer would come. They were told to "rest a little while longer." Why? Because there would be other saints that would join them in martyrdom, completing the number that would give their blood in death for the sake of the Word of God. The Lord spoke peace to them in spite of more blood-shed to come. John witnessed Jesus fulfilling, again, His promise: "Come . . . all you who labor . . . and I will give you rest" (Matthew 11:28 NKJV).

Surely John the Revelator correlated the prophecy that Jesus spoke to him and the disciples on earth with the vision He imparted from heaven. "They will deliver you up to tribulation and kill you, and you will be hated by all nations for My name's sake. And then many will be offended, will betray one another, and will hate one another . . . but he who endures to the end shall be saved. And this gospel of the kingdom will be preached in all the world as a witness to all the nations, and then the end will come" (Matthew 24:9–10, 13–14 NKJV).

For the Christian believer, the return of Christ is comforting, for at last men and women of faith will be exonerated. They will be avenged. The nonbeliever will see and understand why true Christians marched to the sound of another drum. But for the sinful unbeliever, the triumphant return of Christ will prove disastrous—for Christ's return ensures final judgment.

God has promised this planet to His Son, Jesus Christ. He will bring an end to all the injustice, the oppression, the wars, the crime, and the terrorism that dominates every facet of life. So we see that the fifth seal speaks of martyrs at rest and the sixth seal reveals the unrepentant—in their time of great unrest—trying to flee the hand of the Lord, but cannot.

THE SIXTH SEAL

"I looked when He opened the sixth seal," John wrote, "and behold, there was a great earthquake; and the sun became black as sackcloth of hair, and the moon became like blood. And the stars of heaven fell to the earth . . . Then the sky receded as a scroll . . . and every mountain and island was moved out of its place. And the kings of the earth, the great men, the rich men, the commanders, the mighty men, every slave and every free man, hid themselves in the caves and in the rocks of the mountains, and said to the mountains and rocks, 'Fall on us and hide us from the face of Him who sits on the throne and from the wrath of the Lamb! For the great day of His wrath has come, and who is able to stand?" (Revelation 6:12–17 NKJV).

How would the people on earth know to say this if they had not heard Christ's plea? How would they know about the throne of God had they not been told?

As John considered all that was before him, he must have been shaken to the bone as the universe convulsed. An earthquake shakes the entire planet. No Richter scale could measure its fury. There is a complete eclipse of the sun. The moon turns red, and the stars fall to the earth, just as Jesus had said. The world is trembling with terror. The great cities collapse. John sees the citizens of the world, from kings to slaves, fleeing to the mountains, but there is no escape—none. Their day of wrath has come.

There will be a day of reckoning when God closes His books on time and judges every creature, living and dead. This vision of the judgments leading to the final judgment permeates the sixty-six books of the Holy Scripture—this is the Great Tribulation.

As we review the history from the beginning of time, God's voice has been heard through His servants and it has fallen on deaf ears and hardened hearts. Noah warned of the coming Flood—and people scoffed. The angels warned of the destruction of Sodom and Gomorrah—but only Lot and his daughters escaped. Moses warned the children of Israel about idolatry—and an entire generation was prohibited to enter the Promised Land. John the Baptist warned of the coming judgment—yet few believed. Jesus came in the flesh to warn, with great woe, of eternity without Him—and many turned their backs and walked off the pages of history and into hell. The apostles preached the Gospel and were killed by those they hoped would be saved. Historical records tell us of the brave men and women who suffered horrific deaths before and after the reformation. And today we continue to hear about the blood of the saints flowing through the treacherous hands of those who refuse to believe that He is the great I AM, and that He is coming again.

Jesus had also told the disciples, "Let those who are in Judea flee to the mountains. Let him who is on the housetop not go down to take anything out of his house . . . Pray that your flight may not be in winter or on the Sabbath. For then there will be great tribulation, such as has not been since the beginning of the world until this time, no, nor ever shall be" (Matthew 24:16–17, 20–21 NKJV).

Amid the thunderous destruction from earthquakes, and underneath a blackened sky because the sunlight was out, John caught a glimmer of light from heaven. "And I heard the number of those who were sealed. One hundred and forty-four thousand of all the tribes of the children of Israel were sealed" (Revelation 7:4 NKJV). Imagine how John must have felt to finally see Christ's beloved Israel respond to His salvation message. John witnessed the Lord putting a covering of protection on them, sealing them from harm. His purpose for them is what God the Father has longed for: that His chosen people would speak His Holy name in belief and obedience.

These 144,000 are marked for perhaps the greatest evangelistic mission ever to be. Made up of twelve thousand from each of the twelve tribes, these would become the tribulation evangelists, proclaiming that Jesus Christ is indeed the Messiah and the very Son of God. Israel will heed, finally, the voice of their God and speak boldly His everlasting truth. The Bible does not tell us the number of the harvest reaped from their proclamation; it is not for us to know, but I rejoice that it will be the greatest outpouring of the Gospel that redeems the sinful heart.

To just ponder this vision is glorious. Even in God's wrath, demonstrated by full fury at the end of the age, God's heart will surely be full of splendor to see His people proclaiming His Son, Jesus Christ the Savior, as Master and Lord. How wonderful to dwell on the grace and mercy of God the Father. In the midst of the grievous scenery that the sixth seal revealed, the Lord gave this marvelous reprieve for John to see and write down.

John's heart must have pounded like hoofbeats to be in the presence of such glory, remembering the day that Jesus promised they would "see the Son of Man coming in a cloud with power and great glory. When these things begin to take place, stand up and lift up your heads, because your redemption is drawing near" (Luke 21:27–28).

Whenever one looks closely at the prophecies of the end times, inevitably questions surface that trouble the soul. That is as it should be, and that is why God has given us such pronounced warnings of this coming storm that John wrote about. But let me also remind you of God's promise. In the midst of the pessimism, gloom, and frustration, and in this present hour of grave concern, there is still the overarching hope—the promises made by Christ.

Jesus told the disciples before His crucifixion:

I am going away and I am coming back to you. If you loved me, you would be glad that I am going to the Father, for the Father is greater than I. I have told you now before it happens, so that when it does happen you will believe. I will not speak with you much longer, for the prince of this world is coming. He has no hold on me, but the world must learn that I love the Father and that I do exactly what my Father has commanded me." (John 14:28–31)

This vow made by the Lord Jesus is recorded in John's gospel. I am sure those words crossed John's mind many times as he sat in the damp, dark cave documenting the vision of such doom to come. But John did not lose sight of the promise, the pledge, and the assurance that Christ would indeed return for His own.

John's own eyewitness testified of the Lord's death at Calvary, His burial in a borrowed tomb, and His resurrection day. John also witnessed Jesus leaving the Mount of Olives, not on a donkey and not on the back of a white stallion. No. He stood in the midst of His beloved disciples and assured them of all that He had promised. Then He looked toward heaven and "before their very eyes," the Bible says, "He was taken up . . . and a cloud hid him from their sight" (Acts 1:9). John's account of the Revelation was certainly not the first miraculous vision he had seen. Imagine what it must have been to stand at the pinnacle of the mountain, overlooking Jerusalem, talking to the risen Lord, still able to see His pierced hands and feet, and suddenly Jesus the Savior is taken up through the clouds and into the presence of His blessed Father. My friend, that is a vision that bursts with hope. That is a vision that one would never forget. That is a vision that would cause Paul to write, "While we wait for the blessed hope—the glorious appearing of our great God and Savior, Jesus Christ, who gave himself for us to redeem us from all wickedness and to purify for himself a people that are his very own" (Titus 2:13–14). This is the hope that the apostles have passed on to us. We are partakers of such a glorious hope. But even as we are waiting for this marvelous event to take place, we must be on alert because of the hold that the prince of darkness has on this world.

It has been said that "the world is disorderly and dangerous; ungoverned, and apparently ungovernable. The questions arise: Who will restore order? Who can counter the danger of nuclear holocaust? Who can bring an end to all the epidemics of our time? Who alone can govern the world? The answer is Jesus Christ only."

The psalmist asked centuries earlier, "Why do the nations conspire and the peoples plot in vain? The kings of the earth take their stand and the rulers gather together against the LORD and against his Anointed One. 'Let us break their chains,' they say, 'and throw off their fetters.' The One enthroned in heaven laughs; the Lord scoffs at them. Then he rebukes them in his anger and terrifies them in his wrath, saying, 'I have installed my King,'" (Psalm 2:1–6). He promises the Anointed One, "I will make the nations your inheritance, the ends of the earth your possession. You will rule them with an iron scepter . . . Therefore, you kings, be wise, be warned, you rulers of the earth. Serve the Lord with fear and rejoice with trembling" (Psalm 2:8–11). Then He encourages mankind, "Blessed are all who take refuge in him" (v. 12).

The Bible teaches that there is deliverance from the things that are about to come upon the world for those who put their faith and trust in Jesus Christ. In Christ alone there is deliverance from the world's tortured thoughts, healing for weakened minds and bodies, and freedom from the sordid, destructive, and immoral habits that are destroying mankind.

We hear so much today about a new social order coming. We see elements of such being put into place; yet, the world is in a state of chaos. Government officials, politicians, world leaders, and false prophets can banter back and forth and proclaim they know how to bring peace on earth, but the more they try, the more entangled it becomes. Satan is the sower of compromise—weaving a bit of God's truth into the dirty rags of sin. He promises utopia but cannot deliver. Satan is the commander in deceit. Satan is the ringleader in rebellion against the faithful. Satan is the sly serpent of temptation.

Satan is the false hope of security. Satan is the great pretender, persuading that his way will give mankind pleasure and satisfaction. Satan is the great spoiler of everything good. And Satan wants to destroy you. Scripture has warned us of him: "Be . . . alert. Your enemy the devil prowls around like a roaring lion looking for someone to devour. Resist him, standing firm in the faith, because you know that your brothers throughout the world are undergoing the same kind of sufferings" (1 Peter 5:8–9).

What coat of arms do you bear? What weapons are in your hands? Jesus warned us to be watchful, and said, "I am coming soon" (Revelation 22:20). I trust that you will not be found wanting, but suited up, with your helmet of salvation, your sword of truth, and your shield of faith. This is the position we should have in the world: watching, waiting, and working. May we be found about the Father's business on earth so that we can be found faithful when we stand before Him in heaven.

The idea of "watchfulness" is presented throughout Scripture. We, as earth dwellers, are watchful people. Oftentimes, unfortunately, we are watching the wrong things. Thankfully, there are those in the world who keep watch for us—to some degree. Meteorologists, for example, watch radar, monitoring the signs for approaching storms. We should be grateful when their warnings are issued about dangers ahead.

A tornado, considered nature's most powerful and violent storm, is an example. Because of its rapid development, it can come upon us without warning. But forecasters have learned to read the patterns that help formulate their predictions about the conditions that may spawn a surprise from the sky. Following violent thunderstorms, an eerie calm may settle in the air for a brief time. The sky may turn dark and gray with brushstrokes of greenish hues; the leaves on the trees may become quiet and still. Often, just before a tornado moves in with the sound of a roaring freight train—there is silence.

For most living east of the Rocky Mountains, we have experienced tornado watches and warnings. Television programs are interrupted with a series of obnoxious and persistent distress signals; a runner at the bottom of the screen warns viewers to "remain alert," "watch the sky," and "be prepared." When the alert changes from a watch to a warning it means "take shelter immediately—the approaching storm is on its way." We consider ourselves fortunate to get the warning before the power shuts down.

I heard reports of a tornado touching down in Minneapolis several months ago. Our ministry, the Billy Graham Evangelistic Association (BGEA), was headquartered in this beautiful city for fifty years before relocating to Charlotte, North Carolina. Minnesotans were surprised by the tornado that destroyed everything in its erratic path and wanted to know why they had not been warned. The safety officials said, "The storm pulled off a sneak attack." The headline read: "Surprise Storm Didn't Give Officials Time to Sound Sirens." The article reported that "workers with the Hennepin County Sheriff's Office push a button to activate the signals when the weather service issues a warning. But there was no warning." The Sheriff's Department stated that "this event should serve as a reminder that . . . residents should be ready to seek shelter . . . When weather conditions seem threatening, they should not wait to hear sirens."

It is stunning to observe how people respond to weather forecasts—particularly when one of great magnitude is sighted. Most people pay attention, at least to the degree of taking some kind of action. They also make advance preparation so that they have equipment to keep them informed. Shortwave radios and emergency gear have become big business. Many are religious about keeping their batteries fully charged and emergency supplies easily accessible in case of power loss. It seems as long as people can stay abreast of conditions, they feel better equipped to "weather" a storm. But if their batteries run down and they are cut off from communication, panic sets in. Human beings today do not want to hear "silence." Neither do we like the dark—especially during a storm.

The parable of the ten virgins illustrates this point. Jesus gave warning to those who wanted to know about the end times and when they could expect His return. Ten virgins were told to keep their oil lamps trimmed (filled with oil and wick). Five did so faithfully. Five were careless and let their oil and wicks burn out. When the careless five realized that their lamps were empty, they begged the others for some of their oil; but the five who were waiting and watching refused to give them oil lest they be found unprepared when the bridegroom called for them. When the bridegroom appeared at midnight, he took the five virgins with him to the banquet. The Bible says, "And the door was shut" (Matthew 25:10). When the other five returned from buying oil and realized they had been left behind, they knocked on the door where the bridegroom was, but he replied, "I tell you the truth, I don't know you" (v. 12). Jesus finished the parable by saying, "Therefore keep watch, because you do not know the day or the hour" (v. 13).

THE SEVENTH SEAL

This, I believe, is depicted in Revelation when we read this astonishing revelation from the apostle John. He said, "When [the Lamb] opened the seventh seal, there was silence in heaven for about half an hour" (Revelation 8:1). The day and the hour had come.

Imagine the flurry of action unleashed when the six seals were lifted from the scroll. Four horses with their riders stampeding to earth, and the martyrs crying out for justice while the earth churns. Suddenly, the commotion is swallowed up with silence that permeates the abode of God.

John does not write about this peculiar silence. He does not give us a blow-by-blow of what transpired in those thirty minutes. Perhaps no earthly words could describe such a pause. There are many theories about this heavenly hush, but I do wonder if the Lord was granting John some moments of reflection, or perhaps the Lord was once again holding back the final stroke of the clock in order to add to the number of the redeemed. It is even possible that the Lord may have hushed all of heaven in moments of reverence for the martyrs and those not yet martyred. Or maybe it was simply the quiet before the surge—when the seventh seal was peeled back. I can just imagine that silence was demanded as Jesus the Savior prayed for the faithful to endure to the end. Yet another reason might be the fact that God commanded total silence so that all could hear His still, small voice.

This reference is made in the story of the prophet Elijah when he was discouraged by what he witnessed among God's people—the falling away from belief. The Lord told him to go out and stand on the mountain in the presence of the Lord, for the "LORD is about to pass by" (1 Kings 19:11). "Then a great and powerful wind tore the mountains apart and shattered the rocks before the LORD, but the LORD was not in the wind. After the wind there was an earthquake, but the LORD was not in the earthquake. After the earthquake came a fire, but the LORD was not in the fire. And after the fire came a gentle whisper . . . Then a voice said to him, 'What are you doing here, Elijah?'" (1 Kings 19:11–13).

We think of God's voice as a sonic boom, but here we have a wonderful description of the tenderness of the Father. God knew that Elijah was weary. God knew that Elijah felt alone. God knew that Elijah needed encouragement, so the Lord met him in his time of need and encouraged him by revealing that Elijah was one of seven thousand in Israel who had "not bowed down to Baal" (1 Kings 19:18). Just as He gave Elijah rest, He told the martyrs to rest a while longer.

This passage should always comfort believers when they take a stand for the things of the Lord and are ridiculed. So with John, here he was the only eyewitness to the end times. He was taking in these remarkable sights and sounds—and now the silence gives great pause for reflection and perhaps a little rest before the climax of the mighty vision.

John must have considered those in the seven churches. He must have thought about all those he had preached to that had turned away. His heart must have felt great sorrow for those who would see the full fury of God—the gathering of roaring funnel clouds, hurricane-pounding winds, jolting earthquakes, thunderbolts of judgment—the culmination still cannot sufficiently describe the proportion of climatic horror that will come. So this pause of silence could have been to quiet his soul.

Are there times in your life that God seems silent? Don't hide from God. Don't try to shut out His silence. Embrace it, for in His time God will provide what you need: a rebuke, an answer, and a little rest.

In John's case, the silence moves him into the next phase of the vision where he beholds the seven angels standing before God. They follow the warnings of the four horsemen and represent the fulfillment of the judgments of which the earth's inhabitants had been duly warned.

Can we do anything to halt this sequence of events? We may, like Elijah, be used to slow their approach. We should pray for such a time of silence so that others may hear the warning that speaks of God's judgment, but it also speaks of His tender mercies.

Let's not miss the wonderful thought of Jesus passing by, for just as Satan roams the earth "to and fro" (Job 1:7 NKJV), so the Lord passes by. May we not miss His presence. May we not be found with our lamps dimmed. May we be found waiting, watching, and working for His glory. May we be found faithful in answer to His prayer before God's throne: "Righteous Father . . . I have made you known to them, and will continue to make you known in order that the love you have for me may be in them" (John 17:25–26).

For those of us who abide in Him, we are enriched and greatly blessed. Our calling is great and mighty—to extend God's summons to the brokenhearted who need a touch from the Savior. His coming will take the world by storm. Will you be in the midst of the storm?

Or will you find safety in the shelter of His mighty arms? This is your hour of decision. Don't be silent before the Lord of heaven. If He is knocking on your heart's door, answer with gladness. Invite Him into your life to take up residence. Do not delay. His coming is very certain. His coming will be soon. I trust you will be mounted on a white horse riding behind the King of Glory.

16

THE SAVIOR REIGNS

There before me was a white horse,
whose rider is called Faithful and True.
—REVELATION 19:11

Palm Sunday—the triumphal entry into Jerusalem. Throngs of people who had come into the city for Passover lined the road from the Mount of Olives through the gates of the city of God. Shouts of jubilation filled the air. Multitudes of worshippers cut palm branches from the trees and blanketed the dusty and craggy road with fronds and their own cloaks. "Hosanna to the Son of David!" (Matthew 21:9) they shouted. "Blessed is the king who comes in the name of the Lord. Peace in heaven and glory in the highest" (Luke 19:38) they proclaimed. Jesus, King of the Jews, was riding by, seated upon the back of a colt—one that had never been ridden.

At first glance, this scene appears rather humble—Jesus riding a borrowed donkey. But this picture is a fulfillment of prophecy. Its symbolism should not be missed. Jesus entered the city in this way to claim the fact that He is the Messiah. He is the Son of God. He is not only the King of the Jews; He is the Savior of the world.

Palms grow heartily in Israel and are, still today, a national symbol—they speak of peace. Throughout Israel's history, palm branches were spread along the pathway as royalty passed by. "Behold, your King is coming to you; He is just and having salvation, lowly and riding on a donkey, a colt" (Zechariah 9:9 NKJV). The cry from the people acknowledged Him as their Liberator. Hosanna was their way of saying, "Grant salvation now!" They acknowledged Him as Savior.

Less than a week later, many of these same people cried out for His death. How could they have been so mistaken? Their quickened about-face demonstrated their insincere belief in Him. They had seen Him perform miracles and wanted to elevate His status because of the great power He displayed. But when they saw Him re-entering the city from the Garden of Gethsemane as a prisoner a few nights later, they turned on Him immediately, angry that He would not do for Himself what they believed He would do for the people—free them from the bondage of Rome and exalt the Jewish people to kingdom status. They were thinking of themselves—not the Lamb slain before the foundations of the world. They felt betrayed, so they shouted: "Crucify Him!"

When they saw Jesus hanging from a Roman cross on crucifixion day, His body drained of blood, they knew for sure that He couldn't be the Messiah—the One who would come in great glory and honor. This was not glory and honor; this was gore and humiliation. The faith they had claimed was only as deep as their understanding of the Scriptures. They missed the symbolism of Christ's entry on the back of a donkey. They also missed the profound truth that He would overcome execution on the cross. They missed the fact that no borrowed tomb—no grave—would hold His pierced body in death. They believed His miracle-healing power for others but did not believe He could be victorious over death. On Palm Sunday, they believed He could conquer an evil empire. On Preparation Day—the day before Passover—they shouted, "Crucify Him," even as the lambs were being slaughtered on temple grounds, signifying the bloody sacrifice that would cover sin.

This atonement for sin had been practiced among the Jewish people throughout the Old Testament. They understood this, but did not correlate Jesus as the One final sacrifice that would bring such brutality to an end. Nor did they seem to understand the significance of His triumphal entry. A colt that had never been ridden was reserved for holy purposes. The donkey was also traditionally the animal that carried kings into their kingdoms in times of peace. But the people did not want peace; they wanted a warrior king to overthrow their oppressors. When a powerful wartime king rode into a city to conquer it and its people, he was seated on a mighty stallion. Now, instead of following Jesus into the temple to see Him seated on His throne, they saw Him imprisoned by an old rugged cross. They forgot their rich heritage. They forgot their national victories in the face of their ancient enemies. They forgot the lessons God had taught them. They forgot the words of their prophet Isaiah, who recorded: "He was wounded for our transgressions, He was bruised for our iniquities; the chastisement for our *peace* was upon Him, and by His stripes we are healed" (Isaiah 53:5 NKJV; emphasis added).

They also forgot what the Scriptures said, "For a mere moment I have forsaken you, but with great mercies I will gather you . . . My kindness shall not depart from you, nor shall My covenant of *peace* be removed" (Isaiah 54:7, 10 NKJV; emphasis added). The Jews revolted against the One who had ridden a lowly donkey carrying the hope of peace. They wanted war. They wanted to see their King ride through the corridors of the great walled city and slaughter every enemy. Instead the enemy slaughtered their would-be Savior.

THE KING REIGNS VICTORIOUS

Centuries have now passed, and the drama about to be displayed is more in step with what Israel expected the day they heralded Jesus as King of the Jews. This is what they were looking for—the great white stallion serving the warrior King.

Whenever I come to this marvelous passage in Revelation 19, I wonder if John's memory took him back to these scenes—Jesus being acclaimed by vast crowds and then rejected. John the beloved, as He was known to Jesus, must have grieved at the memory of such an awful Passover season. The heart-wrenching remembrance of Peter's denial must have gripped John's heart. No doubt the apostle John recalled every glorious aspect of Jesus being hailed by the people on Palm Sunday, followed by each painstaking detail of Him being nailed to the tree. Now he finds himself standing near this majestic white stallion, looking into the face of the Man called Faithful and True—Jesus the mighty King controlling the reins of His mighty beast of war.

"I, John, am the one who heard and saw these things," the apostle wrote (Revelation 22:8). "The angel said to me, 'These words are trustworthy and true'" (Revelation 22:6). John's countenance must have reflected a somber spirit as he contemplated the mighty acts of God in dealing with the final blows of sin. The Lord shined bright as John saw heaven standing open, and "there before me," John said, "was a white horse, whose rider is called Faithful and True. With justice he judges and makes war. His eyes are like blazing fire, and on his head are many crowns. He has a name written on him that no one knows but He himself" (Revelation 19:11–12).

Now God is about to make His final move. The pages of Scripture come alive—quickening the soul—when the identity of the rider of this white horse is revealed. It is none other than the Lord Jesus Christ, Israel's Messiah, Head of the church, King of kings, Lord of lords, Savior of the soul, Master of the redeemed, and Prince of Peace.

This, of course, is in stark contrast with the white horse of deception that appeared when the first seal was broken. The horse carrying deceit in its saddle takes on its true color—a dismal gray—a horse of a different color. He is *overshadowed* by the immaculate white horse, seen standing inside heaven's gates, whose Rider will strike the false prophets and pagan gods. The red horse that inflicts war to kill and defoliate, is *overcome* by this lively white horse—its Rider, draped in a blood-stained robe, who is victorious in war against the enemy and brings a lasting peace. The black horse that delivers disease and famine is *overpowered* by the pure white horse that brings healing and the Bread of Life. The pale horse of death and hell is *overthrown* by the resilient white horse that brings life to all who place their faith in the One who conquers—the Lord Jesus Christ. The Bible says, "The horse is made ready for the day of battle, but the victory belongs to the LORD" (Proverbs 21:31 ESV).

END OF THE DEMONIC REIGN

When will the Man on the white horse appear? The Word of God clearly teaches that He will come when the human race has sunk to its lowest and most perilous point in all history—the time when the four horses riding on the storms of Apocalypse have run their course and driven mankind to the very edge of the precipice.

Jesus warned us not to speculate on the date of His return, but He also warned that there is coming a time in the future when a counterfeit ruler and world system will establish a false utopia for an extremely short time. The economic and political problems of the world will seem to be solved. But after a brief rule the whole thing will come apart.

The antichrist will emerge as a monstrous impostor, the incarnation of iniquity. People the world over will say, "We've been had!"

During this demonic reign, tensions will mount, and once again the world will begin to explode with a ferocity involving conflict on an unparalleled scale. Even the grip of world leaders will be unable to prevent it. This massive upheaval will be the world's last war, the battle of Armageddon. According to secular and scientific writers, there is inevitability to humanity's date with Armageddon. The Bible says, "He who pursues evil pursues it to his own death" (Proverbs 11:19 NKJV).

I believe this coming storm will be a time of nuclear conflagrations, biological holocausts, and chemical catastrophes spilling over the earth. History will bottom out on the battlefield of Armageddon. We already see agitated clouds gathering over the earth.

Will the human race exterminate itself? Not completely. The demonized leaders "of the whole world" will have mobilized both as antagonists and protagonists of a coming anti-God system, headed by the antichrist. They'll be gathered, we're told, "to the place that in Hebrew is called Armageddon" (Revelation 16:16). The Bible says, "To him who rides the ancient skies above, who thunders with mighty voice. Proclaim the power of God" (Psalm 68:33–34). Christ will come back before man tries to obliterate His creation.

Until that day when Christ shall come "with shout of acclamation," there is still hope for the human race. While there is yet time, we must earnestly seek Him.

The more I learn of the realities of the book of Revelation, the more I realize there are still many mysteries yet to be unveiled. From the unfailing accuracy of biblical prophecy, we have evidence of the faithfulness of Scripture and its often stunning relevance to the circumstances and events of our lives. Thus we know His Word is true.

Woodrow Wilson spoke of "the war to end all wars," and Ellen Goodman, the columnist, wrote of the possibility of an ominous war ahead "to end all life." But rest assured it won't happen. God has other plans for the human race. Life is not going to be brought to a catastrophic end. God's intervention will overturn the evil plan of the human heart.

I do not want to linger on the who, what, why, how, or when of Armageddon. I will simply state my own belief: the time is near. A sudden and massive worldwide revival of God's people and a return to the morality and the values set in place by the Word of God could perhaps hold it off, but already the earth is under the condemnation of God, and its judgment will be swift, unavoidable, and total. In the face of this approaching storm, we have only one sure hope: Armageddon will be interrupted when the Man of Righteousness charges through the lowly ranks of human forces. Behind Him will follow armies from heaven also riding white horses. You may ask: what will this Man on the white horse do?

No description can document this battle scene better than the Author of this revelation. When He stampedes through enemy territory the rivals will recognize the General Almighty. John wrote, "His name is called 'The Word of God'" and with this mightiest of weapons John says, "out of His mouth goes a sharp sword, that with it He should strike the nations. And He Himself will rule them with a rod of iron. He Himself treads the winepress of the fierceness and wrath of Almighty God." John declares that there will be no mistaken identity, for "on His robe and on His thigh a name written: KING OF KINGS AND LORD OF LORDS" (Revelation 19:13–16 NKJV).

John saw "the beast, the kings of the earth, and their armies, gathered together to make war against Him who sat on the horse and against His army. Then the beast was captured, and with him the false prophet who worked signs in his presence . . . the rest were killed with the sword which proceeded from the mouth of Him who sat on the horse" (Revelation 19:19–21 NKJV). The prophet Isaiah predicted this moment: "My word that goes out from my mouth . . . will accomplish what I desire and achieve the purpose for which I sent it" (Isaiah 55:11).

The oldest quotation from literature concerning this event is found in the book of Jude. "Enoch, the seventh from Adam, prophesied: 'See, the Lord is coming with thousands upon thousands of his holy ones to judge everyone, and to convict all the *ungodly* of all the *ungodly* acts they have done in the *ungodly* way, and of all the harsh words *ungodly* sinners have spoken against him" (Jude 14–15;

emphasis added). Notice the repetition of the word *ungodly* in just one sentence. The most ungodly man and his system ever to exist will be embodied in the antichrist. Paul wrote to the Thessalonians, "The Lord Jesus will overthrow [the lawless one] with the breath of his mouth and destroy [him] by the splendor of his coming" (2 Thessalonians 2:8).

The Scripture says, "The government will be on his shoulders. And he will be called Wonderful Counselor, Mighty God, Everlasting Father, Prince of Peace. Of the increase of his government and peace there will be no end. He will reign on David's throne and over his kingdom, establishing and upholding it with justice and righteousness from that time on and forever" (Isaiah 9:6–7).

There is a statue across from the United Nations building in New York bearing the inscription "They will beat their swords into plowshares." Where does that quotation come from? From the Bible! In Micah 4:3, only one of many scriptural prophecies that deal with this catastrophic drama, we read that the world's "nations will come and say, 'Come, let us go up to the mountain of the Lord . . . He will teach us his ways'" (Micah 4:2).

From time immemorial, mankind has longed for a combination of true law and order, of peace and prosperity, of freedom and fulfillment, of health and happiness, of godliness and longevity on this earth. It will happen when Christ comes again to establish His kingdom.

MESSIAH REIGNS ON HIGH

The Scriptures have a great deal to teach us about the world of the coming Christ. The Messiah will take complete charge of the peoples of the entire earth. He "will stand as a banner for the peoples; the nations will rally to him, and *his place of rest* will be glorious," assures Isaiah (11:10; emphasis added). "The Spirit of the Lord will rest on him—the Spirit of wisdom and of understanding, the Spirit of counsel and of power, the Spirit of knowledge and of the fear of the LORD" (11:2).

Throughout the world there are people who crave a society of peace and provision, but also one of goodness and justice. The Messiah Christ will implement all these: "With righteousness he will judge the needy, with justice he will give decisions for the poor of the earth," as "righteousness will be his belt and faithfulness the sash around his waist" (Isaiah 11:4–5). Will it work? Yes! "They will neither harm nor destroy . . . for the earth will be full of the knowledge of the LORD as the waters cover the sea" (11:9).

So transformed will the prevailing order be, that even the animal world will be completely tame. "The wolf will live with the lamb, the leopard will lie down with the goat, the calf and the lion and the yearling together; and a little child will lead them. The cow will feed with the bear, their young will lie down together, and the lion will eat straw like the ox. The infant will play near the hole of the cobra, and the young child put his hand into the viper's nest. They will neither harm nor destroy" (Isaiah 11:6–8). This is the promise of the coming King. This will be in complete contrast to the savage beasts, scavenger birds, devouring insects, and raging diseases that have been among the most ferocious foes of primitive and civilized man from the Adamic to the atomic ages.

THE SAVIOR OF THE WORLD

This leads me to consider what the Scriptures have said about that future era under the reign of the Savior. The storms will all have passed. The sky will be clear. The oceans will be calm. The winds will blow softly. Sickness will be remedied by Christ. There will be no blindness, deafness, muteness, paralysis—no need for eyeglasses, hearing aids, speech therapy, wheelchairs, crutches, or white canes. "No one living," assures Isaiah (33:24), "will say, 'I am ill.'" "I will restore you to health and heal your wounds, declares the LORD" (Jeremiah 30:17). "I will bind up the injured" (Ezekiel 34:16). The horsemen will ride no more.

Isaiah prophesies:

> *Be strong, do not fear; your God will come . . .*
> *Then will the eyes of the blind be opened*
> *and the ears of the deaf unstopped.*
> *Then will the lame leap like a deer,*
> *and the mute tongue shout for joy.*
> *Water will gush forth in the wilderness*
> *and streams in the desert.*
> *The burning sand will become a pool,*
> *the thirsty ground bubbling springs.*
> *In the haunts where jackals once lay,*
> *grass and reed and papyrus will grow.*
> *And a highway will be there;*
> *it will be called the Way of Holiness.* (Isaiah 35:4–8)

"Surely the day is coming," prophesied Malachi (4:1–2) in the last chapter of the Old Testament, when the peoples of the world will finally "revere my name, the sun of righteousness will rise with healing in its wings." We will journey on the King's *skyway* someday.

In the last chapters of the New Testament, John gives us a glimpse of the beautiful place we desire to go:

> The city is laid out like a square . . . The wall was made of jasper . . . the foundations . . . were decorated with every kind of precious stone . . . the twelve gates were twelve pearls . . . the great street of the city was of pure gold . . . I did not see a temple in the city, because the Lord God Almighty and the Lamb are its temple. The city does not need the sun or the moon to shine on it, for the glory of God gives it light, and the Lamb is its lamp . . . its gates

will never be shut . . . there will be no night . . . nothing impure will ever enter it, nor will anyone who does what is shameful or deceitful, but only those whose names are written in the Lamb's book of life. (Revelation 21:16–27)

Just as God created a perfect environment for Adam and Eve, He will *perfect* the environment of heaven with Himself. The human imagination, as magnificent as it is, is only a foretaste of what God has in store for His people. John must have had long hours of praising and worshipping the Savior as he sat in his prison cell doing what the Lord Jesus had instructed him. So he kept writing of the magnificence of the vision:

Then the angel showed me the river of the water of life, as clear as crystal, flowing from the throne of God and of the Lamb down the middle of the great street of the city. On each side of the river stood the tree of life . . . and the leaves of the tree are for the healing of the nations . . . The throne of God and of the Lamb will be in the city, and his servants will serve him. They will see his face, and his name will be on their foreheads. They will not need the light of a lamp or the light of the sun, for the Lord God will give them light. And they will reign for ever and ever. (Revelation 22:1–5)

I, John, am the one who heard and saw these things. And . . . I fell down to worship at the feet of the angel who had been showing them to me. But he said to me, "Do not do it! I am a fellow servant with you and with your brothers the prophets and of all who keep the words of this book. Worship God!" (Revelation 22:8–9)

John now confirms the vision that he witnessed, and the message he heard was from the Lord Jesus. He must have been filled with joy to hear the angel mention John's brothers—the prophets. He documented every detail under the scrutiny of the Holy Spirit as his heart raced with expectation. Then a most glorious command was given to this apostle of revelation. "Then he told me," John wrote, "'Do not seal up the words of the prophecy of this book, because the time is near'" (Revelation 22:10).

REIGNING WITH HIM

What a picture this is. We have learned about the seven seals peeled from the heavenly scroll. With tension and anxiety at times, we learned about the darkness that would be unleashed by the four horses and their riders. So many aspects of the end times had been sealed; now we hear the instructions given to John: "Do not seal up the words of the prophecy." The Godhead, consumed with love for His creation, allows us to peer, with John, into His future plan already marked out. The unknown can frighten us, but the Father in mercy calms our fears. Christ in His fullness of grace grants us assurance of abundant life with Him. The Spirit, who brings great comfort, imparts to us the hope of His coming. We are given the blueprint of our heavenly home. Man could not be offered a more wonderful care package than this. The Bible says, "Cast all your anxiety on him because he cares for you" (1 Peter 5:7).

During life on earth one of the most difficult tasks we are faced with is what to do with our earthly goods when we die? Many simply write out instructions directing where their meager possessions should go. Others engage attorneys to work out complicated estate disbursements. This, often, can turn into family feuds, igniting jealousy and greed. Then there is the Living Will, authorizing measures to prolong life by artificial methods or let life slip away naturally.

Jesus Christ clearly stated His plan for our provision. "In My Father's house are many mansions . . . I go to prepare a place for you . . . I will come again and receive you unto Myself; that where I am, there you may be also. And where I go you know, and the way you know . . . I am the way, the truth, and the life. No one comes to the Father except through Me" (John 14:2–4, 6 NKJV). When Jesus prayed to His Father for His children (all true believers), He said, "They know that everything you have given me comes from you. For I gave them the words you gave me and they accepted them. Father, I want those you have given me to be with me where I am" (John 17:7–8, 24).

The greatest gift ever offered is the salvation of man's soul from the benevolent hand of Almighty God—His Son—the Lord Jesus Christ. The invitation to accept this gift is written with His precious blood and He extends it to every man, woman, and child by His outstretched arm. "His hand is stretched out still" (Isaiah 5:25 NKJV).

"The Lord is . . . not willing that any should perish but that all should come to repentance" (2 Peter 3:9 NKJV). This is Christ's "living will": "God our Savior . . . desires all men to be saved and to come to the knowledge of the truth" (1 Timothy 2:3–4 NKJV).

And the Revelation of Jesus Christ is His will and testament. It contains the title deed to earth, given to Him by His Father in heaven. In it He grants to each of His children a share in all that belongs to Him. Included in such an estate is the most wonderful provision— that we can share in the service of the King for eternity.

How I long to join the throngs of people as Jesus holds out His pierced hands to welcome us home; to thank the Father for the sacrifice of His Son; to bow at the Savior's nail-scarred feet; to sing around the throne of God; to sit at the Bridegroom's bountiful table; to feast on the Bread of Life; to praise the Lamb in all of His glory; to walk with the Master along the river of life and drink of the water that will never run dry; to look into the face of the Holy One who died for me—and worship Him.

THE SAVIOR OF OUR SOULS

Yes, I am watching and waiting and praying for His return. But I must also keep working until He comes. And so as I write the last pages of this book, I cannot possibly conclude without doing what I have done for nearly seventy years—extend His invitation to you. It would be completely futile for me to preach the Gospel if the Holy Spirit were not convicting the hearers of their sin and prompting them to open their hearts to Christ. Your reading of this book is entirely in vain if, in doing so, you do not sense the Holy Spirit drawing you into a deeper knowledge of Him; or if you are not a believer, to give your life to Him. Ask yourself right now if the Holy Spirit is calling out to you, "Come!"

The same Gospel message God the Father gave to Jesus, He passed on to His disciples. This is the same message I have tried to proclaim and pass on to generations after me, just as the Bible has commanded. Someday we will see all things through the Father's eyes.

If you do not know this Man from heaven who loves you, listen to the plea He makes to you in conclusion of this Revelation of Himself. It is the most compelling invitation given in the Holy Scriptures.

"I, Jesus, have sent my angel to give you this testimony," (Revelation 22:16). Jesus Christ Himself issues this appeal. After envisioning a panorama of the past, the present, and the future; after peering high into the heavens, observing sinful life on earth, and looking deep into hell itself—The Word of God calls lost souls to Himself. Why? Because, as we read, "Jesus Christ, the faithful witness . . . loved us and washed us from our sins in His own blood" (Revelation 1:5 NKJV). He who testifies to these things says, "Surely I am coming quickly" (Revelation 22:20 NKJV). John's compelling close of the letter declares, "Amen. Even so, come, Lord Jesus!"

On that day, the hoofbeats will fall silent. On that day, the apocalyptic whirlwind will cease to churn. On the day of His coming, He will once again "still the storm to a whisper" (Psalm 107:29).

AUTHOR'S NOTE TO THE REVISED EDITION

T he task of researching and editing a book of this scope has involved many people, and I am grateful for the contribution of all those who have assisted me in this effort. In addition to those listed in the first edition (1992), I am thankful for my son Franklin's strong encouragement for me to undertake this revised and updated edition of the original volume (which was based in part on my earlier book, *Approaching Hoofbeats*, published in 1983).

I am especially grateful, however, to Donna Lee Toney, who gave invaluable editorial and research assistance to this second edition and coordinated its final editing and publication. Without her dedication and literary skill this project would never have been brought to completion.

Billy Graham
February 2010

WORKS CITED

Augsburger, Myron S. *The Christ-Shaped Conscience*. Wheaton: Victor, 1990.

Augustine. *Confessions*. Translated by Edward P. Pusey. New York: Macmillan Co., 1961.

Barclay, William. *The Revelation of John*. Philadelphia: Westminster Press, 1959.

Barrett, David and Todd Johnson. *World Christian Trends, UPDATED AD30—AD 2200*. Oxford: Oxford University Press, 2001 (1991).

Bible Treasure Chest (booklet), 1925.

Bin Laden, Osama. "Transcript: Bin Ladin video excerpts." *BBC News*. http://News.bbc.co.uk/2/hi/middle_east/1729882.stm (accessed March 7, 2010).

Bonhoeffer, Dietrich. Quoted on ChristianHistory.net. http://www.christianitytoday.com/ch/131christians/martyrs/bonhoeffer.html (accessed March 7, 2010).

Bush, President George H. W. State of the Union Address, January 28, 1992. http://www.c-span.org/executive/transcript.asp?cat=current_event&code=bush_admin&ye (accessed February 2, 2010).

Bussell, Harold. *Unholy Devotion: Why Cults Lure Christians*. Grand Rapids: Zondervan, 1983.

Buttrick, George A., et al,. eds. *The Interpreter's Bible*. New York: Abingdon Press, 1957.

Chandler, Russell. *Understanding the New Age*. Dallas: Word, 1988.

Cohen, Elizabeth. "Centers for Disease Control (CDC): Antidepressants most prescribed drugs in U.S." www.cnn.com/2007/HEALTH/07/09/antidepressants/index.html (accessed July 9, 2007).

Dobson, James C., and Gary L. Bauer. *Children at Risk: The Battle for the Hearts and Minds of Our Kids*. Dallas: Word, 1990.

Dylan, Bob. "Blowin' in the Wind," copyright 1962; renewed 1990, Special Rider Music.

Eisenhower, Dwight. "Chance for Peace." Speech to American Society of Newspapers, April 16, 1953. http://www.eisenhowermemorial. org/speeches/19530416%20Chance%for%20Peace.htm (accessed February 24, 2010).

Elliott, Elisabeth. *Through Gates of Splendor*. New York: Harper & Brothers, 1957.

Faidley, Warren. Storm Chaser. www.stormchaser.com (accessed May 5, 2009)

Feinsilber, Mike. "Despite Signs of Hope, America Rings With Sound of Griping." Associated Press, April 26, 1992. *Los Angeles Times* Article Collection. http://articles.latimes.com/1992-04-26/news/mn-1395_1_cold-war (accessed March 7, 2010).

Fraser, Malcolm. *Melbourne Declaration of Human Rights*. Melbourne: University of Melbourne Press, 1981, 1983.

Gelb, Leslie. "Foreign Affairs; More Arms, Less Aid," *New York Times*, May 8, 1992, Editorial Section.

Gorbachev, Mikhail. Westminster College, Fulton, Missouri. NBC Evening News, May 6, 1992.

Graham, Billy. *Hope for the Troubled Heart*. Dallas: Word, 1991.

———. Moscow Address, May 1982. Personal Papers.

———. *World Aflame*. New York: Doubleday, 1965

Graham, Ruth Bell. *Clouds are the Dust of His Feet*. Wheaton, IL: Crossway Books, 1992.

Hamblen, Stuart. "How Big is God?" Copyright 1960. Hamblen Music, ASCAP.

Hearing Loss Web. "Noise-Induced Hearing Loss." http://www.hearing lossweb.com/Medical/Causes/nihl/nihl.htm (accessed March 7, 2010).

Hough, Lynn Harold, et al,. eds. *The Interpreter's Bible*. 12:414. New York: Abingdon Press, 1957.

Johnston, Jerry. *The Edge of Evil: The Rise of Satanism in North America*. Dallas: Word, 1989.

Kramer, Larry. "We Have Lost the War Against AIDS." *USA Today Magazine*, Vol. 120, issue 2564.

Kreyche, Gerald F. "The Decay of Morality." *USA Today Magazine*, Vol. 120, issue 2564.

Ladd, George Eldon. *A Commentary on the Book of Revelation of John.* Grand Rapids: Eerdmans, 1971.

Latham, Mark. quoted in Christopher S. Wren. "New Mozambique Ordeal: Drought Comes Atop War." http://www.nytimes. com/1992/05/15/world/new-mozambique-ordeal-drought-comes-atop-war.html? (accessed March 7, 2010).

Lavey, Anton. *Satanic Rituals.* New York: HarperCollins, 1976.

———. *The Satanic Witch.* Port Townsend, WA: Feral House, 1986.

Lewis, C. S. *The Weight of Glory and Other Addresses.* Grand Rapids: Eerdmans, 1965.

Library Index. "The Economics of Overweight and Obesity: The High Cost Of Losing Weight." http://www.libraryindex.com/pages/1220/ Economics-Overweight-Obesity-HIGH-COST-LOSING-WEIGHT. html#ixzz0hYlb973D (accessed March 7, 2010).

MacLaine, Shirley. *Out on a Limb.* New York: Bantam, 1983.

Marien, Michael and L. Jennings, eds. *What I Have Learned: Thinking About the Future Then and Now. Future Survey.* Westport, CT: Greenwood, 1987.

Markowski, Joseph. "AIDS: Anatomy of a Murder Charge." *Time*, July 13, 1987. http://www.time.com/time/printout/0,8816,964944,00. html (accessed February 10, 2010).

Matthews, John. "When I Stand with God."Gospel Quartet Music Company, Evergreen Copyrights, Inc.

McClung, Floyd. *Holiness and the Spirit of the Age.* Eugene, OR: Harvest House, 1990.

Meyerson, Harold. "America's Decade of Dread." *Washington Post*, December 16, 2009.http://www.washingtonpost.com/wp-dyn/ content/article/2009/12/15/AR2009121503382.html (accessed February 2, 2010).

The National Foundation for the Deaf (NFD). "Listen Loud and Lose It." www.nfd.org.nz/?t=156 (accessed March 7, 2010).

Nahm, Becky. "Surprise Storm Didn't Give Officials Time to Sound Siren." KSTP TV. http://kstp.com/news/stories/S1097087.shtml?cat=206 (accessed 8/20/09).

Nietzsche, Friedrich. *The Gay Science.* Cambridge: Cambridge University Press, 2001.

Petersen, William J. *Those Curious New Cults.* New Canaan, CT: Keats Publishing, 1973.

Samuelson, Robert J. "How Our American Dream Unraveled." *Newsweek*, March 2, 1992. http://www.newsweek.com/id/118553 (accessed March 7, 2010).

Security World. "The Safety of Cosmetics." http://www.securityworld.com/ia-208-the-safety-of-cosmetics.aspx (accessed March 7, 2010).

Segal, George. *The World Affairs Companion.* New York: Simon & Schuster, 1991.

"The Shadow of Armageddon." *London Times*, March 14, 1974, Editorial section.

Sullivan, Dr. Louis W. "Jonathan Edwards." Lecture, Yale University, November 1990. www.ncbi.nlm.nih.gov/pmc/articles/PMC1473137/

Taylor, Mrs. Howard. *Borden of Yale.* Chicago: Moody Press, March 1988.

Vitz, Paul. *Psychology as Religion: The Cult of Self-Worship.* Grand Rapids: William Eerdmans Publishing Co., 1994.

Walvoord, John F. *The Nations, Israel and the Church in Prophecy.* Grand Rapids: Academie Books, 1968.

Wilkerson, David. "A Call to Anguish." Sermon, Times Square Church, New York, NY, September 15, 2002. http://www.worldchallenge.org/node/2621 (accessed February 10, 2010).

———— with John and Elizabeth Sherrill. *The Cross and the Switchblade.* New York, NY: Spire Books, 1963.